The Efficiency Playbook

Your Tactical Game Plan to Getting More for Less

Michael Andrew

The Efficiency Playbook - by Michael Andrew

Your Tactical Game Plan to Getting More for Less

Address all business inquiries to:

Michael Andrew – support@michalethemaven.com

www.michaelthemaven.com

ISBN: 9780983830016

Library of Congress:

Editors: Lex Hogan, and Tyler Tichelaar and Larry Alexander/Superior Book Productions

Cover Design: Alexander Vultchev

Interior Layout: Larry Alexander/Superior Book Productions

Author Photo: Michael Andrew

Every attempt has been made to source all quotes.

Printed in the United States of America

First Edition

2 4 6 8 10 12

Dedication

This book is dedicated to you. Yes **YOU**.

When I began writing, I imagined you opening up this book, reading it just as you are now, gleaning lessons I've learned the hard way, applying those lessons to your life, and then chasing down your dreams. I saw infinite success. You have graciously supported me already by taking a chance on this book, and I feel a desire to connect directly with you.

I've often also wondered, if this book can help you, what the impact would be if everyone in the world read it? An insane and impossible idea on its own, yet it would lead to a much more peaceful and efficient world nonetheless! Ideas that have the potential to change the world are worth pursuing, and therefore, it felt right to swing for the fences, despite impossible odds.

It was these two ideas that fueled this project to completion. It was my *why* for writing it: to help you specifically, and to try to make the world a better place. I believe this book will do each of those to different degrees, long after I'm gone. Everything else is secondary.

This book is also self-published, which means it faced tremendous friction to bring about. One of the greatest challenges in self-publishing is marketing. Without great marketing, it won't matter what is written on these pages.

I have a simple and efficient idea for solving this problem, as well as allowing me to connect with you: I'm asking you to write an honest review of this book on Amazon.com.

In return for your honest review, I will commit to the following:

I will **personally respond** to each of the first **1,000 reviews on Amazon**. You may have some questions or suggestions or even feedback, and this gives us and other readers a way to share. This is a lofty but not impossible goal. If I do not know the answer to your questions, I will say so directly, but I will personally connect with you there regardless.

Should the book do well enough to gain **1,000 reviews**, I will launch and maintain a workday efficiency podcast for **1 full year**. There, I will share the chapters I didn't include in this draft, as well as answer selected questions, scenarios, and situations to the best of my ability.

That is a scary and uncomfortable thought for me, but I am willing to commit to it if it allows me to connect with you and there is such a demand.

If you think the book is useful, I would be honored to have you refer it to friends and colleagues. This is the book I wish I would have been given as a seventeen-year old about to face the world.

Thank you for being part of my journey. I am so honored that you would consider me to be part of yours!

Michael Andrew, Tuesday March 21, 2017

Acknowledgments

I would like to express the deepest gratitude to my Heavenly Father, who has blessed me with unique talents and impressed my mind with the importance of efficiency, and for giving me the desire to share it in order to help others looking to improve their lives.

I am grateful to my family and true friends for their unwavering support and encouragement. A shout out to all my teammates, in football, my church mission, work, and in the disaster field. Some of my most valuable lessons were learned with you guys and gals in real-world situations. You know who you are.

To each of my faithful customers, students, subscribers, and supporters, I am so honored and humbled to have had you in my corner over the years. Your belief in me has given me the freedom required to put my thoughts down on paper.

There have been a number of additional people who were instrumental in bringing this book forward, including my editors Lex Hogan, Larry Alexander, and Tyler Tichelaar, as well as several proofreaders who spent many hours and made many critical suggestions.

I have made every effort to correctly cite all references, including other authors and individuals whose teachings I have taken to heart. It is possible I may have inadvertently missed or not known a specific reference which impacted me, but will update as necessary. I am so grateful to all those authors and teachers who have inspired me.

This book would not have been possible without each and every one of you—and I thank you all so much!

Contents

Introduction

I – Speed

II – Information Systems

III – Simplicity

Introduction

How to Use This Book

1. **Start with an open mind.** There are flaws with my writing, inconsistencies, and even contradictions. There will be exceptions to every piece of advice I offer. If you are looking for mistakes, you will find them. However, if you are open-minded about improving your personal efficiency, this book will be a powerful resource for you. Dig for gold, not coal, and you will discover solutions to problems you face daily.

2. **Pace yourself.** I suggest reading one chapter each morning. Some of the material is dense and will take time to sink in. A fast read of the entire book will be less effective.

3. **Apply what you learn.** Try to find real-world opportunities throughout your day to apply the principles you read about. The tactics will have greater impact when you are looking for chances to test them.

4. **Use the Nicknames.** I have gone through great trouble to give nicknames to most of the principles, including a small icon. This is for the sake of memory, helping you to link a complex idea to a single image. When you recognize the characteristics or situations of these tactics in real life, identify them out loud or to yourself using these nicknames. Many of my friends and I frequently refer to entire chapters like "a river of focus" to express something we are working on. I tell myself "no sandbagging" when packing. I often verbalize the binaries such as "knowns are greater than unknowns" and "big thoughts are better than little thoughts" when decision-making. Using the nicknames is a gentle, effective reminder that makes the principles' application feel more real.

5. **Answer the questions.** I'll occasionally include questions to help stimulate thought about a concept or principle. It will be well worth

your time to write your answers down on paper, either in the book itself or in a notebook or journal.

6. **Review as needed.** Some of these tactics will stick immediately; others might take more time. I've organized them into seven core groups, in no particular order of importance, to make them easier to find. They are:

1. Speed
2. Information Systems
3. Simplicity
4. Automation
5. Communication Skills
6. Emotional Management
7. Gap Management

An Introduction to the Study of Efficiency:

1 – The Staircase

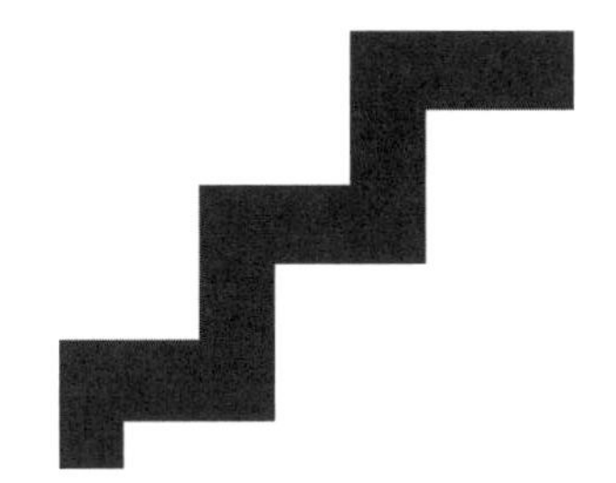

AKA—Process Refinement

IT WAS THE burn that started this all. That searing, painful *burn*. Climbing up one of Brigham Young University's notorious, mountainous staircases after football practice. The stairs weren't that big of a deal; it was climbing them after practice that commanded my attention because of the fire in my legs.

It was during one of these stair-climbing sessions as a young freshman that sparked my personal twenty-five-year study of efficiency as I wondered to myself, *Would it be more efficient to go one, two, or three steps at a time? If I leap, I may be able to get four, but that would require more individual exertion, as would three steps over two. It seems one step would require the least exertion, but then more cycles would be required.*

From a physics perspective, in a measurement of "work," which is defined as force times distance, it was all the same for each one-, two-, or three-step process. Each process resulted in the same amount of mass going the same distance, which led to even greater confusion. My question was, which of the processes was most energy efficient, or were they all exactly the same?

I decided to conduct my own experiments. For weeks, every time I climbed those steps, I would try something different, attempting to gauge my exertion in every possible manner. At first, it was how tired I felt on a scale of 1-10. Then it became how fast I was breathing, then my heart rate, then the actual time to go from bottom to top. I tried to gauge the strain on each individual leg per step. To the bewilderment of passersby, I tried every conceivable way to go up and down those stairs—sideways, backwards, and on all fours.

With time, I would learn that nearly all of the best players on the team, the players destined to play in the NFL, had secret lists—bits of information they had learned over the years.

I remember listening to a radio interview with a defensive lineman whose words exploded in my mind like an information bomb when he said, "Most offensive linemen stop breathing immediately before the snap." To the casual observer, this may not make a lot of sense. To a defender tasked with pressuring the quarterback on every down, it was a goldmine of information. In the game of football, it is believed that the offense has a split-second advantage because it knows the snap count. The defense does not, and therefore must wait until the ball is physically moved before rushing.

If there was a clue that the snap was about to occur, the defense could in theory attack at the very moment the ball is snapped, instead of a half-second later. Play after play, both sets of linemen begin to breathe heavily, and for whatever reason, there is a natural, human tendency for offensive players to hold their breaths immediately before the snap. Uncorrected, these breath-stopping linemen signal the timing of the snap count and allow the defense a full-step advantage in their attack. Not an easy thing to overcome over the course of a game.

The defender who knows this secret has an *advantage* over players who do not. *All elite athletes, in every sport, have secret lists.* All of them. They are doing something that unsuccessful players are not doing. These secrets are consciously applied.

If you were to think and do everything that another successful person is thinking and doing, you would enjoy the same success as he or she does. This assumes that all the conditions in both cases are identical (which is impossible), but this is an incredible concept. There are people out there who know how to be successful, so all you need to do is apply that same knowledge in the same circumstances and you can be successful too.

Never take advice from someone who is doing worse than you are in a particular subject. If you get a B on a chemistry test, it wouldn't make a lot of sense to take advice from a student who got a C because you are already doing better than him. If you know an A student, and trust her, listen to her advice on how to prepare and study, and watch your performance improve.

What you hold in your hands is my personal efficiency playbook. It contains twenty-five years of observation, experimentation, and study. The principles are true and powerful. If you learn just a few of them, you will have the tools to solve many of your daily problems and these tools will remain in your toolbox for the rest of your life.

And what about the steps of BYU? Turns out there was an answer, and it came from another question: *Is it possible to make climbing the stairs less efficient?*

If you can make any process less efficient, it usually means you can also make it more efficient by doing the opposite of that very thing.

There was no doubt in my mind that I could make my stair-climbing rituals much more difficult. I visualized things such as:

1. Carrying one of our 300-pound linemen up the stairs on my back.

2. Climbing the stairs with broken knees.

3. Covering the stairs in broken glass, sharp metal, and sewing needles sticking straight up.

4. Wrapping my head in a plastic bag.

5. Instead of having 100 regular-sized steps, what about 5,000 really, really small ones and being required to step on each one?

That was when it dawned on me: The question was not about force over distance; it was about how many individual tasks are required to complete a goal, and it applied to all processes. *The greater the number of steps required, the less efficient a process becomes, and therefore, the more you can remove steps from a process, the more efficient the process becomes!*

I also learned that when climbing steps, there are at least two actions:

1. Lifting your leg to the next step.

2. Transferring your weight to that leg and standing in order to lift the other leg up.

If this were true, going one step-at a time up a 100-step staircase would require 200 actions on my part. Going two steps at a time would require 100 actions. Going three steps at a time, would require 66.66 actions. For every additional required action per step, there was an enormous compounding interest over the task of climbing the staircase.

1. This was a profound revelation to me as a young man. I immediately understood that any time I could reduce the number of steps, transitions, distance, shifting of inertia, middlemen, decision makers, costs, rules—while maintaining the goal—I could improve my efficiency.

2. The number of steps required to complete a task is a form of friction. *Friction, for the most part, is the opposite of efficiency.* I'll be mentioning friction throughout the book, but for now, keep in mind that the greater the resistance to your goals, the less efficiently you will perform.

When we understand the nature of our enemies, we are able to defeat them.

Friction is your enemy.

2 – Friction

AKA—Resistance to Your Dreams

THOSE WHO ARE unaware of friction's nature will spend most of their lives being pushed around by it in every direction, like a rowboat in the rough sea, flailing to stay afloat. It is cold, wet, and windy. The passengers are tired and hungry. Sharks are in the water, waiting to devour them. These voyagers cannot pursue and will never realize their greatest dreams, as they are too busy just trying to stay afloat. While bailing out water, fixing holes, paddling frantically, panicking, arguing with each other, some go into shock, becoming helpless, awaiting their fate at the hands of a merciless sea. The forces of friction are real and are not to be ignored.

However, once people understand the nature of friction, they can defeat it and even harness it to their advantage. They can become like a sailboat, using what others consider resistance to generate power and steer their craft, heading anywhere they want to go. One can even use it as a weapon to defeat his or her foes.

If you could have anything in life that you do not already have, what would the top three things be? (Write your answers here or in a note book)

Now think about what prevents you from having these things, and write them here: (These are most likely the variants of friction you are facing)

To the common person, friction is bad because it is *resistance to goals*. If you look in the very back of this book, you will find my "Appendix of Friction"—a short list of the things I constantly find myself working against. They are things that will probably affect you as well, but what is more important is that we are able to see and recognize *the pattern of friction* in its many forms.

As we keep our eyes peeled for friction, we get into the habit of identifying it and finding its patterns. Like the breath-stopping linemen, or steps in a process, once the pattern is discovered, a weakness can be exploited. Play after play, that tiny advantage will yield huge returns over the course of the game, if you apply the principles.

Once your boat is steady, it will be time to construct a means to harness the energy of friction to your advantage.

To illustrate this point, list the top five companies in the world you are aware of here:

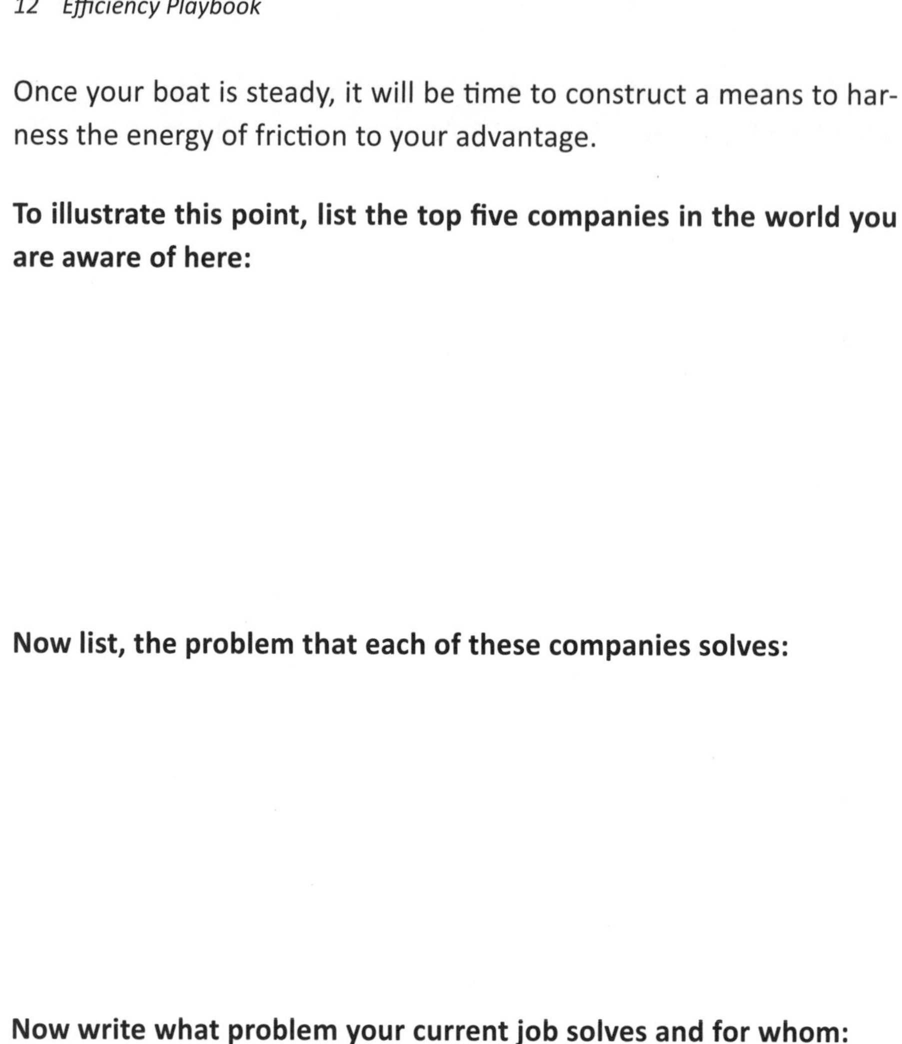

Now list, the problem that each of these companies solves:

Now write what problem your current job solves and for whom:

The reason I ask these questions is to illustrate that there is tremendous opportunity in friction. In other words, friction creates the opportunity for business and profit!

How valuable is the bucket to the rowboat owner who is quickly sinking!

How priceless is a more steady boat!

How sought after is that warm, waterproof coat!

How delicious is the warm cup of soup on a cold rainy day!

These are the two sides of the fence in dealing with friction. On one side, you are a victim, and on the other, you are a conqueror. On one side you are defensive; on the other, you are offensive. One side is a consumer; the other is a producer. As you go through your daily life, yes, notice the friction, but also notice someone, somewhere is probably making a fortune off that same headache.

The greatest entrepreneurial minds are able to see when friction or demand can be exploited to their advantages.

There is value and opportunity in friction.

3 – What Is Efficiency?

Eta—The Symbol for Efficiency in Physics and Engineering

THE SHORT DEFINITION of efficiency is: *the ability to achieve a specific goal with minimum waste.*

Efficiency is often confused with being effective. Effective is the ability to achieve a specific goal. You can be effective and less efficient. For example, if it was your goal to illuminate a dark room, you can do so by burning a large pile of one-hundred dollar bills or by turning on an energy-saving light bulb. Both methods are effective, but because the latter costs so much less, it is more efficient. Efficient is being effective at a cost savings.

As an equation, at least in electrical engineering, efficiency is defined as:

$$\textbf{Efficiency} = \frac{\textbf{Useful Power Output}}{\textbf{Total Power Input}}$$

It basically means, in order to accomplish something, what are you spending to get it? "Bang for your buck" is a common, everyday phrase that describes efficiency. An hourly wage is a real-world way to measure income efficiency. For every hour of your time, what are you getting in return? $8 an hour or $100 an hour?

Efficiency is so important because every day we needlessly waste valuable resources, often overspending what it would take to get the same thing through another method.

The epitome of inefficiency is the waiting line. Here you are, ready to give a company money, and it is literally making you stand there, wasting your time, before you give it your hard-earned cash. That's like paying twice!

Many years ago, we received checks, drove to the bank—only when it was open—filled out a deposit slip, stood in line waiting for tellers to serve us, and then, finally, deposited the check. With all these steps, the entire trip could take forty to sixty minutes. Shortly after my stair-climbing revelation, I found myself going bananas every time I had to go to the bank or post office because of this knowledge.

Then banks started accepting deposits at the ATM. This added flexibility to making deposits, and in many cases, there was no waiting in line, making it more efficient.

Today, you can deposit a check with your phone. You open a banking app, take a picture of the check, hit send, and voila! Check deposited. You just saved forty minutes of your life—no travel time, no waiting. You should definitely feel *good* about finding shortcuts to life like this. *Technology has a way of introducing more efficient means to accomplish our goals.* Sometimes, all we need to become more efficient is to educate ourselves about what is available.

Any study of efficiency is only valuable in respect to the goal.

To illustrate, let's pretend that you commute to work every day, and it takes you about forty minutes each way.

1. If your goal is to save *time*, you might be willing to try a few different routes to work. Perhaps there is a non-direct free-

way with less traffic that would consistently get you there ten minutes sooner. With respect to time, this would be a 25 percent increase in efficiency (one way). You could calculate that this route would save you twenty minutes a day, one hundred minutes a week, or roughly eighty hours per year. (Congratulations...that is like getting two extra work weeks of time!)

2. If your goal is to save *money*, you might consider car-pooling with a coworker and splitting the cost of gas, even though it may take an extra fifteen minutes each way.

Another example is the number of different ways we can rent a movie compared to just a few years ago. We have various options: streaming, mail-order rentals, and vending machines.

1. If your goal is to save ***time***, streaming is usually the way to go. Within seconds, you can be watching a release that was in theaters just weeks ago in your home, without going anywhere to pick up a DVD.

2. If your goal is ***selection***, then something like Netflix's DVD rental program might be a better choice because not every movie is available as a streaming rental.

3. If your goal is ***cost-savings***, you might consider Red Box, since it is only $1.50 to $2 dollars per night. But its selection isn't that extensive, and you have to travel to the nearest location.

In order to measure your true efficiency, you must always keep in mind what the end goal is. If you are unaware of what it is you are trying to get more of, be it time, money, or opportunity, you will not be able to improve accurately and consistently.

Changing the goal changes the measure of efficiency.

It also helps to look at a study of efficiency from the position that there are many paths to reach the same end goal. When the end goal is identical, *the most efficient path should become your priority.*

List 2-3 goals you would like to solve with efficiency. Keep these goals in mind as you read, and ask yourself how the principles of this playbook might apply.

When you find a principle in this book that might help you reach your goal, return to this page and write down your strategy next to the goal you wrote earlier. Doing this will help you think tactically about efficiency, as well as help you commit to your plan on paper.

I – Speed

4 – Test Tubes

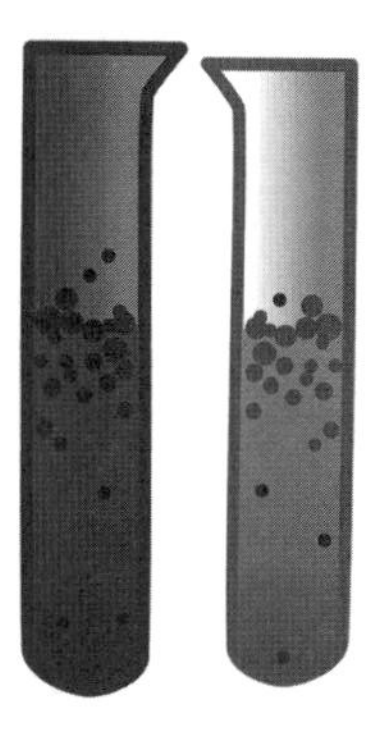

AKA—The Value of Efficient Workflow

IN 1932, RUSSIAN scientist Georgii Gause published an important paper about competition between similar species. He showed that when two similar, non-sexually compatible organisms share the same limited space and resources, one would always eventually out-compete the other.

He learned that the species *that was more efficient* would reproduce at a higher rate over time. The fate of the less-efficient species was extinction.

Organisms that utilize similar resources with greater efficiency will always enjoy greater success than their competitors.

I have been a professional photographer for over thirteen years. A photographer's workflow consists of all the processes from start to finish of any job. Workflow includes preparing for the shoot, shooting the client (with a camera of course), post-production, blog posting/ social media, delivering the images, backing up the images, and other deliverables.

The photography industry is also highly competitive, and Gause's Law of Competitive Exclusion is applicable. Two photographers in a given area will compete for the same resources—clients.

How could *workflow efficiency* allow one photographer to dominate another completely? One of the core efficiency tools is *speed*. When one photographer has a faster system for product delivery, he or she has a distinct advantage.

Let's pretend we have two photographers who are identical in every aspect except workflow. Assume even the end product is identical. Both photographers shoot for one hour. Photographer A uses an *automated system* in Lightroom or Photoshop to prepare images after the shoot and, therefore, has a one-hour post-shoot workflow.

Photographer B does not use an automated system to process and prepare images so he has a nine-hour post-shoot workflow. This really happens, by the way. Photographer A uses two hours to every ten hours photographer B uses. We can say that photographer A is five times more efficient than photographer B.

Over the period of many months, or even years, photographer A will out-compete photographer B simply because A's turnaround time is so much quicker. This gives photographer A more free time, which can be used to shoot more clients, make more money, or even take more time off, preventing burnout. Also, it is important to note that at least in this hypothetical situation, the success of photographer A has *nothing* to do with the quality of images, time on location shooting, gear or lens used (assuming they are the same), or price charged. Photographer A was simply *smarter* about workflow; photographer B was more in the "work-hard" mind-set.

A similar example would be if two Subway Sandwich Restaurants were operating side by side. (Note: this would be highly unlikely in real life, but I use it to illustrate "two goals being equal.") If Subway

A is able to move customers through the line five times faster than Subway B, Subway A will produce considerably more sales, bringing in much greater profit. Subway A will dominate and thrive as a business, not because its product and location are better, but simply because it is more efficient with its resources, time, and customers who are in a hurry.

Any repeating system of workflow that you control can and should be exploited for efficiency gains. This is true whether it is a business system or something you do personally, such as preparing for the day, studying, making meals, or even exercising.

5 – The Spark

AKA—The Faster You Start, the Sooner You Finish

"In limitation, the master reveals himself."
— Goethe

WHICH IS FASTER, a state-of-the-art helicopter, or a man on foot with a fifty-pound backpack? Such was the question I faced as an aid worker in Kathmandu, Nepal, in late April 2015. In the aftermath of a devastating earthquake and its aftershocks, reports arrived of dozens of villages short on supplies and days away by foot, hiking the treacherous Himalayan Mountains. My task was to get aid to these villages. As I sat planning with two local Sherpas, I had to weigh the question: Is it better to start immediately on foot or to wait for an available helicopter?

Based on previous disaster aid experience, I knew that helicopters were always in short supply after disasters. I could see them flying about, but getting access to one was a long shot. My disaster aid partner, Craig, and I called it "riding the unicorn" because it never actually happened. Still, rumors circulated that some might be available soon—just not for certain.

Hiking was risky since landslides were common and sometimes lethal. The hike would be hard and require camping overnight in devastated areas. If I fell or was seriously injured, there would be no rescue plan. Yet the idea of competing with other aid groups for a limited number of helicopters seemed unwise. The most immediate opportunity was on foot. While not ideal, we could start as soon as we were ready.

Hiking in on foot was an asset that was *known.* We controlled everything about it and when it would happen. Access to the helicopter was an *unknown.* We didn't control it, nor would we be able to say where and when it could be used.

In the disaster aid situations, information is king. The better and fresher your information, the easier it is to get limited resources, like a helicopter. This is especially true when you have images, data on populations, needs, and GPS coordinates to share.

The next morning, two Nepalese locals and I started that risky three-day hike. Along the way, we GPS-tagged eight villages in need of aid. We found a woman who needed immediate medical evacuation, and we were able to arrange it with real-time information using a satellite phone (the medical team ironically came by helicopter). Making contacts at the villages, we were able to arrange for hundreds of thousands of meals, tarps, and other aid to be delivered to the area partnering with the Salvation Army and other groups. The most amazing part about the experience was that we finished the first major deliveries before we even got our own access to helicopters.

Lesson learned; sometimes going on foot *is* faster than by helicopter.

This is "**heuristics,**" which in my own terms means finding a solution that isn't perfect, but gets the job done well enough anyway. In my experience, most problems can be solved with a "good enough" solution and rarely require a perfect one.

As a binary, a tool I will describe in a later chapter, "heuristics now > perfection later."

While going on foot was not the fancy answer, it was by far more preferable because we did not waste time and resources pursuing an asset that may appear to be the only solution. Try not to fool yourself into thinking there is only one way to get something done.

Don't get me wrong; there are definitely times when only the right tool for the task will do. However, human nature is such that we often tell ourselves we need this to get that, when many times, we already have everything we need to get the job done if we are creative and apply ourselves. If we are able to find a way to accomplish what we need to get done with what we already have, typically we can reduce our expense and still achieve our goals sooner. The belief that it can be done with what we have often makes the difference.

If you can foster that mind-set, always believing that you *can* do it now, the creativity will come. Force yourself to believe that if someone put a gun to your head and ordered you to find a way, your motivation would force you to find a solution. You might be surprised by how powerful that thought is: *I already have a way; I just need to figure it out,* instead of allowing yourself to be defeated before you even start.

You must use wise judgment to know when starting something immediately can actually hurt you. Sometimes, patience and waiting for the right window is a valuable part of being efficient. As a general rule, however, once the path is known, starting early will give you an advantage.

Speed in the correct direction, toward the right goal has no substitute. From football players to cars, from cashiers to your Internet connection, the faster something works, the sooner it finishes its task. Yes, exceptions exist, but for the most part, *speed is good*.

The *spark* represents the act of beginning and finishing an important, required task as soon as possible, with what you have now. The sooner you start, the sooner you finish. In many instances, starting early makes the task feel easier, as opposed to waiting until the last minute. In college, I knew the sooner my projects were finished, the less stress I felt.

Starting a required task now is usually more efficient than starting later.

In regards to a set process of required steps, for me, a minute now is worth more than a minute later. I've had many arguments over this with close friends, and it comes down to: If you *have* to do something, it is almost always better to start earlier than later because:

1. You will also lose time and energy thinking about it over and over, a procrastination tax if you will.

2. Being forced to start the task later can inhibit your ability to pursue other opportunities.

3. In some cases, the same amount of work will actually be harder when you start later. If you have washed dishes by hand, you know *The Spark*. Wait a few hours and once easy-to-wash dishes become a scrubbing nightmare. Starting earlier makes the washing itself *easier,* and so it is when we are inspired or excited to act. *We have greater momentum and freshness earlier on.*

If you cannot start immediately, pre-visualize yourself starting and finishing. See the end result. Feel good about it. Then begin as soon as you can.

Avoid talking with others about your plans, dreams, and goals for vanity purposes. It is a trap and will rob that spark of initiative. Yes, you can do your research and homework to gauge whether the idea is worth pursuing, but talking about it just to talk about it? No. Do not do that. Your subconscious can be confused between talking about something and actually doing it. If you talk too much about it, you will trick yourself into believing you are making progress. Many people—family and friends included—will poop on your idea and excitement. Cast your pearls of excitement before enough poo-pooers and watch your hunger die.

Spilling your future plans and trade secrets can come back to haunt you. The world is full of talkers. Be a doer. Pull the trigger early and often. Talking about it doesn't matter until it is done because, otherwise, you too are just a talker. Once it is finished, then talk and market as needed.

Something interesting you will see is that, with discipline and success, resentment will grow, even among close loved ones. They don't want you to be successful; they want you to be mediocre. Why? Because with each success you have, they will self-compare and feel empty. I advise friends not to talk about or volunteer stories of success if they can help it. Learn to self-congratulate if you need to celebrate, even verbally if necessary. Those who are truly happy for you will initiate it. Those who are jealous will also become known. The more you experience success, the more resistance you will find from haters. It's inevitable. Continued success is the best revenge for those doubters, so ignore them. Focus on that one task in front of you until the process is complete.

Once you know your plan of action:

Start early, start fast, start cheap, start smart, start often, start with what you have now and with what you can control.

Whenever you finish something you considered might be difficult, say to yourself:

"That was all there was to it?"

"That was easy."

"That was fun!"

6 – Ballast

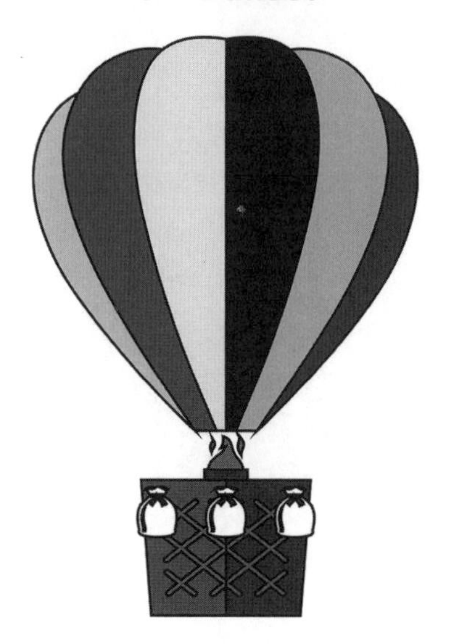

AKA—Pre-Stressing

IN MID-NOVEMBER OF 1996, our BYU football team was preparing to face the Utah Utes, our archrivals from the north. They had beaten us the year before. You could never take the Utes too seriously; they could lose every game of the season up to the BYU game and then come out and play against us like it was the Super Bowl.

I prided myself in my role as a prep-player (like Rudy in the film of the same name). My role was to play the part of opposing offenses, specifically running back, to give our defense the best preview of what it would face. I knew that the more serious and realistic I was about mimicking opposing running backs, the better our defense seemed to play—and I felt tremendous pride when it played well.

Utah had a very unusual running back; mad props to you if you can both remember and pronounce his name. He was 6'0" and weighed a whopping 270 pounds. Despite this, he was nimble, agile, and had an explosive burst of acceleration not common for men his size. I was 6′2″ and closer to 230 pounds, and I was concerned that I couldn't adequately portray what it was our defense was about to face. The Utah back was notorious for delivering violent hits and had an ability to break tackles and turn short gains into long runs.

I'm not exactly sure how I got the idea, but I figured if I could somehow add twenty-five to thirty pounds of weight under my pads, it would be a much closer simulation. Mick Hill, our equipment manager, had access to all kinds of strange gear, so I asked him whether he had an extra weight vest like the ones I had seen some of the track guys wearing. He did. He loaned me one without asking what my intentions were.

I put the weight vest on and stood on a scale with all of my gear on—266 pounds! Close enough. Somehow, I felt that if I didn't say anything to anyone about what I was doing, especially my prep team coaches, no one would really catch on and interfere with my experiment. The vest was easily hidden under my pads. The only thing I really noticed was the extra effort required to start accelerating at the snap. Once I got a full head of steam, it wasn't so hard to run with the extra weight. I was curious to know whether our defense would notice the extra force of the impact when they hit me.

In the beginning of our practice, we had a drill which is essentially running plays without receivers. The idea is to let the offensive linemen and running backs go head-to-head against the defensive linemen and linebackers. Everyone on the field knew that each play was a run, whereas with full team drills the defense doesn't know whether the play will be a run or a pass.

This drill was a battle of wills to see whether our starting defense could stop the run. I was shocked by how much success I was having with the vest on. It seemed like nearly all of my runs were five yards or more, and when there was contact, *I fell forward*. The simple process of falling forward is always worth an extra yard or two. The defense never picked up on why this was happening.

My legs were absolutely burning running play after play carrying that extra weight, but I was having so much success, I was starting to feel both thrilled for myself and worried for our defense—that the Utes monster back was going to destroy them on Saturday.

Before you all run out and buy weight vests, the story gets better....

During a water break, I had lifted up my jersey to adjust the strap that held the weight vest close to my body. One of my coaches saw it, squinted in disbelief, shook his head as if he couldn't believe his eyes, laughed, and then commanded: "Take it off, Mike!"

Despite my attempts to persuade him, he would hear nothing of it. I was upset that I had to remove it, but I did as I was told.

Perhaps it was psychological, or maybe physiological—perhaps my mind was still in full-power-mode from running with the vest on, but for whatever reason, I felt *super-fast* once it came off.

That practice was the best football performance of my career. I broke multiple thirty-yard runs that would have been touchdowns in a game, ran over several of our defensive starters, and simply could not be tackled on first contact. Nearly every time I was tackled, it required two or more defenders to drag me down.

During goal line drills, I found myself literally leaping over the top of our offensive linemen for the score. It was like I had caught on fire. The defense was getting mad I was making them look bad, and they wanted it to stop. It didn't. When practice ended that day, I felt I had earned the respect of my teammates and coaches like I hadn't before.

We would later go on to beat the Utes that year, 37-17, but I've never forgotten the lesson I learned that practice about *ballast*.

***

When I first dropped out of grad school, I had more than $100,000 in credit card debt. I had no job and was facing bankruptcy. For the next year, I had to live on an extremely strict budget and be financially disciplined in a way I never could have imagined before. I had to count every penny, know exactly where my money was going, and pay off all those bills.

Over time, I was able to develop the financial discipline (and hate for debt) to remain frugal once I had paid off all those credit cards at 27 percent interest. Being strapped with that much debt and burden made my financial discipline stronger than it had ever been. Once the burden was lifted, being disciplined was easy. I pay for everything with cash now. While this was something I was forced into, through it the principle of *Ballast* became clear.

Ballast is the principle of artificially burdening yourself with some kind of weight during a non-critical time, learning to function and perform with that weight, and then at the critical moment, removing that artificial weight. If your body and mind have acclimated to the ballast, you will have much greater power and the ability to deal with the things that matter.

Any form of exercise could be considered a form of ballast. When we subject ourselves to weight lifting or resistance, our bodies and minds have to develop a resolve to get through the routine.

The result is mental and physical conditioning to stressful tasks. Once this conditioning sinks in, the perceived stress when under real-world duress becomes minimized because it is already familiar. This is a huge advantage to have over those who have not been conditioned to similar stressful environments.

Police officers and soldiers often go through "stress inoculation," which creates combat-like situations, including close proximity gunfire and explosions so when real world conflict finally does happen, they are already acclimated and do not panic. Some football teams are known to play crowd-like noises when preparing to play in large stadiums to simulate game-time conditions, and practice non-verbal ways to communicate.

Usually, stress is something that finds us naturally. Often after we have made a mistake that needs to be corrected. I feel far more motivated to work when I have less money. I feel hungry to learn when I feel stupid or do not know something. I feel more drive when I have been humbled. Why wait for life to force you into these situations to grow?

Ballast is the principle of *artificially* creating stress so you will thrive in real-world situations. It is disciplined mental and physical conditioning preparatory to the point of conflict. Those who do it will generally have a distinct advantage over those who do not.

Stay green (meaning believe you have much to learn), stay broke, stay hungry, stay stressed, stay humble, *but do so because you choose to be—not because you have to be.*

7 – Sandbagging

AKA—The Over-Preparedness Principle

AS A PRODUCER and videographer, much of what I do for video production requires very specific types of gear. I might need a particular tripod for a camera, a special light stand, or a constantly lit video light. I might also need flash systems and triggers for stills and different sets of lenses for different perspectives. I might need a microphone—don't forget to check the batteries—and a headset to monitor the audio as it is being recorded. I might also be tempted to take my steadi-cam, but I'll also need to bring my wide-angle lens if I want to use it.

My camera bag is quickly filled, and then I remember something else..."Wouldn't it be great to bring the slider and get some new set up shots?" So I stuff that into the bag, too.

Sandbagging is the principle of thinking or preparing to do much more than possible, *all for the sake of trying to become more efficient*. It means you are weighing yourself down to the point where you cannot perform any task at all. There is a fine balance between these two ideas: Be prepared and have backups, but don't overdo it.

My situation as a camera guru is unique. I may have five or six different cameras with me at a time that I use for specific reasons. I have over thirty different lenses, each with their own strengths. I have to be really careful not to sandbag by bringing more cameras and lenses than I can actually use in a given shoot. The "nothing more" principle is the idea of bringing just what you need to get the main goal done, and leaving everything else behind.

Shooting weddings has taught me that I must bring at least two cameras, in case one breaks. The nature of event photography is to have a longer zoom on one camera and a wider, general purpose zoom on the other, so I can switch back and forth quickly without changing lenses. I'll wear both cameras at the same time, using a special harness, and bring only an additional wide angle and fast aperture lens for portraits. Two cameras, four lenses, and *nothing more* because of the weight to carry and the time it takes to switch lenses takes me away from shooting.

If I am shooting for fun, or doing a more casual shoot, I only need one camera and one or two lenses—*nothing more*. It is a faster and far more enjoyable shooting experience.

If I am the cinematographer for a feature-length film, I will bring a full arsenal of lenses, the difference being, I will also have two full-time assistants to help manage all this gear.

The same can be said for clothing and shoes. There comes a point when one acquires so many articles of clothing that there is no possible way to wear them all. If one does not or cannot wear all the shoes and clothing one owns, what good is owning it? Sandbagging can also be seen since some individuals will bring several suitcases of clothing for a weekend trip.

I have a gear bag that stays packed year-round in the event of a disaster. On my first disaster trip, that bag weighed about seventy pounds. I have learned the hard way the importance of keeping my bags light, having carried them through many airports. Over time, I have found better, lighter gear. My original water filter weighed several pounds. The current one weighs a few ounces. Instead of larger flashlights, I use tiny head lights. Instead of a thick sleeping pad, I now use a very light, inflatable mattress. Instead of a larger tent, a smaller hammock. Instead of heavy MREs (meals ready to eat), lighter dehydrated meals. Over time, the bag has become much lighter, making it easier to carry, reducing the amount of work I have to perform. This is an important consideration for anyone who has any kind of gear bag: *Find a way to make it as light as possible*.

Over-preparing or overstocking a resource to the point where it cannot possibly be used *reduces your efficiency.* Because of the speed factor, going light has clear advantages, especially over longer periods and distances.

If two gear bags are loaded with similar performing tools needed to complete identical tasks, the lighter one will result in greater efficiency.

Find ways to lighten your assets, without diminishing your capacity or resources to complete the primary goal.

8 – Wheel Size

AKA—The Relationship of Size to Speed, Capacity, and Momentum

"The Parable of the Apple Orchard"

ONCE UPON A time, there was a boy whose parents planted an apple tree. When he was younger, the tree would only produce a handful of tasty apples, which the boy loved to eat. He couldn't pick them himself, so he carefully watched the tree and the ground around it, waiting for a ripe apple to fall. When one did, he would pick it up and eat it before his mamma noticed.

By the time the boy was a teenager, the tree was producing plenty of apples, which, if unpicked, would soon rot. While he still enjoyed eating them, there were way too many to eat, and he felt bad that the tree's apples were going to waste.

The young man knew that he could sell the apples down at the farmers' market, so he picked a few of the nicest, most perfect apples, loaded them into his basket, and headed for the market on his bike. He was elated when he sold his basket of apples almost immediately. This really got the young man excited and thinking. He had made nearly a dollar! The next step seemed so simple—pick more apples, sell more apples. So he did the same thing the next day and got the same result. This made the teenager even more excited! He did some math and realized that if he could pick even more apples, and bring them to market, he should be able to make double or triple the amount of money he had made on the first two days. He needed to borrow his dad's truck to execute his plan. His dad was happy to see his son becoming an entrepreneur, but he thought it would be a good lesson to ask his son to cover the cost of the gas, which he did. By the end of the summer, the teenager had made several hundred dollars. He could buy the boots he'd had his eye on, ask Mary Ann out for a shake, and even pay for the gas to pick her up in his dad's truck. Heck, he thought he might even soon buy a used truck of his own. Imagine that!

But wait...not so fast! The single tree barely had enough apples to last to the end of the summer. The next year, *he'd need to have many more trees.* While planting some of his own apple seeds would be economical, it would take many years for the trees to mature. The faster route would be to buy a few younger apple trees and have them transplanted. And he did just that. The problem was this process was expensive, and he had to take out a small loan to make it happen.

While the next few summers were not as productive as he had hoped, with time, he soon had several dozen mature trees. But now there were way too many apples to pick on his own and unless he hired help, he wouldn't be able to capture his product's value. So the young man hired a few helping hands. This created some issues. Not only did he have to pay them minimum wage, which to the young man was a fortune, but he was completely confused about all the paperwork he would have to fill out to pay the income taxes. *What the heck is a W-9?* he wondered. His mother knew an accountant in town who could help with that, but he would have to pay this number cruncher as well.

Furthermore, he learned that he needed to pay a number of other unexpected fees, such as worker's compensation and insurance. To make matters worse, some of the employees became unreliable just a few weeks after hiring them, by showing up late, working slowly, or even taking naps after lunch if they were not closely monitored. The young man had great difficulty finding perfectly reliable help, so he hired a part-time manager to help look after the employees. The manager helped resolve this, but he was also expensive. All of them demanded free coffee and a breakroom too.

The young man then realized he needed a second truck, even though he was still using his father's and nearly all of his profits were going toward expenses.

He racked his brain until he came up with two solutions:

1. Sell the apples for more money, creating more profit.

2. Plant even more trees, making more apples, therefore, also making more money.

When he tried to raise the price of the apples from five cents to ten cents, he noticed that he had a hard time selling them at that price, simply because Farmer Jane sold her similar type apples for five cents. The young man would have to sell at five cents per apple, so the only option was to increase volume, thus plant many, many more trees.

Fifteen years later, the (less) young man looked over his massive apple orchard. The volume of his apple production was the best in the county; he had a fleet of trucks, automated picking and packing machines, and a couple of hundred workers. He had his own pilot, who sprayed his fields with insecticides. A massive irrigation system watered the orchard regularly. He had his own accountant, legal team, and all the insurance he would need. He realized he felt tired—running a business wasn't easy, and it was not as profitable as he had imagined. In fact, for the work he was doing, sometimes twelve to sixteen hours a day, he questioned whether it was worth it.

It seems like the larger the orchard grows, the more the expenses and headaches grow, he thought to himself.

As he walked back to the house, through the yard, and past the original tree that had started it all, a perfect red apple fell to the ground. He picked it up as he had done as a child and took a bite—he smiled, missing the simplicity of the days when he'd been too small to pick apples from the tree and had just waited for the ripe ones to fall.

***

If you were to place a small, light wheel next to a very large, heavy wheel on the top of a hill and let them go at the same time, you would notice that the very small wheel begins to move and accelerate much more quickly than the large, heavy wheel.

The small wheel can accelerate quickly because it has less inertia. It takes the large wheel longer to move because anything at rest tends to stay at rest, *especially* when that inertia is large. Its activation energy is greater.

This principle has greatly influenced me in doing disaster aid work. There are many aid organizations out there; some have just a few people, others, like the Red Cross, can have tens of thousands of workers. It is easy for me to get moving; I am solo. I have an emergency disaster aid gear bag packed and ready to go. All I have to do is book a flight, grab my bag, and I am on my way. A larger organization will take a little more time to get moving, simply because of its size—more people, more equipment, more costs, more logistics.

In biology, the surface area of a cell is critically important to its efficiency. Typically, the greater the surface area, the easier it is for that cell to exchange gases and nutrients. So the question is: What has greater surface area, an orange or a bundle of grapes of the same weight?

If we were to peel all the skin off of the grapes and the orange, and measure the surface area of that skin, we would see that the grapes will have much more surface area, and this is due to their relative smaller size.

The same is true with blood vessels, particularly our capillaries—vessels that can be so tiny that only a single red blood cell can move through one at a time. I have watched through microscopes in amazement as long lines of single red blood cells march through capillaries at high speeds. The length and surface area of our capillaries dwarf the length and surface of our arteries and veins. It is said that if we were to connect all of our blood vessels end to end, they would be 60,000-100,000 miles in length!

These examples allow us to make some very important generalizations about the relationship of size to efficiency:

- The smaller an organization, the more potential it has for efficiency and the more rapid its rate of acceleration. Smaller organizations can usually make decisions faster when there is less bureaucracy. Smaller organizations also typically have *less overall capacity*.

- The larger an organization, the less efficient it becomes. But larger organizations typically have *larger capacity*.

While I am able to get to a disaster quickly, what I can do and how long I can stay is limited. A larger organization can work in an area for years. I last about three to five weeks.

As any system gets larger, it naturally becomes less efficient due to the nature of its size.

II – Information Systems

9 – The Radar

AKA—The Time Value of Information

IN THE EARLY morning of December 7, 1941, a small Japanese submarine was spotted, attacked, and sunk just outside of Pearl Harbor. A message was relayed immediately to Naval Command, but the message took time to prepare, encode, and de-code. The process by which this information was transmitted took so long that by the time it was received, much larger problems were at hand.

Shortly after the midget sub was sunk, a radar operator on Oahu's north shore spotted what appeared to be a convoy of planes some fifty miles north of the island. This message was likewise relayed to supervisors who would dismiss it as a fleet of B-17s returning from a reconnaissance mission.

Again, another opportunity was missed when a message from Japan to its embassy in Washington was intercepted prior to December 7, 1941. The message was intended for the Japanese ambassador, who was then to transcribe and deliver it to U.S. officials. The message announced an end to negotiations and formally opened the possibility of war. The delivery of the message was to occur approximately one half hour before the planned attack. While the Japanese ambassador was unable to transcribe the message quickly enough, United States code-breakers had already intercepted and delivered the message to Washington, and a last minute warning was sent to Naval Command at Pearl Harbor. It would not arrive on time.

At approximately 7:48 a.m., the first of the Japanese Zeros penetrated the clouds above Pearl Harbor. "Tora, Tora, Tora!" they cried over their radio, meaning "Tiger, Tiger, Tiger!" It was the code for having achieved the element of total surprise, catching the United States unprepared. Once the Japanese destroyed American planes neatly parked on the runways, they would have the advantage of nearly full air superiority during the attack.

Two thousand, four hundred Americans were killed that day.

The failure to heed the early warnings of December 7, 1941 is a powerful illustration on the "Time Value of Information," meaning that a piece of critical information is always more valuable the earlier it is received. That same information, as seen above, can be priceless one moment and absolutely worthless the next. A huge advantage exists in getting accurate information early.

What would have happened had U.S. Naval Command received information from any of those three sources that an attack was imminent, which would have given U.S. forces an hour, or even a half hour to prepare? One can only speculate as to the number of lives it would have saved.

I watched the 2014 college football national championship game with great interest. In the first half, Auburn's defense dominated Florida State's unstoppable-before-that-game offense. Then, something strange occurred in the second half.... Florida State seemed to regain its offensive mojo so it could march up and down the field at will. What happened that could explain the change?

Shortly after the game, it was revealed that one of Auburn's coaches, who had worked at Florida State the previous year, was deciphering Florida State's offensive play calls, *allowing Auburn to predict exactly what Florida State intended to do in the next few seconds.* I don't care how good of a football team you are, if the opposing team knows what play you are running, that knowledge will allow it to create a lot of problems for you. Florida State adjusted in the second half by using towels to block the view of the Auburn coaches. The result? Florida State rallied to a thrilling win.

The importance of maintaining secrecy when facing an intelligent opponent cannot be overstated. The ability to keep secrets is valuable; it directly translates into efficiency on the battlefield because there is less resistance from the enemy to your specific plan. If your enemies do not know where you will attack, they must prepare for all scenarios. Once they know your specific plan, all of their resources can work to prevent it. ***It is always more efficient to deal with knowns, than unknowns.*** You want be operating in knowns; you want your enemy to be operating in unknowns.

The phrase, "Loose lips sink ships," means that when sailors are on shore, they are not to speak about their fleet's intent. Doing so could allow the enemy to devise a trap or provide an opportunity for sabotage.

Getting the right information before others is so powerful that in many cases it is illegal. Think Martha Stewart and insider trading. When a person, who has intimate knowledge of a company's workings or potential downfall before others, acts on that knowledge by selling or purchasing stock, she has an unfair advantage over the public.

When you have the right information about a critical situation, it allows you to prepare, plan your next move, limit damage, and exploit opportunity. It allows you to steer your car, ship, or plane in the right direction. Many of our technological advances revolve around what and how information is shared and how we can improve the speed at which that information travels. We have radars, sonar, and real-time search engines; we can gather information about just about anything in a matter of moments.

Get critical decision-making information early, often, and fast, and you will have a competitive advantage over those who do not.

10 – The Magician's Handcuffs

AKA—Why Cheaters Cheat

"The only rules that really matter are these; what a man can do, and what a man can't do."
— Captain Jack Sparrow, Pirates of the Caribbean

SHORTLY AFTER FINISHING my collegiate football career, I had the opportunity to enter an "all natural" bodybuilding contest. The rules stated anabolic steroid use was not allowed, and there would be random testing performed for the participants, as well as the overall winner. I was confident of my chances, having dropped from 245 pounds to 202 in an eight-week period. Long story short, I would end up fifth in the Light Heavy Weight Division.

The winner was nineteen years old, and far more developed than I, who at twenty-six years old had been working out consistently throughout all my adult life. It wasn't even close. Strangely, no actual drug testing took place. The overall contest winner was supposed to take a polygraph test (not an actual blood test), but I later learned that this polygraph test also never happened. It didn't seem fair to have worked so hard only to lose to someone who probably had been injecting himself with steroids, especially when even the sub-standard means of testing was not enforced.

Piracy is not a happy, feel-good topic, but it is reality. The day I realized my training videos were being pirated by the thousands was a tremendous blow. To this day, I receive only a fraction of what I would be earning if everyone who watched my training videos actually paid for them. It defies logic because most of these pirates can afford a camera worth several thousand dollars, yet will steal a training video worth a fraction of that cost *simply because they can.* I am so fortunate and blessed to have a certain percentage of customers who are honest and have supported me over the years. I estimate my honest customers to be about 5 to 10 percent of the total number of those who watch my videos. Without them, I would have closed shop years ago.

Because video pirates are taking advantage of me, I have implemented a number of defenses, some of which have been successful. My DVDs are now encoded with anti-piracy software, and I have a company that monitors illegal downloads of my products. I register my work with the United States copyright office and have an attorney on retainer to sue pirates or Internet companies who harbor them.

When someone is cheating you, you must take action or it will continue.

It is unsettling but true: *Efficiency is improved when one evades debts, costs, and burdens.* That's precisely what those pirates are doing—being efficient in how they save or make money.

While I believe most people are honest, it is safest to assume your competition, some of your friends, and, unfortunately, even some of your family will cheat if they believe they can get away with it.

Sometimes it isn't so black and white. For example, someone might not be breaking the law, but he may be using dishonest tactics and playing on false assumptions. For example, I know of a popular fish restaurant that goes to great lengths to give its customers the impression its fish is fresh and locally caught, when in fact, it is imported and frozen. The restaurant does not necessarily lie, but it will say everything short of that in order for its customers to perceive incorrectly that the product has more quality than it actually does. Not illegal, but a sketchy way to trick its customers into believing they are buying something much more expensive than they really are, allowing the restaurant to charge more and be more profitable.

Cheating is a way to tilt the scales of competition in your favor. But I have often been on the losing end because it is important for me to be honest and play fair.

Adding to this complex issue is the fact that those who enforce the rules are human—they are going to make mistakes. For example, in football, pass interference occurs when a defender impedes an offensive player's movements downfield, typically five yards beyond the line of scrimmage.

In college football, when a defender breaking this rule is caught, it is an automatic first down for the offense, and the ball is placed at the spot of the foul, within a maximum distance of fifteen yards from the line of scrimmage. This is a significant penalty when enforced.

In the NFL, it is still an automatic first down, but the ball is placed at the spot of the infraction regardless of how far from the line of scrimmage, which can be the length of the field within two yards of the goal line, and it is often a devastating blow to any defense.

Over the years, coaching staffs have made some important and clever observations:

1. In college, where the penalty is limited to a maximum of 15 yards, coaches will sometimes teach defensive players to in-

tentionally grab the receiver and hold them on deeper patterns, preventing an easy touchdown.

2. Some teams of referees are much less likely to call pass interference than others. This fact can be measured statistically. If a coaching staff knows the referee team *is less likely to call pass interference,* it can instruct its players to break this rule more, *without getting caught.*

3. Defensive coaches also know that if the interference is *not* flagrant, they can often get away with it—no penalty called. So they avoid a full grab or push, but make just enough contact to break receivers' momentum, knock them off course, or interrupt the timing of their routes. They know it will prevent a successful offensive play and it is effective.

To summarize, teams will *intentionally cheat in regards to rules if:*

1. The penalty is more desirable than the consequence of fair play.

2. The means of rule enforcement are lacking. (Or there is no penalty for breaking the rule.)

3. Minor infractions are not enforced, even if they should be.

These three principles will help you identify when and where cheating is likely.

The take home message here is there will be cases where your competition will be able to take advantage of a situation because there is no or little penalty, *even when there should be*. Assume their mindset requires all options to be on the table. Many can and will break the rules, as well as the law if they think they can get away with it. I am not encouraging you to cheat, but if you are directly competing with someone, chances are your opponent will. Count on it and **never rely on your enemies' virtues to show you mercy.** If you have a tendency to show weaknesses, expect to be taken advantage of, even if it is against the "rules." There are far too many bullies in the world to believe otherwise.

I am a firm believer in honesty and in being a good sportsman. In no way am I advocating breaking rules or being dishonest. But I also am a believer in not allowing myself to be unfairly penalized or cheated by the competition, and I will take action if I feel that is the case.

So you may be asking yourself, "How do I deal with cheaters?"

I played on a lot of special teams, in particular punt coverage, which meant I had to block a defender long enough to keep him from getting to the punter, then get around him and get downfield to make a tackle.

On occasion, the player I was blocking would grab my shoulder pads and hold on to me, which is illegal. If the player was good, he would pull my shoulder pads close to his, making his hands impossible to see. Once they latched on like that, it was very difficult to escape in time to make a play downfield.

I found an easy escape when someone latched on to me like this. At the top of my lungs, I would yell, "Hey, Ref—Holding!" Meaning "Mr. Referee, look at this punk holding me. We want a ten-yard penalty!"

The result was instantaneous and as sure as a reflex every time I used it. The player would immediately let go to avoid being detected by the referee; I could then push him aside and run down field. It worked because *when cheaters are cheating, they are very nervous about being caught*.

When your competition is cheating, sound an alarm and reveal his misdeeds to the authorities.

All this being said, there is still an eternal truth for those of us who like to play by the rules:

The lower your debt, taxes, costs, friction, constraints, or burdens are, the easier it is to become more efficient.

It can be something as simple as standing in the shade on a hot day, paying a lower interest rate (or none) on a loan, living in a state that has lower taxes, having a car with better gas mileage, rolling with the punches instead of into them, or it can be much more complex. Many opportunities will arise for you to reduce your burden, both legally and lawfully, so exploit them every chance you get.

11 – The Spyglass

AKA—Copy and Improve

WHAT IS YOUR biggest (most painful) problem right now? Write your answer here:

When faced with a challenge, one common strategy is to experiment on your own with random or somewhat calculated solutions. Some may work; some will not. I call this working in "unknowns."

Even if you find the correct solution, it will take time, resources, and energy to develop. Chances are, friends, foes, and even strangers have faced similar challenges. Allow their lessons learned to become yours. Reinventing the wheel is always less efficient because you carry the expense related to trial and error even when others have already found solutions.

Instead, use what I call the Spyglass.

Here's how it works: When you are facing a difficult situation like the one above, ask yourself these questions:

1. Who has faced this problem?

2. How does that person currently deal with the problem?

3. What hidden techniques or technologies is he or she using?

4. How can I duplicate or improve that person's strategy and carry it out in a similar manner?

The Spyglass Rules of Consideration:

- Be humble. To use the Spyglass, you must concede that whatever you are doing is inferior and you lack knowledge.

- Seek those who *excel* at whatever it is you are battling and find out how they solved the problem.

- Once the secret is learned, strengthen it. Most strategies, no matter how good, can be improved. That is where your creativity comes in. Use tried and true methods as a starting point and slowly build upon them, making them better. By starting from an established strategy, you have saved considerable time and avoided some of the chance of failure.

- Do not copy tactics or techniques of those who are doing worse than you in a particular area. That does not mean to ignore other things they are doing well.

- Do not become a copycat. When you do, you risk being labeled as inauthentic and a thief. You must use your judgment to know when you are borrowing problem-solving ideas versus plagiarizing someone.

- Those performing at a high level will often be willing to share their secrets. Approach them and ask for them to share. Be frank and honest when you ask: "Hey, Jim, I'm really impressed with your work! What tips can you give me to improve?" You may have to pay them for their advice, but it may be well worth the cost.

- Many experts have published their secrets in books. Reading the insights of the masters is an excellent way to be more efficient if your path is similar to theirs. I constantly have a great audiobook playing whenever I can—driving, flying, walking, doing errands around the house. I typically do not advocate *multi-tasking* because it creates complexity and more things that can go wrong, but listening to a great audiobook is an exception to this rule.

- Equally important, be willing to share your strategies when appropriate. By teaching others, especially those doing worse than you, your capacity to find a partner and alliance can usually be increased. Make allies wherever possible.

- The Spyglass is equally valuable for instruction when learning *what did not work*. We are doubly efficient when we can learn from others' mistakes.

A true life story: As a football player, I overheard a comment made by a wide receiver who excelled in escaping man-to-man coverage. "It's the little things," he confided. "If they are playing me tight and I am about to make my break, I will touch them. Not a push or a shove...no...that will draw a penalty. I touch them with just a finger, maybe two; it's enough to disrupt their balance so they cannot break when I do."

In practice, I decided to try this strategy against our star linebacker, who would later go on to have a successful career with the Indianapolis Colts. He was by far the most difficult player for me to go against, and he was very good in pass coverage. I had tried everything against him. He was too big to try to muscle through. Deception? I lost. Running away from him? I lost. Misdirection? I lost. Two little fingers on his shoulder before I made my break on the corner? It worked. I was not a stellar college football player, but the experience of using someone else's strategy to solve my problem was seared into my mind forever.

Finally, the spyglass should not be used to duplicate others' intellectual property. Examples include—school papers, test answers, copyrighted material such as music or movies. Be careful *not* to copy things you know you should not. I would never recommend breaking a law, and I despise media pirates because I have been burned so badly by them time and time again.

Exercise a degree of caution when using the Spyglass on intelligent enemies whose weaknesses have been exposed by others. If they are worthy opponents, they will correct and strengthen exposed flaws where others have successfully attacked.

In summary, if you are dealing with a difficult problem, find those who have dealt with it before, and adapt and improve the solution, making it yours.

12 – The Abacus

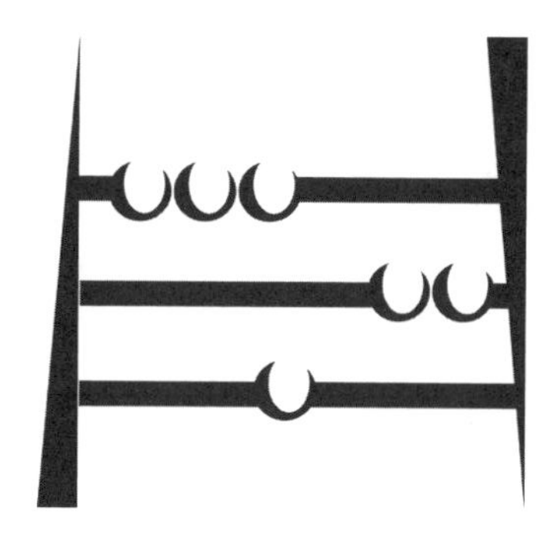

AKA—Measuring Opportunities in Numbers

HERE IS ONE of my favorite Abacus calculations of all time (in regards to expense).... It applies to you!

How much time will you have spent watching television (or on social media) in your lifetime? Write your guesstimate here:

I've learned the hard way that your information is only as good as your accuracy to measure. The truth of it is, we probably waste far more time than we imagine, so let's try to get a better idea. As an example, this is how I would calculate it, and I would encourage you to calculate your numbers accordingly:

The average American watches four to five hours of television per day. Let's assume you watch just two.

2 x 7 = 14 hours per week

14 x 52 = 728 hours per year

The average life of an American is about seventy-six years. Granted, you probably aren't watching television as a newborn.... Then again, maybe you are.

728 x 76 = 55,328 hours in a lifetime

55,328 hours in a lifetime ÷ 24 = 2,305 days of television

2,305 days of television ÷ 365 = 6.31 years

This is the kicker because this is straight—we would have to adjust for sleeping time. Say the average night's sleep is eight hours or one-third of the hours in a day.

6.31 x 1.33 = 8.21 effective years in front of the television

Keep in mind this calculation is just for two hours a day of television!

What if you are among those who fall into the four-, six-, or eight-hour category?

Sometimes, just knowing the expense is all that is needed for change.

All strategic measures of efficiency begin with an objective calculation. The Abacus is the idea of using numbers to measure how efficient a course of action may or may not be.

Let me give you another scenario that has two parts. Answer honestly, truthfully, and as quickly as you can:

Part 1

Let's assume you are about to purchase your dream car for $30,000. It is amazing in every way and everything you hoped and dreamed it would be. Then the salesperson confides to you: "I know I'm not really supposed to tell you this, but if you walk ten minutes down the street, our other dealership has the same exact model on sale for ten dollars less. That's right, it is only $29,990!"

Would you walk to the other dealership, ten minutes away, to save that ten dollars?

Mark your answer:

___No, I would not walk to the other location to save $10.

___Yes, I would walk to the other location to save $10.

Part 2

Let's assume you are about to purchase the most amazing bath soap in the world for fifteen dollars. The smell alone is incredible; you wonder how it can possibly be legal to sell such a bath soap without a medical license! The cashier confides to you: "I know I'm not really supposed to tell you this, but if you walk ten minutes down to the end of the mall, our other store has the same exact bath soap on sale for ten dollars less. That's right; it is only five dollars!"

Would you walk to the other store, ten minutes away, to save that ten dollars?

Mark your answer:

___No, I would not walk to the other location to save $10.

___Yes, I would walk to the other location to save $10.

Interestingly, most people answer each of the above questions differently. They typically buy the original car at $30,000 and then walk to the other lotion store to save ten dollars. However, when a computer is asked these same questions, it sees the cost-to-benefit ratios as exactly the same.

Both scenarios are asking: **Is it worth ten minutes of your time to save ten dollars**?

Answer that question here:

This exercise implies that human decision-making is not always objective or consistent. We make many decisions based on ever-changing emotions. Computers do not use emotion to calculate. They look at numerical values to determine differences. Human decision-making is often inconsistent and illogical, so it introduces inefficiency. The more we can teach ourselves to look at decisions objectively, the more efficiency we can enjoy.

The Abacus is any tool that allows you to measure numerically what would be gained or lost in a particular transaction, before it happens. This is referred to by some as a "cost-to-benefit" analysis or CBA.

Consider using the Abacus (CBA) if:

- You find yourself saying: "But I just don't have any time."
- You are unaware of your monthly expenses, within twenty dollars.
- You are unaware of how much money you spend on clothing per year.
- Your debt is steadily growing.

- You are gaining more weight than you are comfortable with.
- You find yourself depressed or thinking negatively.
- You find yourself surrounded by people who make you feel unhappy.

Most people would like to make more money, have more spare time, or have more opportunities which they believe will bring them more happiness. Successful entrepreneurs know it's okay to spend hundreds of millions of dollars on something if it will earn at least that much or more. They understand the Abacus.

Since the mid-1990s, we have heard countless stories of celebrities and lottery winners who were worth millions of dollars but suddenly declared bankruptcy. While some of these same celebrities might generate speculation about their judgment by tattooing their faces, how is it possible for people to squander hundreds of millions of dollars and end up broke?

The answer is simple: Their expenses exceeded their income.

How someone could spend that kind of money is mind-boggling!

Time is a little different. You cannot get more than twenty-four hours in your day. Because your *time income* is fixed, the only chance you have of regulating it is by controlling your *time expense*.

Consider the following equation:

Income – Expense = Total Gain

I know what you are thinking. "Duh, I know that." It's a simple and powerful equation. Let's look at the laws associated with this equation:

1. If income is maintained, and expense decreased, *total gain* goes up.

For this law, I will include an example; you can make up your own for the rest. Try them. They are solid.

Let's pretend you are a world champion heavyweight boxer and you make about 100 million per year. You are taxed fifty million, and your living expense is about seventy million. The equation of *total gain* would look like this:

$$100 - 120 = -20 \text{ Million}$$

You are now twenty million dollars in the hole.

If you know you will make another 100 million next year, and you decide to quit buying BMWs for all your friends (true, that is a very nice thing to do), you may be able to *squeeze by* on forty million a year in expenses, plus the 50 million in taxes, or ninety million total. The equation now looks like this:

$$100 - 90 = +10 \text{ Million}$$

Your income or taxes didn't change, yet you have more total gain. While we all aren't making 100 million a year, I use this illustration to point out that, while your income is important (I often call income "offense"), your expenses ("defense") must be managed. Same income, very different final score.

(Note: Great success has the ability to really mess people up. Sometimes the worst thing for a person's happiness is to have a whole lot of time, money, and food and not know what to do with it. Often our sense of increased income far exceeds our mental restraint. Another tendency I see time and again.)

Other inferred laws of this equation:

- If income goes up, and expenses stay the same, you will have more total gain (obviously).
- The fastest way to have a large total gain is to increase income and decrease expenses simultaneously.
- You will experience the greatest net loss when expenses go up and income goes down. This is a good thing when it has to do with caloric intake (where income is what you eat and expense is what you burn off in exercise). It is bad if you are used to an NFL salary and suddenly retire.
- If both income and expense decrease, you can have more total gain if expenses decrease faster than income.
- If both expenses and income increase, but expenses increase faster than income, you will still eventually be broke.

This total gain equation can also be rewritten as:

Benefit – Cost = Worth It?

It basically means, if you want something, what do you have to give up, and would it be worth it? I prefer to use this equation more than anything else because it can include many kinds of variables: time, emotion, social benefits, or even experience, not just money.

The simplest example I use to teach this to children is in regards to ice cream.

Most children love ice cream, which is the *benefit*. Almost everyone would be willing to pay one dollar (the cost) for an amazing scoop of ice cream. Giving up a dollar for an amazing scoop of ice cream is definitely worth it.

What about five to ten dollars? Maybe in rare circumstances, where certain exotic flavors and higher ratios of fat content are involved—yes...*sometimes,* it's worth it.

What about fifty dollars? Never. Not even for the best ice cream in the world. *It just isn't worth it.* The benefit of delicious ice cream hasn't changed. It was the expense to benefit that changed and, therefore, made it undesirable.

In summary, the Abacus is simply the idea of measuring income minus expense to show what you will be left with. Its applications are infinite and powerful, because it allows us to come up with a numerical value to measure the probability of success before we even begin. By using a measurable number, we are less likely to make impulse mistakes based on whims, subjective information, emotions or "unknowns." It helps us predict the chances of success.

A calculated plan of financial efficiency begins with the prospect of gain or loss, in terms of measurable numbers.

13 – The Money Clock

AKA—Personal Time Value or PTV

BECAUSE TIME IS a valuable, irreplaceable resource, you can, and should, apply a monetary value to every hour of your time. This is what I call "Personal Time Value" (PTV). Determining your PTV is one of the essential exercises I share with photographers at workshops because it helps them determine how much to charge clients for varying types of jobs. If this principle is the only one you learn from this book, it will be worth the cost (price to buy the book + time it took to read it) a thousand times over.

If you are paid by the hour, it is safe to estimate your PTV at your hourly wage. This is essentially your price for giving up your free time. In reality, it will be less than your hourly wage because you have prep and travel time involved.

If you work on salary, the fastest way to determine your hourly rate is to take your weekly wage and divide it by the number of hours you spend working at, commuting to, preparing for, and thinking about your job. Be sure to factor in your traveling expenses as well. The resulting number should give you a pretty solid idea of what your time is worth.

For example:

As a grad student, I was making about two dollars an hour for my time in the lab as well as teaching. I was willing to do this because my tuition was also covered, but in terms of a paycheck, this is what I was actually bringing home for my time invested.

Then I started cleaning swimming pools in my spare time, making about twenty dollars an hour. Then I started doing wedding videos making about thirty dollars an hour. Then I started doing photography, which earned me about forty dollars an hour.

By knowing my PTV, I had a measuring stick for each new opportunity from a purely numerical perspective, and it made my decision-making process faster and easier. When I started a new job where I made more money, I stopped doing the work that paid less.

However, it also told me what one hour of my idle time was worth. If I wasn't doing anything at all, that one hour should be worth forty dollars to me now, because that's how much I could be earning if I *were working.*

Think of your time as currency because it is your most valuable resource. When you look at your time as having an actual monetary value attached to it, you tend to waste it less. You will also begin to see the value of your time when deciding whether or not to take on certain new opportunities, and reject most of them.

Your PTV will also allow you to calculate the value of "lost time." With photographers, I would teach my students to include their editing time, travel time, shooting time, prep time, etc. in creating a custom quote for a new job. If their PTV is forty dollars an hour, and the total workflow was eight hours for a particular job, plus expenses, then they should bill $320 plus expenses *minimum, or reject that opportunity.* Setting a benchmark related to your PTV can make these types of choices simple and automatic because you know where your time is best spent.

Many people will take up your time for various reasons. Just make sure the benefit they are offering is worth the time and effort you are losing.

Calculate and write your current PTV here:

You now have a benchmark by which to reject all less-efficient employment opportunities. Focus on creating a job or opportunity that pays more than this per hour of your time, and you will be increasing your income efficiency.

Your PTV will also serve as a valuable tool to determine daily CBA calculations by allowing you to convert your time into a financial value:

PTV & CBA Example 1A—The Car Wash

Is it more efficient to wash your car by hand, or more efficient to pay for an automated car wash? The answer will vary depending on your PTV. Let's keep it simple and assume the "cleanliness" of the finished car in both cases is identical, and the car wash is nearby.

If you washed your car by hand, it would take a total of forty-five minutes, with an expense of $1 for soap and supplies.

A car wash will take three minutes through the wash, with an additional total of twelve minutes to drive there round-trip, and it will cost $12 for a similar quality wash.

In such an example, I would draw up a comparison table that would look like this, listing relative expenses under each choice:

Wash by Hand	Automated Car Wash
45 Minutes $1	15 Minutes $12

I like to line up similar resources, in this case, time, followed by money. I then subtract the lowest common similarities from each side, giving what the differences in cost are for each situation:

Wash by Hand	Automated Car Wash
30 Additional Minutes	$11 More Dollars

In this case, we are essentially giving up thirty minutes of our time to save $11.

If I am a struggling high school or college student, I might only be making $8/hr. In such a case, thirty additional minutes of my time to wash by hand would be worth $4. If so, it would be more cost-efficient to wash the car by hand, instead of paying $11 more dollars for the car wash. Thus saving $7 in cash.

If I am a successful wedding photographer, and I am making $40/hr, thirty more minutes of my time (to wash by hand) would be worth $20. If so, it would be more cost-efficient to wash the car with the car wash being $11 more, saving $9 in time.

This is the heart of PTV in a CBA analysis. You treat your time as money, and calculate accordingly. (Note: this exact type of analysis can also be used to determine whether it is more efficient to dine in or eat out).

PTV & CBA Example 2—When It Is "Worth It" to Fly First Class!

I was recently traveling to Hawaii with three heavy bags. Originally, my one-way ticket was $350, but there was an upgrade option of $250 for a first class seat. The catch was that in economy, I would have to pay for each bag, but I noticed that first class passengers get three bags up to 70lbs free. I also saw the benefit of sitting in first class as quite valuable for the six-hour flight.

Economy Class charges the following:

1st Bag: $25

2nd Bag: $35

3rd Bag: $125

But each bag over 50 lbs., would require an additional $50 charge.

I had three bags, two under 50 lbs., one just under 70. I could, therefore, calculate my total baggage fees for Economy to be: $25 + $35 + 125 + $50 = $235 in baggage fees.

This is how my table was then set up:

Economy	First Class
$235 more	$250 more

I then subtract the lowest cost from each side:

Economy	First Class
	$15 More

Who wouldn't pay an additional $15 to fly in first class?

I initially balked when I saw the upgrade fee of $250, but quickly crunching the numbers proved to me what the better choice was. I look for this opportunity every chance I get when flying with many heavy bags.

PTV & CBA Example 3—Is It More Efficient to Travel by Car or Plane?

Let's say you and your business partner need to travel from Utah to Hollywood to meet with agents interested in your latest film. As part of your agreement with your partner, you need to pay all the travel expenses for the two of you. You have two options:

1. You can drive in your Prius hybrid, which will cost about $180 in gas for the round trip, as well as a full day (about eleven hours) of driving each way. Or twenty-two hours of total travel time.

2. Or you can fly. Round trip tickets are $150 each, or $300 for the both of you, and you will spend about four hours traveling. You will also need a rental car once you arrive, which will be about $150 total.

You will also need a hotel once in Hollywood in both cases.

This is how I arrange my CBA Chart:

Drive to Hollywood	Fly to Hollywood
22 Hours of Travel $180 in Gas Hotel	8 Hours of Travel $300 in Tickets $150 Rental Car Hotel

Hotels cancel each other out because the cost is the same in both situations. So we can reduce the charts to...

Drive to Hollywood	Fly to Hollywood
22 Hours of Travel $180 in Gas	8 Hours of Travel $300 in Tickets $150 Rental Car

Then add up our costs to fly:

Drive to Hollywood	Fly to Hollywood
22 Hours of Travel $180 in Gas	8 Hours of Travel $450 Tickets/Rental

Giving our total expense in time and money each option.

I then subtract the $180 it would cost to drive from the $450 it would cost to fly...

Drive to Hollywood	Fly to Hollywood
22 Hours of Travel	8 Hours of Travel $270 More

$450 Airfare - $180 Fuel = $270

I then subtract the eight hours it would take to fly from the twenty-two hours it would take to drive...

22 – 8 = 14

The chart becomes...

Drive to Hollywood	Fly to Hollywood
14 More Hours of Travel	$270 More

14 Hours vs. $270

This narrows it down to a *binary decision.* Is traveling an extra fourteen hours worth $270? If you know your PTV, in my case forty dollars an hour, and multiple that by fourteen hours, it would be the equivalent of $560 in time for me.

Once we narrow it down like this, we can see flying would be much more cost-efficient.

Despite starting with discordant assets, these are simple ways to make them comparable, and one of the most common ways to do this is to convert your time into a monetary value using PTV.

These types of CBA and PTV calculations are at the heart of making cost and time efficient decisions.

Keep in mind, this book's purpose is not to turn you into an efficiency freak, or someone who spends so much time thinking about efficiency that he or she becomes *wasteful* in doing so. Instead, it is aimed at helping you create healthy habits so you can quickly determine which option is more efficient in a given situation.

P.S. A word about self-sabotage:

Self-sabotage is your ability to make your life worse if you don't carefully calculate the consequences of your planned actions. Self-sabotage happens to us daily, sometimes intentionally. It can also be the result of carelessness (saying what you think in the heat of the moment) or forgetfulness (wasting time trying to find something you misplaced).

I recently read a story about a professional football player who was kicked off his team for fighting. Apparently, this player was upset with his teammates because they received a free pair of headphones when he did not. The headphones probably cost a few hundred dollars at most, and he could have purchased as many as he wanted with his salary. This is a great example of self-sabotage because this player was unable to consider the CBA of complaining over a free headset that he could have just purchased. He lost a contract worth hundreds of thousands of dollars because of his ego. Not a smart financial decision.

If you believe that every decision you make has an investment (cost) as well as a result (benefit), you will be much more careful to measure the consequences of your actions in advance.

14 – The Coin

AKA—Binary Decision-Making

AS WE JUST saw, *binary decision-making* is the strategy of removing the variables common to both choices until you are only considering two simple factors. Then you simply weigh these two choices against what is most important to you and the decision should become much easier.

But what if there aren't numbers to measure, or what if one of the choices has to do with money or time and the other something abstract, such as a feeling or experience? What about those rare times when you are faced with a decision about an unfamiliar topic, and the more you think about it, the more unsure you are? Having a systematic way to cut to the heart of the matter will greatly enhance your decision-making ability, saving you valuable time and increasing your efficiency. Let's explore binary decision making further.

A simple example might be deciding where to get a great burger for dinner tonight: 5 Guys or Red Robin.

The core variables in this decision are:

1. Find a great burger for dinner.

2. Don't spend a fortune.

3. Have a great dessert with it.

Both restaurants offer fabulous, equally tasty burgers. Therefore, variable one can be eliminated from consideration, unless you are looking for a very specific-tasting burger.

While 5 Guys is more affordable, Red Robin has a better selection, and *both have reasonable prices*. I would, therefore, eliminate variable two from consideration.

When we start looking at the dessert menu, the differences really start to become apparent. While 5 Guys has delicious milkshakes, Red Robin has an entire arsenal of desserts, including shakes, mud pies, and bottomless root beer floats.

In this case, the binary decision would be:

- Would I rather have a simple shake or an assortment of choices?

I can make my decision from there since all other factors are eliminated because they are *similar enough.*

However, let's say the speed of service was one of my core variables instead of dessert selection. In that case, 5 Guys would have the edge.

This is the heart of binary decision-making. Eliminate common traits of each choice, find out what the real differences are, and compare them with what is more valuable to you.

Let's look at another example:

Kearstin is considering summer employment. Her key variables are:

1. Make as much money as possible
2. Have fun over the summer at work

Job A pays ten dollars an hour and is at a super-fun waterpark.

Job B Pays twelve dollars an hour and is at a boring office.

Even though fun is not something that can be measured in numbers, it is still valuable for consideration and should be included in our chart:

Work at Water Park	Work at Office
$10/hr FUN!	$12/hr No Fun!

I subtract ten dollars from both sides because it is common:

Work at Water Park	Work at Office
FUN!	$2/hr More No Fun!

Because the experience is for the entire summer, I would try to estimate the total financial value of that extra $2/hour, at 40 hours per week, for about 12 total weeks:

$2/hr x 40 hours x 12 weeks = $960 before taxes

$960 – 15% tax, or $144 (assuming Kearstin is in this tax bracket) = $816

Work at Water Park	Work at Office
FUN!	$816 More No Fun!

In this case, the binary decision comes down to either having a fun job or getting $816 more over the summer. Kearstin should choose depending on which core variable is more important to her, either money or fun. If she is trying to buy her own car, that extra $816 might make a huge difference.

Let's consider a final, more complex example:

You are about to publish a book, and you are considering two highly-recommended editors:

Editor A will cost $3,000, has multiple bestselling books, lives far away, comes highly recommended, and needs two months to edit your book.

Editor B will cost $1,500, has never edited a book, lives in your town, comes highly recommended, and says it will take three months to edit your book.

Your core variables are:

1. Quality
2. Cost
3. Speed of delivery
4. Recommendations

I would create a table of variables, just as I did in my CBA + PTV examples:

Editor A	**Editor B**
$3,000 Experienced Lives Far Away Recommended 2 Months	$1,500 Inexperienced Lives Nearby Recommended 3 Months

In this case, I would eliminate the recommendations as well as the distance—distance is not a core variable when publishing a book:

Editor A	Editor B
$3,000 Experienced ~~Lives Far Away~~ ~~Recommended~~ 2 Months	$1,500 Inexperienced ~~Lives Nearby~~ ~~Recommended~~ 3 Months

I would then subtract $1,500 from both sides because it is common:

Editor A	Editor B
$1,500 More Experienced ~~Lives Far Away~~ ~~Recommended~~ 2 Months	~~$1500~~ Inexperienced ~~Lives Nearby~~ ~~Recommended~~ 3 Months

Next, I would subtract two months from both sides because it is common:

Editor A	Editor B
$1500 More Experienced ~~Lives Far Away~~ ~~Recommended~~ ~~2 Months~~	~~$1500~~ Inexperienced ~~Lives Nearby~~ ~~Recommended~~ 1 Month Longer

I would then re-create the table with the remaining variables:

Editor A	Editor B
$1,500 More Experienced	Inexperienced 1 Month Longer

So in this case, the decision would come down to spending *$1,500 more for a faster, more-experienced editor, or adding an additional month to the process with the more-affordable, less-experienced editor.* If quality is more important than cost, then Editor A is best.

Eliminate any decision-making variables that are:

1. Similar
2. Beyond control
3. Irrelevant

And then weigh the decision based on only those variables that are both *unique* and *valuable*. This skill set will take some time to develop, and in some cases, it can become extremely complex. But if you are willing to spend a few minutes going through the process, it can simplify the most difficult decisions.

15 – The Flashlight

AKA—Known > Unknown

"A sparrow in thy hand is better than a thousand sparrows flying."
— Proverbs of Ahiqar, sixth century BCE

AS A YOUNG man, I spent many weekends hiking and camping with my scout group. When playing capture-the-flag in the late nights, we would all carry flashlights, but turning them on would reveal our position to the opposing team, so we used them as seldom as possible. The problem with this was we would often end up tripping over things, running into bushes, losing the trail, or even getting lost until we had no choice but to turn our lights on and find our way back to camp. As we became more sophisticated, we would carry red-filtered lights, so we could see the trail, but the other team couldn't see us. Oh, what a difference in performance when we *knew* the path to follow instead of stumbling into *unknown* directions!

I also use this real world example to introduce a set of tools that build on binary decision-making that I call "binaries." These are a set of "either this or thats" that have a predetermined measuring stick as to which of the two choices is more efficient. By using binaries and even developing your own, you will know immediately which sets of information or choices are more valuable, without having to do any heavy thinking or calculating.

My most used and favorite binary is *Known > Unknown*. I use it several times daily, in countless applications, to guide my decisions. It is my go-to. Let me give you some examples.

Known vs. Unknown Example 1:

Let's assume you earn a $1,000 unexpected bonus. You have a credit card bill for that amount, but your uncle Tony also suddenly has a great idea for a business that he says "will make you rich if you invest just $1,000!"

Write down here which of the two opportunities are best for you, either pay off debt or invest with Uncle Tony. How would you spend that money?

Using the binary "known vs. unknown," I personally would *always* pay the debt off, because it is something I can be absolutely sure of. There is a 100 percent chance of its existence both before and after if I do not pay it. The speculative business opportunity is an *unknown,* and is, therefore, devalued. Without getting into tangents, every new business opportunity usually has not one, but a number of unknowns, and therefore, it is even much less probable than debt. From this concept, I have always advised friends to pay off debt (all of it) before investing.

Known vs. Unknown Example 2:

Let's pretend you are a professional portrait photographer who is asked to do a family session. The client says:

"I don't have much money, but all of my friends and family will see your images on Facebook, and you will get so much referral business from it!"

Let's assume you are an experienced photographer, and the client has no extenuating circumstances and is not your friend; he just wants a free session in exchange for "free exposure" among his family and friends.

Do you shoot the family for free or not? Why? Write your answer here:

You would be astonished by the number of times I have been asked to work for free as a photographer. Like other professionals, photographers spend many thousands of dollars on gear, training, marketing, and countless hours before and after a shoot, yet we are constantly asked to shoot for free. The most common tactic used in pitching this "photos-for-free strategy" is the *promise of exposure on social media.*

The problem with the promise of exposure is that it is uncertain what exactly that exposure is, as well as how much business it will bring. It is an unknown, and from experience, I conclude it is an empty promise and should be discounted immediately. They are offering nothing. By identifying the unknown and immediately discounting it, I have saved significant time and energy by avoiding the shoot.

If a photographer is just beginning and needs practice, I think there is value in doing the right kind of free work, and I even recommend it to certain students struggling with confidence. A skilled professional photographer, however, will be insulted by such a proposal because he or she knows that paying customers refer paying customers, not more strangers who want free photos.

Note: Good professional photographers also know to collect a down payment to schedule and get the final payment *before* the shoot, because demand is *known.* A photographer will always be able to charge and collect more before the wedding than after. The demand for services is *known* before the event, but it becomes *unknown* right after that same big, expensive event because the need has been met. Any photographer who has had to collect payment after the wedding knows it is much harder.

What you *know* is almost always more valuable than what is *unknown* and, therefore, knowns should automatically be given greater consideration and precedence.

Once you get a decision down to a binary choice (either this or that), fifty-fifty, one way or the other, it is very easy to *tilt the scales* in one direction or the other, *based on what is known, or what new information can be learned for certain*.

A friend recently asked me whether I thought his son should accept a football scholarship offer from a smaller college or try to walk-on (no scholarship) at a Division I school and maybe earn one there.

"Go where the offer is; it is certain" was my answer. "You have no idea whether your son will even earn a spot, stay healthy, get playing time, or earn a scholarship at another school." The scholarship at the smaller school was the better offer—*it was certain his tuition would be paid, thus avoiding debt*—that wasn't the case at the other school.

The more unknowns you have in a given choice, the more speculative that choice becomes and the more the unknown choice should be discounted accordingly.

Another play on "known vs. unknown" is the "Control > No Control" binary, which refers to situations where one choice offers an opportunity to maintain control (known) of a situation/project and another gives control away (unknown). This is very useful when working with new employees or vendors, something that is critical if you ever decide to upscale a business.

If no previous data exists about a person's ability to get a job done (an unknown), I'd be extremely cautious about hiring them. Instead of investing a lot of time and money into a first-time hire, do a fast, inexpensive test with them first so that their tendencies will become *known* before going down a long road.

The video production industry would be an example. Most editors promise fast turn around services. I have given editing jobs to a range of professionals. In one case, it took nearly two months for an editor to turn a project around. It slowed everything down. On the next project, we went with someone who was proven, who finished the same sized project in less than a week. If someone is *known* to be reliable, the relationship has a greater chance of succeeding than someone who is unproven. In my world, unprovens are at a disadvantage until I know more about them.

I cannot tell you how many times I consult with friends who are so completely focused on the unknowns; they lose their direction on what they are really trying to accomplish.

"Borrowing trouble" means to assume the worst without any real data to support that conclusion. It will hinder your efficiency because you are not *focused on the task at hand, what you know for sure, or what you can control*, which is where your attention and resources should be.

Efficiency increases when you dismiss the doubts and hesitations that are not based on facts. It's like being afraid to go swimming in a lake for fear there might be sharks present, when it is biologically impossible. Or that your parachute might not open when skydiving (nearly impossible). "Borrowing trouble" or creating stressful, imaginary unknowns is a natural human tendency that should be immediately dismissed.

When faced with a decision that requires any kind of heavy thinking, bias your decisions in the direction of what you know for certain. Even if it is just a little bit of truth, like shining a dim red light on a trail at night, it will be much better than aimlessly walking into pitch black.

Exercise: I have included a list of my favorite and most commonly used binaries in the back of the book. I want you to start looking for your own sets of binaries in your daily life, be it work, travel, relationships, or recreation. Look for opportunities to find these general truths, where one option is almost always more favorable than another, test it out, and when you find a good one, add it to your own personal list of binaries.

Write your first original binary here:

16 – The Surveillance Camera

AKA—The Burden of Proof

"I THINK MY assistant is stealing from me," my good friend Sarah confided. She worked very hard operating a day care out of her home. Sarah has a strange habit of leaving big wads of cash in various places, a kitchen cupboard, the closet or in a desk drawer, but she also had an equally strange ability to keep track of how much money was in each pile.

"Sarah, I would be really shocked if a grown woman, someone who has worked faithfully for years, would suddenly decide to steal money from right under your nose," I replied.

"I *don't know* for sure, but I have this hunch it is her."

There are going to be times you will be faced with a binary decision, as my friend Sarah was—either her assistant was stealing or she was not. It is one or the other, and both possibilities are unknowns because there simply isn't enough data.

The burden of proof is the responsibility to provide irrefutable evidence to prove an idea in opposition to a general assumption.

Proof, for me, means hard evidence that supports an idea. It can be images, video, information, data, witness testimony, or demonstration of skill sets. It is any legitimate content not available to other parties, such as a judge or jury, who would change their opinions if they had this information.

In law, the accused are assumed to be innocent until proven guilty. Therefore, the prosecution assumes the *burden of proof* to provide evidence beyond a reasonable doubt that demonstrates the defendant is, in fact, guilty. It is much more work to assume the burden of proof; however, if you have proof, it is a competitive advantage.

Defendants, who do not assume the burden of proof, carry the *benefit of assumption*. Defendants have the right to plead not guilty. Children, even at a young age, instinctively know: "It wasn't me." **Denial**, in the absence of proof, is usually effective, whether it is true or not. I like to imagine it as a wall that can only be penetrated by truth. Sometimes, defendants will try to **shift the blame** toward another possible culprit to draw attention away from themselves. In the end, without some kind of proof, we cannot and should not say someone is guilty because we may be wrong and it would be a terrible thing to convict an innocent person.

Proof is almost always universally accepted when it can be supported beyond a reasonable doubt. Proof >> Unsupported Assumption.

If proof is provided, there are still some common ways for the defendant defeat it:

1. Provide opposing proof that the evidence, methods used, or those gathering it are flawed.

2. Provide superior evidence to the contrary.

On my YouTube Channel, MichaelTheMaven, I specialize in head-to-head camera tests, which I call Epic Shootouts, usually between competing brands. In my videos, I provide the actual test results to my viewers. I assume the burden of proof intentionally because it gives me a competitive advantage over channels unwilling to do the tests themselves.

Telling someone his camera is flawed or doesn't perform as well as another model is like a punch in the gut, so the next thing that person might do is attack me as being a flawed tester. My opponent's thinking is, *If the test is flawed, the proof here is wrong.* At that point, I refer the person to the evidence I provided in the video supporting my claim.

"Awesome," I tell them. "I would be thrilled to see your published tests and results supporting what you are suggesting." At that point, most of my critics give up. In my eight years on YouTube, on only a handful of occasions have viewers actually gone out and repeated my tests. To their surprise, they got the same results. They even published them, providing even more support for my statements.

The reason I am mentioning this here is that the burden of proof, at least when you have it on your side, is much *more efficient* in terms of decision making and persuasion than just talk or assumption. *Showing evidence >> spoken opinion* (this is another binary).

I look at the burden of proof as an opportunity to magnify positions, accelerate persuasion, and intensify focus. It is a recruiting tool that can help build momentum. If someone has a false assumption, you can destroy it with the burden of proof. Once you do, your enemies are at a tactical disadvantage because they now must provide actual evidence to support their opposing position. Never be afraid to knock it out of the ballpark when you can assume the burden of proof!

Let's come back to the example of my friend who was experiencing theft. She decided to ask her assistant about it and...

"She said it wasn't her (denial). Instead, she suggested that maybe one of the older children might be the culprit (shifting the blame). What should I do?" Sarah asked me.

"Sarah, you cannot blame her for this without evidence (assumption of innocence). You have to get some hardcore evidence before accusing her."

"What should I do?" she repeated. "I've lost almost a thousand dollars."

"Assume the burden of proof. Buy some cheap, small video cameras and set them up in the areas where you have money."

Sure enough, within a single day of setting up the hidden security cameras, Sarah sent me a video of this grown woman sneaking around her home, reaching into cupboards and envelopes, taking money out of them. I was shocked, but the proof at this point was irrefutable. Sarah immediately fired her assistant and that was that.

There will be times when, despite your very best resources and attempts, you will be unable to acquire the data and proof you need to make a good "known" decision. If discovering the truth isn't possible, we still have some other tools at our disposal.

17 – The Chart

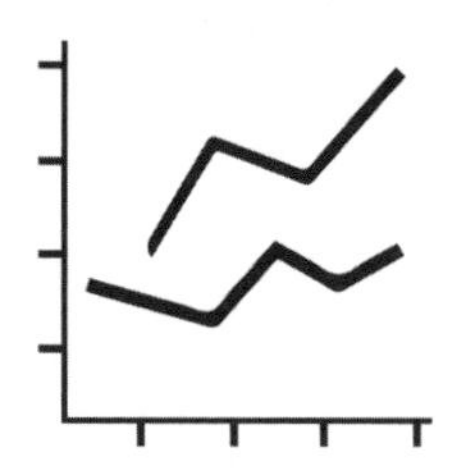

AKA—Inference and Probability

EXPERIENCED POKER PLAYERS know the **probabilities** of what other cards are in the deck *based on what cards have already been played.*

Medical professionals can *diagnose* patients' illnesses based on certain symptoms.

Meteorologists can predict the weather based on previous data.

While none of these examples are perfectly accurate, they still allow decision makers to tilt the scales of a decision in a certain direction, without having all of the data, based on probabilities.

The skill of extracting usable, mostly-reliable probabilities based on limited evidence is referred to as *inference*.

For me, probabilities carry more weight than unknowns, but less weight than knowns when weighing my decision-making processes. The complete scheme follows this order:

Knowns > Probabilities > Unknowns

Inference is coming to a logical conclusion based on something that is assumed to be true. I like to think of *inference* as extracting new information from a fact. We can also extract new information from complete unknowns by performing little tests. In either case, the better *probable* information you have about something, the more accurately you should be able to make critical choices.

(Note: To be technical, deductive reasoning and inductive reasoning are both forms of *inference*. Because I see deductive conclusions as facts (knowns), and inductive conclusions as probabilities with uncertainties, I am focusing on inductive inference as a tool of efficiency in this chapter since it will still hold a degree of uncertainty. Let me give you two quick examples:

Deductive Inference: All of the chairs in this house are blue; therefore, the chairs in the kitchen are blue.

Inductive Inference: In a particular house, chairs in the kitchen, dining room, and living room are blue; therefore, the chairs in the bedrooms are *probably blue.*

Inductive inference is an assumption that still may be incorrect.

Every day, you will have new ideas, opportunities, and even people coming into your life, much like wind blowing seeds into a garden. Soon these seeds start to grow, but the problem is that it is very difficult to determine whether these are weeds or fruit-bearing plants. Fruit-bearing plants can be delicious and wonderful, but they take a lot of time to nurture. Weeds can rob the garden of resources and even kill the good plants already growing. Weeds are also much easier to pull when they are young.

I know that the sooner I can identify exactly what a new seedling is, the faster I can nurture, reject, or destroy that seedling, *which accordingly increases my efficiency.* Much like a gardener who carefully inspects the leaves of a young seedling, so too can we *infer* what something is early on.

For example, when looking for a new programmer, I can usually *infer* how good a potential hire's communication skills are based on *how quickly he or she returns my initial messages.* If I reach out to a programmer about a potential job and I do not hear back for several days, I *know*: he was slow to return my message. From this fact, I can *infer* that either he *probably* has weak communication skills, my communication was not important to him, or maybe a more pressing matter surfaced.

I can further *infer* that because this person failed to return my message promptly, *future communications would also probably be slow.*

I can also *infer* that *if future communications will probably be slow, it will probably take him much longer to finish the project than someone who communicates faster.*

I can also *infer* that because I am a new business prospect, *it will probably be even more difficult to communicate with this individual as time progresses and I am not a new customer.*

While these inferences may not actually be true, my experience has shown that more often than not, they *are mostly accurate.* If the individual is indeed an exceptional talent and communicator, but just missed my call, the burden is on his shoulders to make it up to me. Otherwise, I know this prospect is slow to respond and I can look elsewhere, saving me time, money, and effort in my search, and, therefore, *inference makes my decision-making more efficient*.

This is also a part of what I call the **Honeymoon Test**.

Honeymoons are classically thought of as a celebration of a new partnership. Both parties are hot for each other. They want to make the other person happy, and both are looking forward to the long, yet exciting road ahead. If everything is working right, the relationship should be fun, easy, and mutually beneficial during the honeymoon phase. I also think it is pretty safe to say that problems will arise in time, tempers will be tested, and frustrations will emerge.

When in a new relationship, take any red flags you see and multiply their negative effects by ten. If those effects are bearable at ten times their power, it is a good indication that the two of you will be able to make it work. If they are not, the relationship should end immediately.

I cannot tell you how many times I have been in the following situation: I hire a potential programmer or attorney, someone who has come highly recommended by a trusted friend. After doing what research I can, and when initial contact is made, mutual interests are shown and it seems that the work is about to begin—we both feel excited about the opportunity and it looks like a wonderful relationship will ensue. Then, exactly two days later, I call or email, and for whatever reason, that call is not returned. I wait a day or two. Try again. Nothing. After some time, the person finally calls back, apologizes, and tells me about his busy schedule. If it happens in the early stages of communications, I can infer it will most likely get worse with time.

Flip the scenario around. Pretend you are a wedding photographer and have a new potential client. She was referred to you by a friend, knows who you are, and says she is ready to book. When you ask for the deposit to reserve the day, she says she will have it in the mail tomorrow, and it arrives exactly when it should (at that point, she is a "known"). As someone who has shot a lot of weddings, I know this is a customer you want to keep. From those early indicators, you would be well-advised to focus on her and keep her happy, much more so than the bride who says she "wants to think about it" (an unknown) or tries to negotiate with you. Focus your strengths on the "known" opportunities instead of hard-to-get, "unknown" ones.

Both of these examples are classic illustrations of *inference*, which is to take a fact and extract actionable probabilities, *even though they may not be necessarily true.* This information is far better than not knowing what to expect at all. It will also give you greater chances of success than just flipping a coin.

Inference is also used in the scientific method—something we all use daily. The way I taught the scientific method to my students in college was the acronym, O?HET:

1. We make an Observation.

2. We ask a question (?) about that observation.

3. We form a Hypothesis, which is an educated guess.

4. We Experiment to find data to support or refute the hypothesis.

5. We form a Theory based on our results.

Let me give you an example. A photographer arrived on one of our sets to take some stills for print and advertising to market a film I was working on. He said he was a full-time professional, but:

1. I *observed* he was carrying a low-end, low-resolution, much older digital camera.

2. I *asked* myself, "Is this guy really a professional using that kind of camera?"

3. I inferred, "He probably isn't a pro photographer." (In this case, I used inference to form a *hypothesis*).

4. My *experimentation* was to watch this photographer carefully during his shoot, gathering more data. This is what I observed:

    - He was using a kit lens.
    - He was shooting on too wide a focal length, distorting the subjects.
    - He was using a much too slow shutter speed for handheld work.
    - His compositions were weak.
    - He did not or could not properly set his white balance, even after seeing it was way off on his monitor.
    - He shot JPEGs in mixed lighting conditions.
    - He seemed unaware of the direction of the best quality light.

5. None of these observations were consistent with what would be expected from a professional photographer on a professional shoot. From gathering this data, I *inferred* he was probably not a professional photographer.

It is important to note that despite all of these observations and assumptions, he still could have been a pro. *It was just very unlikely in my mind.* Sure enough, a few weeks later, we learned the advertising company needed new images in order to create the movie poster art.

Inference, when correctly applied, allows keen observers to tip the scales of probability in one direction or another of a binary decision.

Inference is used accurately and regularly in a number of professions and social settings.

There are many statistical tools I use in my camera training video business to know which cameras to focus on and which to ignore, based on their relative popularity. Spending a month creating and promoting a training video for a camera few would purchase would be a tremendous waste of time and resources. These statistical tools help steer my decisions, instead of just making a video for every single camera that comes out.

Police detectives are able to infer evidence based on related facts. The more evidence they gather about a suspect—a motive, a witness, the suspect's DNA at the crime scene, the suspect being in possession of stolen property—the better they can infer, conclude, or offer high probability that a specific suspect did, in fact, commit a crime.

You probably have close friends whose *body language* or *facial expressions* tell you exactly what *mood* they are in.

I lived in Norway with my grandparents as a high school freshman. One time, my grandmother gave me money for the subway to go downtown. It wasn't more than a couple of dollars, and there was some change left over. I came home, ate dinner, and started getting ready for bed. Eventually, my grandmother came knocking on the door. She asked whether there was any change left from the subway money she had given me. I said there was. She then asked why I hadn't returned it to her. I explained that I assumed she was giving the rest of the change to me. I'll never forget her answer:

"No, Michael, I didn't. I gave you money for the fare; that was all."

At the time, I thought my grandmother was being a control freak, but eventually, I realized she was right. The change was minimal, but it was still hers, and I had made an incorrect assumption. I learned a very important lesson.

Many times since then, I have used this same technique to discover the tendencies of someone I am dealing with. I'll give someone an opportunity of pure trust to see whether he or she will take a little more or nothing at all. My longtime assistant Adam has always returned change and receipts when I send him out to purchase something. I don't even have to ask. That is a really good indicator that you can trust someone. Other assistants whom I have sent out on similar errands will sometimes keep the change.

Many times, I have lent out gear, only to have it returned dirty or damaged. I'll have someone ask me for an hour of my time that turns into two or three. Whenever someone takes a little more than he or she should, a little red flag goes up in my mind.

I can infer whether or not a person is sincere by how accurately he does exactly as he says he will. If someone commits to you, and falls short of that commitment time and again, it is probably a good way to infer that he cannot be trusted with greater risks.

Be extremely cautious about exercising too much trust in someone who nibbles away at your trust in him. If it happens, all is not lost; it can be a tremendous learning opportunity. If it is a pattern that goes unchecked, especially after confronting him, the relationship will unravel, so in most cases, the sooner you get out of it the better.

Use caution with inference:

- If your evidence is not accurate, your inferred assumptions will also be inaccurate.

- Be extremely careful about speaking in absolutes when using inference because you are going to be wrong occasionally, even when using the best inductive reasoning.

In summary, while most decisions can be simplified to an "either this or that" type of choice, *the probabilities can often be tilted in favor of one direction by using inference.*

P.S. If you infer, always use disclaimers:

When I was in grad school, we had to give these regular presentations about the research we were doing, and I quickly learned that you never say things like:

"My information proves..."

"The only logical explanation..."

"You would be an idiot not to realize..."

"I now know..."

"This is why you are wrong..."

Instead, we would always leave some room for error, saying things like:

"The data suggests..."

"This leads us to believe..."

"This somewhat implies..."

"The probability is high that..."

"Unless I am misunderstanding..."

"I may be wrong, but..."

This way, if you are ever called out, and you are wrong, you do not have to feel the need to defend an indefensible position. You can follow up with:

"This new information contradicts previous data that led me to believe otherwise."

"That would now lead us to believe...."

"There is now better probability...."

"Yes...it seems I misunderstood."

All of these disclaimers and qualifiers lower the potential for friction you might encounter when using inference and deduction incorrectly.

18 – Know Thy Frenemy

AKA—Not All Friends Are Friends

THE NATURE OF a pure enemy is simple; he wants to destroy you. You set up your defenses, devise counterattacks, or try to avoid your enemy altogether. No benefit exists in interacting with him, and he feels the same way about you. You are always on your guard when it comes to your true enemies, and there is no misunderstanding about your relationship.

You are also surrounded by and interact with a much more dangerous foe: the **frenemy**. *The frenemy is someone (or something) who is simultaneously both your friend and enemy.*

A good friend of mine, Suzi, recently shared an experience she had with a new friend of hers. They both enjoyed dining out, so they decided to have lunch together and split the bill. After some time, Suzi noticed that while she preferred less expensive salads, her new friend would order far more expensive meals, often taking home the leftovers. With more time, her new friend added second meals to go, even while they were still "splitting the bill." Suzi's new friend had found a way to shift at least some of the expense of her eating habits onto Suzi.

You may know about the experiment in which you place a frog in a pot of room-temperature water and gradually increase the heat. The frog doesn't realize it is being cooked, and by the time it does, it is much too late. This situation is typically what happens in frenemy-type relationships.

The nature of such a "frenemous" relationship is confusing and sometimes impossible to identify. True friends are willing to sacrifice for each other without any expectation of return because of sincere love for each other. Frenemies are beneficial, but they demand something in return or sometimes steal it. You both benefit from the relationship in meaningful ways, and yet at the same time, frenemies compete against or even hurt each other. Often, we only see the benefit side of the relationship, dismissing the negative. This seduces us into believing that this person (or thing) is really our friend, period. A really good chance even exists that many of your frenemies are so beneficial that there is no easy way for you to cut them out of your life.

Here are some examples of frenemies:

- The other running back competing for that one spot in the starting lineup. In the locker room, you are buddies. In the gym, you might work out together and even encourage one another. On the practice field, he might secretly want you to fail so he will get more playing time.

- Money is a powerful frenemy. Does it work for you, or do you work for it? It's a beneficial tool that can easily become an unjust slave master.

- Television: Are you watching desired programs for information, or does the device tell you what to watch? Are you being brainwashed?

- Price gougers who invade disaster areas, overcharging locals because they need that tree-cutting service so desperately to make their homes livable again.

- Friends and family members who want to dump their problems into your lap without any cost to them.

- The overly-friendly photographer who occasionally gives you referrals, and likes to pick your brain, but who never wants to pay for your trade secrets or give you credit for teaching her. In a few months, she will be marketing your secrets as her own.

- Social Media: It can be extremely beneficial for both business and social interactions—it can also be extremely detrimental and a phenomenal waste of time. The same applies to many, many other websites.

- And last, but not least...the Smart Phone—probably the most invasive and dominating frenemy of our modern society. We operate them while driving, resulting in fatal car accidents. We cannot walk into a restaurant without seeing a multitude of heads aimed down, typing away. These powerful, miniature, potentially-life-saving, always-with-you, easy-to-access, super-computers/communication devices serve us valuably in many ways, but they also invade our daily lives, depriving us of both time and truly meaningful human interaction.

Chances are you have a handful of frenemies who are causing the most damage. If you have been unaware of the concept, dealing with them is what really matters right now. In fact, I would strongly encourage you to make a list of your top 2-3 frenemies. The first step is knowing who they are and how they take advantage of you.

Who are your frenemies and why are you certain they are? (Write your answer here):

Unfortunately, I cannot tell you how to deal with your frenemies specifically. Although I can give you five helpful tactics to maintain the upper hand in dealing with, and perhaps even ridding yourself of them:

Anti-Frenemy Tactic 1: Control: The first step is to recognize and to establish control over the frenemy. You must actively work toward controlling your interactions with him or her and the results of those interactions. Reducing the amount of power they have over you and shifting more control to your position is critical. More importantly, *your frenemies must feel that they are still the ones in control of the relationship and winning (very important).* This is not an easy balance. We want the frenemy to feel like he has you just where he wants you, knows everything you are doing, and feels confident that you are not a threat to him. You want him to let his guard down. You want him to have a feeling of complacency, without any sense of urgency or inspiration to attack. You want him feeling you are extremely predictable, so when a moment of truth comes, you do the opposite of what he expects.

Anti-Frenemy Tactic 2: Compartmentalization: Frenemies are most dangerous when there are no limits to their access to you or what they feel they can take. When you compartmentalize them—limit their access to you physically, mentally, or financially—it reduces their ability to engage you. The compartment can be opened when you wish, allowing for beneficial exchange. **Example:** Put your smartphone into a drawer or some other inaccessible place when you are trying to work. If the distraction is removed, it won't be able to invade when you are trying to be productive. I have a saying I use daily—"Compartmentalization until completion!" That means my phone is going into a drawer in a different room until I am finished with the task at hand. I have been told by friends using my efficiency playbook that compartmentalization of their smartphone was the single most important piece of advice from this book that changed their lives. Something I often do during big projects, is **I won't even look at my phone** until after lunch. It is amazing how productive I am when I do this.

Anti-Frenemy Tactic 3: Conceal: Hide your intentions and plans from your frenemies, no matter how much that plan may be worth sharing. Secrecy is only beneficial when it is held *unknown* to the targets. Once they have a blueprint of your intentions, they can build a response. Secrecy is much more efficient when it is maintained. **Example:** Avoid advertising your intentions to do something, instead act unsure about your plans and make the decision later. If you must give out your plans, leave the option open to change your mind later.

Anti-Frenemy Tactic 4: Counter: When there is an exchange or offer of an exchange of information or services, make sure it is mutually beneficial. This goes both ways. I knew a certain photographer who was an absolute expert at creating situations where it was never a win-win, but rather every deal was at least sixty-forty in her favor. You simply could not interact with or do any business with this woman unless she benefited much more than you did. She made a terrible mistake in not allowing others to profit as much as herself. This same friend was notorious for offering to join me for meals going "Dutch," yet she always "forgot" her purse so she couldn't pay. Important note—if you have identified someone as a "frenemy," always assume that person is out for his or her best interest first. You will have to fight to keep the score even, but in the end, this kind of relationship is difficult to sustain indefinitely. Frenemies use the word "friendship" simply as permission to take advantage of others.

Anti-Frenemy Tactic 5: Cutoff: When possible, end ties to any and all frenemies who are taking advantage of you. These are the friends who are only interested in what you can provide cost-free to them, but rarely if ever do they return the favor. You can expect the same of them if you are a freeloader or mooch.

The principle of the frenemy doesn't feel good, and it isn't easy to admit. If you have a friend who time and again shifts a burden or expense to you with minimal reciprocation, it might be time to take a closer look at it as a means to improve your efficiency.

19 – The Conduit

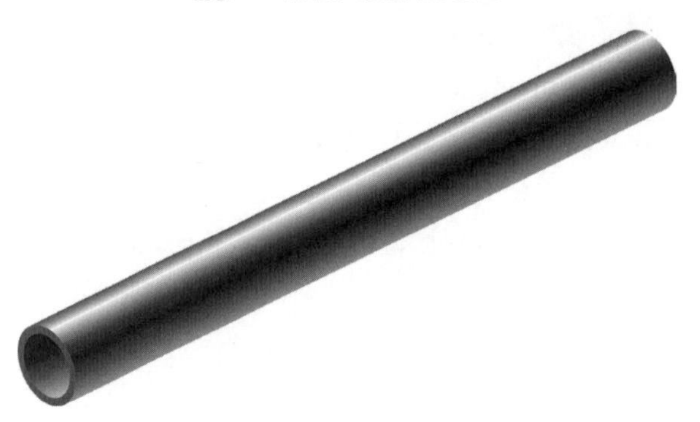

AKA—Information Hot Spots

OUR MINDS ARE constantly receiving ideas, thoughts, and inspirations much like a radio receiver receives a radio signal. Good, bad, and useless signals come in. The more attention we give to certain thoughts, the stronger those signals get. This is true everywhere we are. Anyone who has experienced a moment of inspiration describes it as positive, uplifting, energizing, and exciting. We would love to have access to that possibility twenty-four hours a day, seven days a week. Unfortunately, many of these moments, while useful, are brief and fleeting.

Sometimes, "thought inhibitors" prevent good ideas from entering our minds. With advances in social media and technology and the proliferation of smartphones, many of us face constant inhibition, preventing us from receiving the inspiration otherwise available to us. Our modern age has so many distractions that I am fearful our youth are gradually being more and more limited when it comes to having original thoughts.

What I refer to as a "hot spot" is a set of physical and environmental conditions that allow the human mind to be open and receptive to inspiration and ideas at much greater speed and efficiency than in another location and under a different set of conditions. A hot spot facilitates seemingly endless information flowing directly to the mind.

Chances are you have experienced it yourself. Some will refer to these phenomena as concentration, focus, or lack of distractions. I take it a step further as I believe the geographical location and physical conditions are as important to the principle as the lack of distractions. The location is also context sensitive, meaning that while it may usually work, it can be interfered with by one's surroundings, circumstances, and current state of mind.

A hot spot is different than the flash of inspiration you have probably experienced while driving, going for a walk, or sitting in church because returning to the location and conditions can be exploited intentionally when looking for new ideas. Hot spots can be intentionally initiated, whereas flashes of inspiration are more spontaneous. You know you have a hot spot when you can recreate it anytime you desire, and once you do, you feel overwhelmed by how many specific ideas are coming into your mind. It's like drinking a sip of water from an opened fire hydrant. I do not know whether it is a matter of scenery, sounds, or something magnetic, but I can tell you that when I find a good idea location, I return as often as necessary to benefit from it.

Many of my best ideas in recent years have come while sitting beneath a specific tree at a nearby beach on Maui. I know when I have something important to draft, script, or outline, that is the place to do it. What would take me hours to plan and prepare at home or at my desk takes only minutes under that tree. For whatever reason, it doesn't work as well in other locations.

Here is how you can determine whether you have a hot spot: Take notice of where you are and what you are doing the next time you get a jolt of information, inspiration, or an idea. The next time you have any difficult decision to make, return to that specific location and the circumstances to see whether you can use those conditions so you can intentionally get answers for something else. If the inspiration is repeatable, chances are you have identified a personal hot spot. Bring an empty notepad and pencil, and then exploit the hot spot to your advantage.

While the idea may seem crazy to some, from experience, I know thought processes, planning, consideration, brainstorming, preparing, scripting, and ability to come up with great ideas will all be faster, stronger, and more efficient near a personal hot spot.

Where were you when you had a moment of inspiration, and what were you doing when it happened? Write it down here.

Return to this place and activity the next time you are doing heavy thinking.

20 – The Key

AKA—Fluency and the Efficiency of Languages

"OUR PROFESSION REQUIRES that you learn a new language every six months." My information systems professor made this proclamation with pride. To this day, I cannot see how needing to learn a new language every six months is an advantage.

When I lived in Norway, it took me six months of immersion in a Norwegian-speaking school to pick up the language competently. Those first six months were some of the scariest of my life—going to school and not knowing what the heck my teachers and fellow students were saying to or about me.

I would take several years of German linguistics classes in high school, which I never really learned, and later, when I went on my two-year church mission, I would spend a good four months before I really started to grasp and use Russian.

Learning a new language is agonizing. You feel helpless, stupid, and completely incompetent during that learning phase. In fact, that learning curve *is the friction* before you are capable of doing anything productive with that language.

Imagine how efficient your life would be if you were placed in a new country every six months to learn a new language. Sure, you would tell yourself you were learning and growing, but in terms of actually being an effective member of that society, it just wouldn't be happening.

Now, I want you to think more broadly about what a language is. It shouldn't be limited to spoken languages or computer coding, but rather any set of information or skill sets that are required to master before you are able to produce in a given field.

The more often the core rules governing a system are changed, the less efficient an individual will be in that system.

The less often the core rules of a system are changed, the more efficient an individual will become in that system.

These rules also apply to *additional information* about a language, which will typically increase performance and production in the use of that language.

I think real estate regulations are a good example. Real estate brokers learn a complex series of lending laws, rules, and codes, get comfortable with them, and then, BAM, overnight there is a new set of federal laws and codes to read, learn, and understand. Studying these new rules will take the brokers away from actually doing their work. If the laws are changing every year, how much of their time will be spent learning those new codes instead of working with clients?

Web development is another great example. I know a programmer who built his business on a language called ColdFusion—the language itself is technically ColdFusion Markup Language (CFML). He was fast and proficient with it. However, like all things computer, ColdFusion changed. And just like that, this programmer needed to adapt to survive. Web development and computer programming are professions where the languages are constantly changing and evolving.

Chess is a difficult game the way it is now. Can you imagine how hard it would be if the pieces moved differently from year to year, or worse, month to month? Or every time you played, you had to learn the new moves?

Any situation that requires you regularly to relearn from the ground up will typically be stacking the learning curve against you in such a way to inhibit or slow your ability to flourish. This is a bad thing if it is happening to you; it is a good thing if you impose such a condition on your enemies.

Forcing your enemies to re-learn a required set of skills or information, or making it more expensive for them to do so, decreases their efficiency.

When I first considered getting into photography as a wedding videographer, I met a well-known photographer at a wedding we were both shooting together. I started asking him questions about the photography side of it, and he immediately shut me down. He had zero interest in helping someone with whom he might end up competing against. At the time, I was a little offended, but looking back on it now, he was just protecting his business. I have encountered this many times in my career as a photographer, meeting those who are very skilled and very unwilling to share for fear of losing business.

For a number of years, I coached intramural flag football for men's, women's, and co-ed teams. We never used the typical formations or plays everyone else did. Instead, we had the wackiest, craziest formations and plays imaginable. The more crazy and unorthodox, the better. After seeing each of our plays a few times, the defenses we played against felt they had learned what we were doing and changed their alignment and strategies accordingly.

As soon as they did so, we would start running wrinkle plays, which began by appearing to be the same exact plays as before, but ended up being something else entirely. Our competitors had been baited into believing they had mastered our system.

Every time they adjusted, believing they would stop us, we would throw a new wrinkle out of the same formation for huge gains or even a touchdown. By half time, most of our opponents were so completely on their heels and confused that many times their will was broken and they had mentally given up. The learning curve itself was used to beat them into submission, given the time limit of the game itself.

If you force someone to relearn a new language over and over, without benefiting from the fruits of their labor, they will almost always give up. The same applies to you personally. If steep learning curves are imposed on you, then changed repeatedly, it is impossible to succeed.

On the flip side, some languages are brutal to learn, but their efficiency for the duration of your life after you achieve fluency is so spectacular that it cannot be measured. Learning to read and write, or perform basic math, for example, is huge. Once learned and mastered, you will use these skills to great benefit for the rest of your life.

I remember in junior high school, how I used to tease one of my best friends, P.J., about his typing class. In my mind, it had to be one of the silliest classes ever. I took woodshop instead. P.J. learned to type at blistering speeds, and after taking that short class, he was then able to type anything at those blistering speeds for the rest of his life.

Woodshop has not benefited me since—at all.

To summarize:

1. Be extremely cautious about choosing a profession that requires the learning of new languages or rules on a continual basis.

2. Find ways to defeat the learning curve. For example, if you are learning to use a new camera, invest just a little bit of money into a course designed to make it as fast and easy as possible.

3. Find ways to manipulate your opposition's learning curves. Make it as hard as possible for enemies to make adjustments or learn from their experiences with you.

4. Find the long-term, stable languages that will give you the greatest return for the smallest investment.

21 – The Slide

AKA—Activation Energy, Learning Curves, Catalysts, and Momentum

I NEVER KNEW how much work was involved in making an independent film until I actually helped produce one. The easiest comparison is to imagine shooting twenty-three days of back-to-back twelve-hour weddings with a single day off after two weeks. Then imagine that there will be about twenty to thirty other people working that same schedule. Next imagine there are usually two to three months of pre-production (planning, scheduling, and location-scouting), as well as four to five months of post-production—things like editing, special effects, sound engineering, music, coloring, and titles. Attempting to pull something like this off on your own would be lunacy.

The one reliable way to make a feature film is to have help. And you will need good help. There are plenty of so-called pros out there who do sub-par work. You will have to filter through them. Then you have the people who do great work, but have poor social skills, creating tension and friction with other crew members—or maybe they just aren't team players (meaning they will do what they want even if you tell them to do something else). If you ever attempt to create a film, you will know friction, and you will know what *activation energy* is.

Activation Energy is the total minimal amount of energy required to begin a process.

When we were children playing on a playground, if there was a slide that we wanted to ride down, work had to be done first, which typically involved climbing up a set of stairs. I like the analogy because if you look at a slide from the side, you can see the classical graph view of activation energy:

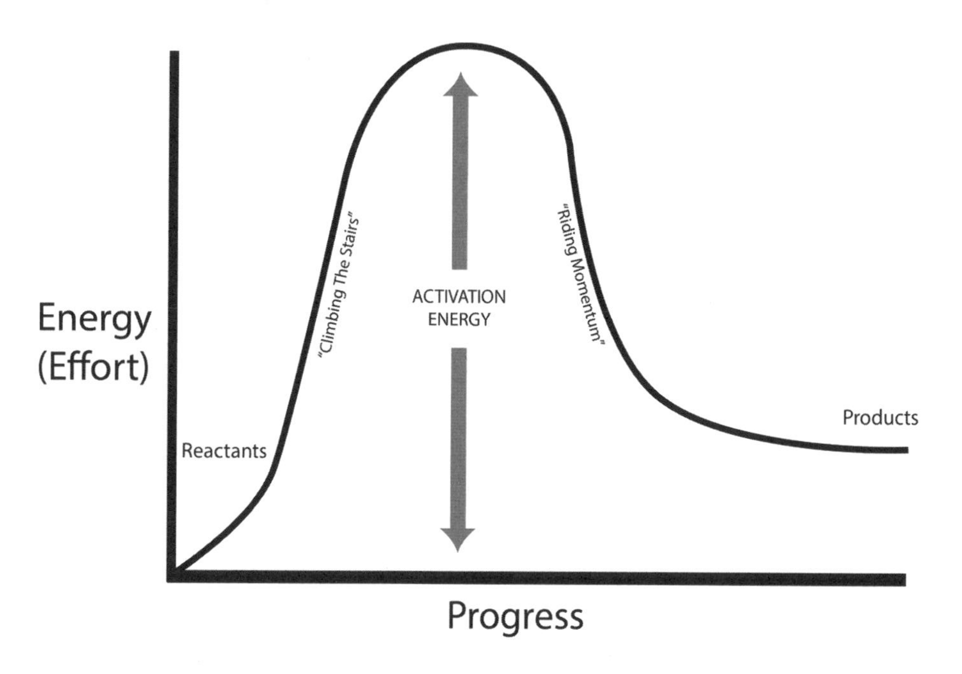

While activation energy usually refers to chemical reactions, the concepts and principles are applicable to nearly all processes or goals. In order to have meaningful progress, a certain amount of *friction* must be overcome.

For some, activation energy is any obstacle you need to overcome to move forward in a goal or endeavor. For example, activation energy is what makes you get out of bed in the morning when you want to sleep just a little longer. It is starting a car on an early freezing morning. It is the funding you need to launch your new business. It is the negotiating before the deal.

If you want to make a peanut butter and jelly sandwich, it is gathering all the required ingredients. It is also that sticky lid on the jelly—the stickier the lid, the harder it will be for this process to move forward.

It is the lost time driving to the gym when you want to work out *now.* It is the surfer who must drive to the beach, paddle out into the break, wait for the right wave, and then try to catch it.

Activation energy is everything you do to get yourself in a position to work or be productive during the day.

If you sell anything (and we all do), activation energy is what is required to overcome your potential customers' resistance to buying whatever it is you are selling.

Newton's First Law of Motion:

An object at rest will remain at rest unless acted on by another force. An object in motion continues in motion with the same speed and direction unless acted upon by another force.

What Newton's First Law of Motion basically means is that any machine or system at rest is going to require some kind of energy to get it going.

The point of this chapter is to *find ways to defeat the friction required for a process or system to begin.*

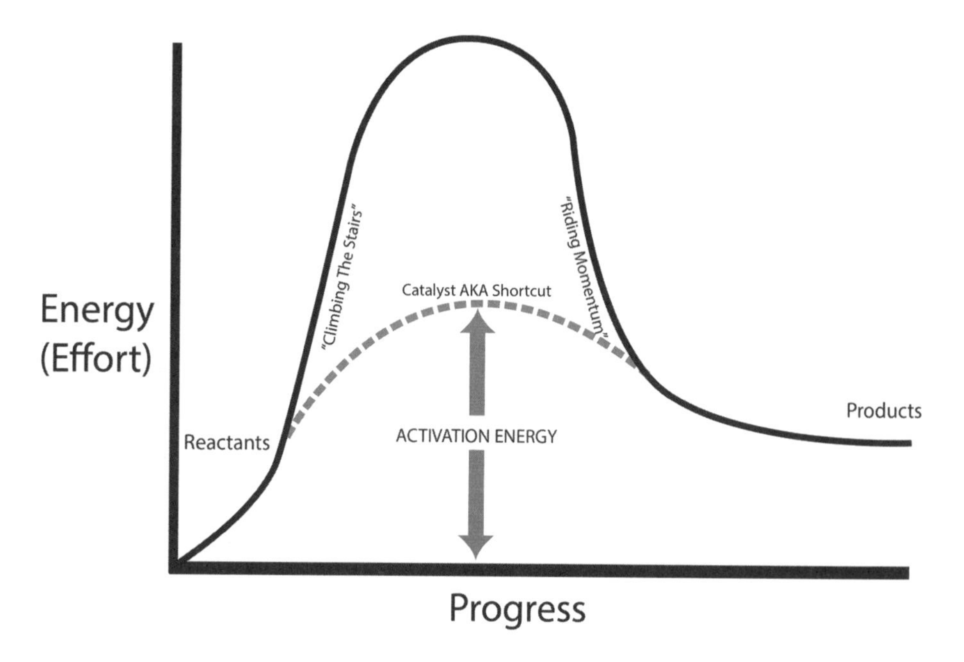

A **catalyst** is anything that lowers a process' activation energy. If the process' activation energy is too expensive to overcome, a catalyst makes it more affordable. Catalysts do not change the results; they make it easier to start. If you find yourself in a situation where you do not have the resources to start a process, the easiest thing you can do is to lower the expense of starting.

Coming back to the example of film making, a catalyst could come in the form of funding. If your film has been financed, you will be much more able to put a team together because you can pay your team members to divide the enormous workload, instead of doing everything yourself. It is even better if you can find crew members who can do high quality work in multiple tasks, such as both shooting and editing, so you don't have to hire as many people. It's even better still if you are able to negotiate payment in such a way that it'll only happen *after* the movie is successful, such as profit sharing. As you can see, while tremendous friction occurs when creating an independent film, many catalysts can also jump-start the process.

Momentum builds upon the first law of motion because once a process begins, it is typically easier to keep that process in motion than it is to restart it because it has already overcome the initial friction point. For example, it is far easier to finish a film with a good crew than it is to get started without one. Once the process has begun, you can typically maintain that momentum with much less effort than was required to initialize it.

When you have momentum, you are more efficient. You are already past your activation energy point. You have less friction to impede your progress, and it is easier for you to advance. When it comes to symbolizing momentum, I like to envision a surfer riding a wave. Most of the hard work is done, so if she just keeps her balance, she can ride it for a very long, enjoyable ride, with little effort, resulting in the product of having fun.

With experience and time, you will know when you have momentum. It will feel like everything is going your way and nothing can stop you. You should tell yourself, "I have tremendous momentum right now," when appropriate to affirm the fact and ride it out even longer.

However, beware of *momentum killers*. For example, computer programming teams always seem to kill progress just as I feel a new app or website project is building steam. On more than one occasion, these coding teams have fumbled at critical moments and, I believe, cost us powerful investors or opportunities. I do not believe this fumbling was something done intentionally. I believe it stems from incompetence issues. If you have a team member who cannot bring his or her A-game, someone who repeatedly interrupts your momentum, that person needs to be fired. You want people on your team who *build momentum with you, not rob you of it.* Sometimes, you can be the momentum killer yourself. It will take humility and discipline for you to realize that.

When beginning any process, analyze the activation energy (calculate the cost) for that process to begin. If the required energy is too much, too expensive, requires too much time or distance, find a way to defeat that friction by means of a catalyst. Once you have momentum, ride it like a wave until your dreams are realized.

III – Simplicity

22 – A River of Focus

AKA—Choose One Thing

OCTOBER, 539 BCE—THE armies of the Persian King Cyrus were advancing to attack the city of Babylon when they came to the Gyndes River. Among Cyrus' army were a set of prized white stallions, one of which decided to make the crossing on his own and was swiftly carried away by the current and drowned. King Cyrus, infuriated with the loss of the horse and that the river dare defy him, decided his army would concentrate its efforts on *killing the river*.

Cyrus' soldiers spent the next year digging 360 trenches that would divert the flow of water away from the Gyndes, reducing its current and dissipating its energy. The effort resulted in the essential death of the river, now just a set of trickling, feeble brooks and streams.

I often quote the story of King Cyrus and the Gyndes River to my friends when they confide in me that they are chasing a difficult dream because it is loaded with lessons. The symbolic analogies are powerful but the take home message is this: **Focus all of your energy on one main goal**.

Cyrus initially set out to defeat Babylon, but he became distracted when he lost a prized possession, something completely unrelated to his initial plan. He let his ego undermine the larger vision. That distraction cost him and his army a year. The river, though initially powerful, was also reduced to weakness through diversion.

The key to achieving any difficult goal is to narrow all of your available resources—your time, talents, thoughts, money—everything should be focused on one goal. As long as your powers are concentrated toward that goal and you do not give up, you will either succeed or die trying, and that is a beautiful thing.

A few years ago, I took a shop class on using water jet cutters to cut through marble or metal to create different products such as tabletops or machine parts. These cutters essentially take water with a little bit of sand, accelerate both, and then concentrate the flow to a thread-like thickness that is moving at supersonic speed. The stream of water mixed with sand will cut right through solid steel, or just about anything else for that matter. Think of the Gyndes River and what it could cut through if all of its energy, speed, and power were focused in a similar manner.

Most children who have played with a magnifying glass on a sunny day understand this principle. Taking just a few square inches of sunlight and concentrating it on a single, sharp pinpoint results in tremendous power and energy.

Unfortunately, our modern life is full of distractions. Social media, text messages, phone calls, app notifications, news, friends, people who want to chit-chat, everyday life friction, all these little diversions that make their way into our main channel of focus and divert our resources in meaningless directions. It happens so often and in so many ways that there is potential for each day to become a total loss if we are not vigilant in maintaining our "river of focus."

Supreme focus is having one dominant thought or goal in mind. *One*. All other concerns, opportunities, desires, everything else in your life becomes secondary. Supreme focus is the mind-set of identifying a single goal and chipping away at each step until the goal is achieved. In some cases, supreme focus may only need to span a few moments, but bigger projects require months or even years of consistent, applied focus.

The most important characteristics of Supreme Focus are:

1. It is an obsession. From the time you wake up, to the time you go to sleep, it is mostly what you think about. No other thought dominates more.

2. You will pay just about any reasonable price to achieve it.

3. It takes priority over all other things. You will find a way to work on it daily, even if it's around an otherwise busy schedule.

4. You are not discouraged by slow progress or negative comments about it.

5. You become an expert at saying "No" to anything else that might possibly interfere with finishing your goal.

6. You spend a significant amount of time pre-visualizing your desired outcome and feel great satisfaction fantasizing about reaching that goal.

Your river of focus is also critical when dealing with other people. They can add to or take away from your focus and momentum. I might add there is a delicate balance in becoming unreceptive to useful feedback and dismissing true naysayers. You never want to become so rigid in your goals and plans that you suspend your critical thinking skills.

Should you let little troughs of distraction divert your flow, your focus will become weaker. Treat your time and resources as you would the Gyndes River. Focus all of your resources on a single point and you will cut through steel.

This analogy should bring up two important questions:

How does one know how large or small his river is in terms of maximum size?

And if one's river is smaller than it could be, *how does one increase the size and power of that "river of focus"?*

23 – The Thought Ruler

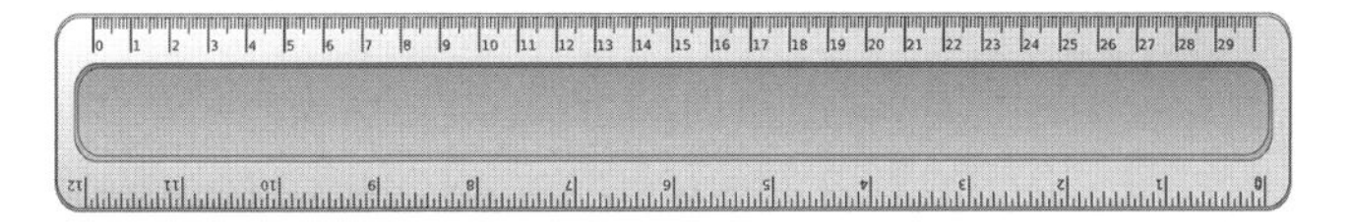

AKA—Measuring Thought Size

HAVE YOU EVER noticed that when discussing things like politics, religion, or sports, you find there are incompatibilities with others? That no matter how hard you try to reason or apply logic, math, or sincerity, there is just no way you can get the other side to see your point? What if I told you that these incompatibilities between thinking go much deeper than the obvious topics? What if I told you that *thought size* or how big a person is wired to think, also greatly influences his compatibilities with others, his earning potential, as well as how much free time he has? Or if there was a way to measure this instantly revealing how big we and others think, and how compatible we are with them, how useful would that be? There are few things that will have greater impact on your productivity than consciously monitoring and adjusting your own thought sizes.

One day a friend of mine shared with me an idea that was so tiny that I couldn't help but to say out loud: "Holy cow, what a little idea." He was struggling financially, had no car, an hourly wage job, yet needed money for a new lens for his camera. His plan was to cut costs from transportation by riding the public bus, resulting in additional travel time of two hours per day. This was mind-boggling to me because photography jobs can pay several hundreds of dollars each, for less than an hour on location shooting. Having a car would allow him to cover a far greater area faster, and therefore, book more clients than if he didn't rely on a bus for transportation. When he responded that he didn't even have enough money to buy a used car, I suggested he go ahead and book the shoots and rent a car as needed, say for $25-30 a day, but he still refused. He was far more worried about the costs needed to buy a lens or to have a car, than he was interested in the prospect of making far more money than necessary to pay for both!

Try as I did, I could not convince him otherwise, even with mathematical proof. My efforts were all to no avail. I was filled with frustration and felt like my time was wasted for even listening to him. He was only looking for confirmation from me that his idea was good, not to get actual feedback. The sad thing about this was I felt at that point I could not give him any referrals (which I constantly have), simply because I doubted his ability to arrive on time and be professional.

It was shortly after this incident that I found myself continuously measuring the size of thoughts from others and myself. I began to notice that some friends and strangers consistently had very small thoughts and aspirations, while others had very large ones.

I also started paying attention to how I *felt* around big thinkers. It was as if my own mind was expanding with each interaction. My problems were minimized. All those stupid little pesky things that bothered me on a day-to-day basis shrunk to such small proportions that they did not even exist anymore.

When I am around bigger thinkers than myself, I feel happy and excited about life and the future. I feel like I too can accomplish great and big things. Big thinkers are the ones who set no limits on what is possible and know that they can. I feel tremendous excitement to seek and be around people who think larger than myself. The more I am around big thinkers and big ideas, the more I begin to think big too. I learned that when big thoughts are put into my mind, I tend to have bigger thoughts of my own than I normally did before. It is as if they are mentally rubbing off on me.

Realizing that some thoughts are bigger than others, I started assigning thoughts a score on a scale of one to ten.

Having a way to measure thought size allows me to have constant feedback of where my thought processes are, what to do with those thoughts, and with whom to speak and about what and why.

Also, knowing the *average* size of a another person's thoughts and actions makes it very quick and easy to identify how big a thinker someone is, what he or she responds to, what you may or may not have in common with the person, and what motivates each of you.

Here are some important disclaimers about this thought-measuring scale:

1. All people have varying sizes of thoughts daily, and all sizes of thinking play an important role.

2. Thought size has nothing to do with happiness, good or bad will, potential, or intelligence. Any size thinker can be happy or unhappy, good or evil, intelligent or not. A state of happiness is more important than an ability to think big, and we all have the potential to do huge things.

3. I use this scale to measure both individual thoughts as well as to average how big a person *usually* thinks, including myself.

4. The thought scale has application to a number of varying subjects, not just income and how we earn money, but I use financial and career examples to explain the list because how we make our income and how much we make will have the biggest impact on our productivity.

5. Each increase in thought size recognizes a critical mental step that needs to be mastered to remain in that state.

The thought-size ruler can be misinterpreted as condescending or judgmental. It isn't, but if it were, it wouldn't matter because your day-to-day efficiency strategies are far more important than offending small thinkers. This is simply a tool for measuring an individual's thoughts and general processes.

If we were to compare the thought scale to our river of focus example, it is how large the river is and what kind of momentum it carries. Small rivers are much more easily diverted at the smallest point of resistance. Huge rivers have tremendous force and mass; the larger they are, the easier they crush resistance and overcome obstacles.

If I were to compare thought size to a muscle, it is lifting power combined with lifting wisdom. I define wisdom as the "application of knowledge." Therefore, thought size is a combination of both thought **force and wise use.** It is mental strength and mental smarts combined. One without the other is less efficient.

Level 1 Thinking: Basic Instinct

Level 1 thoughts have to do with instinct and survival. They include carnal appetites, hunger, desire for shelter, sleep, and stroking the ego. Level 1 thinking includes anger and a willingness to hurt others to achieve goals if necessary. Level 1 thinkers typically do not see their thought or emotion processes as controllable. They justify their actions as a means of survival. All newborn babies, many animals, and even insects are capable of Level 1 thinking.

Level 1 thinkers feel happy when their hungers are fed.

Core Principle: Survival

Weakness: Reflexive thinking only.

How to advance beyond Level 1 thinking: Anything alive will experience Level 1 thinking on a daily basis, as it is required for survival.

Level 2 Thinking: Self-Awareness & Protest

A key difference between Level 1 and Level 2 thinking is the ability to recognize self and the needs and wants of the individual beyond survival. This is what I call the "toddler" level of thinking. The toddler wants something, and she cries when she doesn't get it. The toddler doesn't understand why she doesn't get everything she wants. She couldn't understand even if you tried to explain it to her logically and she finds a way to express those frustrations. This is normal for very young children.

Adult Level 2 thinkers remain in the toddler mentality and have mostly surrendered themselves to being victims of circumstance. To them, the world is after them, despite feeling entitled. Level 2 thinkers are easy to identify because they are problem magnets. They are usually sick, broke, or having some kind of emergency. They need money, *from you.* They have cars that break down often and insist you give them rides everywhere because you are friends.

Level 2 type thinkers sometimes seek employment; however, they are usually fired or quit within a few weeks because they are averse to actually working. They are usually in growing debt and do not have a long-term plan to get out of it. They haven't made the connection that the consequences they face are mostly due to their own lack of planning or foresight. Level 2 thinkers see the government, friends, and family as financial resources to be used. They are perfectly fine with making mountains out of molehills because they see all thoughts as being the same size and worth fighting over. They struggle to overlook small issues because they cannot anticipate the consequences for not doing so. They expect others to provide for them, and they will seek to shift blame and problems to others.

Core Principle: Expectancy

Weakness: Must rely on others.

How to advance beyond Level 2 thinking: Get the Level 2 person off the teat, so to speak, and teach him the advantage of self-sufficiency. Tough love and letting him suffer are important. The very worst thing you can do for a Level 2 adult is to give them what they are asking for, even in the very short-term, even if it is for just this once. You sustaining him is his plan. When I identify a Level 2 adult who is capable of providing for himself but simply chooses not to, I sever ties and communications with him because it is not possible to "talk him out of it." (Believe me, I have tried.) It is a one-way street, and we are a resource for Level 2 people to use and nothing more.

People who use others financially, those who feel entitled, look for handouts, complain about things they feel they have no control over, or seek others to help them when they are able to help themselves, are classic Level 2 thinkers. If they can sustain their strategies indefinitely, they will not change. They are parasitic in nature, so when you cut off their supply completely, they will be forced to evolve to Level 3 thinking.

Level 3 Thinking: Defense

Level 3-sized thought is that all-able bodied people are responsible to and should take care of themselves. I remember as a very young child being taught to tie my own shoes, as we all have been, *so we can manage our own problems.* I believe this applies to all of our needs as adults. Without mastery of self-sufficiency, an individual is forced into Level 2 thinking, complaining to and relying on others, because there is no other way to survive. Level 3 thinking also connects the relationship of self-motivated action to consequence.

Once an individual accepts self-sufficiency whole-heartedly, she begins to focus primarily on defensive thinking. This means that all of her energies are focused on meeting required immediate needs. Running errands is a great example of a size three thought.

As far as employment, Level 3 thinkers tread the waters of survival mostly on their own, making ends meet, but typically, they are living from paycheck to paycheck, without a long-term plan. They usually prefer to work harder over smarter. They are primarily reactionary thinkers, surrounded by stress, putting out fires, and do not have time for much else. Very small problems can cause a big emotional shift in them because their workload is already maxed out. Level 3 thinkers are not afraid to work very hard. I spent a significant amount of my life in Level 3.

Level 3 thinkers find great satisfaction in resting.

Core Principle: Self-Responsibility

Weakness: Burnout is inevitable, no time for anything else

How to advance beyond Level 3 thinking: Learn to anticipate and prepare in advance for all future needs.

Level 4 Thinking: Preparedness

Preparing for an anticipated need is a classic Level 4 thought.

Those who are mostly Level 4 thinkers combine hard work with thoughtful planning. Level 4 thinkers are not working nearly as hard as Level 3 thinkers. Level 4 thinkers have a valuable skill set or education that generates revenue, and therefore, they are typically salaried employees.

Level 4 thinkers are generally prepared; they have found a degree of sustainable comfort and seek to maintain it. They have a job they enjoy, are less stressed out about finances, and can continue in their current lifestyle happily until they die. They love knowing what they can anticipate in terms of a schedule, paycheck, and workload. This security is very important when raising a family. Some Level 4 thinkers know exactly what is required to keep their jobs, and they are not doing a single thing beyond that.

Level 4 thinkers will find ways to reduce personal expenses, or improve their long-term current situation when it is easy, but they are resistant to big changes, especially when it affects their comfort. They will influence individuals on a personal level based on their direct interactions, but they rarely put themselves out there. Level 4 thinkers find great happiness in recreation, fun, and comfort.

Core Principle: Foresight

Weakness: Very little drive or desire to improve beyond a state of comfort.

How to advance beyond Level 4 thinking: Might not be necessary. Level 4 is the comfort zone, and I have often asked myself if it would be a better lifestyle. I think the vast majority of those in this level of thinking are happy, which makes them successful. If a person is deeply happy, there is no need for change. The key to expanding thought size, however, is finding that inner voice that tells you it's time to be better than you are now. Self-initiated drive is the key to becoming a Level 5 thinker.

Level 5 Thinking: A Drive for Success in the Face of Security

Level 5 thought can be summarized as a drive for success. Level 5 thinkers are gainfully employed and are usually more successful financially because they are very driven for success within their work.

These are people who go the extra mile.

Level 5 thinkers are pricked with a sense of wanting more, often without knowing exactly what it is or how to get it. Level 5 thinkers don't tend to sweat the small stuff and can usually cut through to the heart of the matter quickly.

I cap off any employee at a maximum of level 5 thinking because the amount of time required from their daily job will greatly impede their ability to develop and *execute* larger thoughts outside of their employment.

I see Level 5 thinkers as those who have a desire to be entrepreneurs or business owners but do not yet have the courage, discipline, or initiative to make it happen. 5s have endless ideas of what should have or could have been done better when there is failure. Level 5 thinkers are typically successful managers, leaders, teachers, and coaches in a system that has already been established and have been trained by others to be so.

Level 5 thinkers are competitive and find great satisfaction in personal improvement, such as exercise or excelling within a system. They love to win low risk games and will invest time and energy to improve themselves. When someone "chickens out" on a risk that is nearly guaranteed to be successful, it is a Level 5 thought that prevents them from doing so. Level 5 thinkers talk a great talk, but they rarely back it up if it is too risky for them. Level 5 thinkers secretly dislike those who are willing to take the risks they want to, but for whatever reason cannot.

Core Principle: Wanting more, but not more than being secure.

Weakness: Fear of Risk Taking

How to advance beyond Level 5 thinking: A hallmark difference between a Level 5 and Level 6 thinker is the ability to be comfortable with risk and carrying out these risky endeavors.

Level 6 Thinking: The Experimenter or Explorer

Level 6 thinking is the magic tipping point. The Level 6 thinker might still be an employee, but he has taken the jump into developing a side business with the goal to become a full-time entrepreneur. This is someone who will experiment on his own and discover new techniques, skills, and business ideas.

Level 6 is the beginning of offensive thinking. It shows initiative and a high level of self-motivation. Level 6 thinkers are excited to finally be pursuing a dream. They are able to take risks despite fears and are either financially stable or so frustrated they feel they must take action. They spend most of their time thinking about businesses, opportunities, or personal projects that the general population wouldn't consider possible. Level 6 thinkers are driven, hard workers, preferring to initiate it all themselves. They do not wait for others. They are starting to show leadership qualities outside of an established system, meaning they will form a team without any existing connections or established frameworks.

Level 6 thinkers are comfortable with some failure. However, direct personal attacks, negative reviews, or criticism from others can be crushing blows. More often than not, a Level 6 thought will end in failure, not because it was a bad idea, but because it didn't get traction (in front of the right audience) and could not sustain itself.

Level 6 thinkers find great satisfaction in taking an educated risk and succeeding.

Core Principle: Offensive Thinking

Weakness: Failure & criticism can crush their self-confidence.

How to advance beyond Level 6 thinking: Level 6 experiments are often fixed, meaning the new idea must work on its original conception for it to be successful. Therefore, success in risk-taking endeavors will be the most important factor in transitioning between a Level 6 and Level 7 type thinker. If an idea is successful, confidence will come. If a business model cannot be sustained indefinitely, many will revisit Level 6 and revisit it often. The important thing to remember is that a *true* Level 6 thinker is not afraid to fail over and over again. Because of this, he or she will often end up succeeding at something eventually, and then transition to level 7 thinking. *Part-time* Level 6 thinkers tend to revert back to Level 5 once they have failed.

Level 7 Thinker: Adaptability

Level 7 thinking shows the ability to learn quickly from mistakes and make adjustments on the fly. Level 7 thinkers are master improvisers. They are all about adaptability in a self-maintaining system. They are often entrepreneurs who work full-time for themselves, or own a small company, which has endured many years primarily because of their ability to adapt to changing and competitive conditions.

Level 7 thinkers are confident and aggressive about taking calculated risks and see failure as a statistical probability that can be overcome with either learning or greater successes. 7s embrace failure as a learning opportunity. They tend to farm out more of their little tasks and defensive work to others, including their own employees, because they want more free time, but they still do much of the work themselves. They are much less likely to be rattled by others' negative comments and complaints, and they are more receptive to feedback. They see most problems as solvable. When they have sustained their success for long periods, they are often considered leaders of their industry.

Level 7 thinkers find great satisfaction in innovation and business growth.

Core Principle: Ability to learn from errors.

Weakness: Even the best innovators fall short sometimes. If the company is too large and unable to adapt *quickly enough*, it can sink the ship.

How to advance beyond Level 7 thinking: Networking and collaborating with other big thinkers.

Classic Level 8 Thinking: The Collaboration

Level 8 thinking is primarily focused on bringing teams together. Level 8s are also expert networkers and collaborators because they know very big thoughts will require other people. They will typically associate with other 7s and 8s because they know they are all more powerful when they do.

I see these collaborations as many powerful rivers combining to form a super-river focused on a common goal. I have experienced it working as a team member for movie projects. Level 8 thinkers display a high degree of organizational, planning, and networking skills. They sometimes own very large, multi-million dollar companies with hundreds of employees. Level 8s can go completely broke and become millionaires again within a short period because they have mastered certain thought processes that allow them to rebuild from scratch.

Typically, 8s are often very advanced level entrepreneurs, business owners, and investors. They are fearless and have no hesitations using other people's money for their projects. Most Level 8 thinkers have some form of residual income and feel a desire for more free time to pursue their passions. They have an unusual combination of intelligence, discipline, charisma, fearlessness, and self-motivation.

Level 8 thinkers find great satisfaction with the successful completion of a huge project requiring many people.

Core Principle: Team Building

Weakness: Success can bring complacency and boredom (Strange but true!)

These last two levels are quite different, but equally big. I used to call one 9 and the other 10, but I prefer to call them 9A and 9B now because they are similar in size, but completely different in style.

Classic Level 9A Thinker: Philanthropy & Service

Level 9A thinkers are unique in their ability to self-sacrifice. I refer to them as "enlightened." They are emotionally brilliant and are able to set aside their own egos and self-interests for the benefit of others. They do not necessarily need to be wealthy. I know a 9A thinker who runs an orphanage in Haiti who lives on a very modest salary, but her skill and execution to help others is off the charts. She lives within her means so that she may dedicate all of her time and energy to improving her philanthropic cause. 9As typically impact the lives of many, many people for good. Most 9As do not work for money as a motivation, but rather, they are paid residually for doing something they already love, whatever that may be. Full time 9As often give up everything for the opportunity to serve. We can all experience the benefits of being a 9A temporarily by serving and volunteering when we can.

Core Principle: Self-Sacrifice, Charity, Surrender of Ego

Weakness: Hard to sustain indefinitely

Classic Level 9B Thinker: The Visionary

9Bs are extremely rare; I define them as Tier 1, master-level thinkers in their fields. These are individuals who have all of the mental capacities and leadership qualities to bring about repeated change that will affect a large percentage of the world population for many years to come. They can affect the world through art, science, religion, writing, movies, technology, business, politics, and even war. 9Bs have such as huge impact on society that they become household names, even long after their deaths.

Core Principle: An ability to put a dent in the universe

Weakness: Rapid, momentous changes can become obsolete with time and future advances, but even in those cases, the work of visionaries are generally accepted as foundational.

How to use this scale:

If you take just a few minutes to understand fully the thought scale, you will be able to identify different sizes of thoughts instantly, both in your own mind as well as from others. This has some tremendous efficiency applications.

Small thinkers may feel inadequate or overwhelmed when considering big thoughts or listening to the ideas of big thinkers. This often compels them to become naysayers.

Big thinkers may feel frustrated, as if they are wasting time, being mentally suffocated, or being underwhelmed when interacting with small thoughts or small thinkers. They would regard small ideas as "minutia."

The closer in thought size two people are, the greater likelihood they will naturally get along and often add value to one another.

I am very reluctant to label anyone a specific number until I have spent enough time around him or her to know for certain. For example, if someone complains, I might think: *"That is a size-2 thought,"* but I wouldn't necessarily label the person as a Level 2 thinker. If the vast majority of their thoughts are complaints, however, I would not hesitate to label them a 2.

If you can identify the size of an individual's thoughts, it is much easier to engage that person in conversation.

For example, I know Level 3 thinkers are concerned about defense, and therefore, I would speak to them about defensive kinds of things.

I know Level 4 thinkers want comfort and fun, so I would stick to those topics most of the time. Football is a great conversation for 4s and 5s. For 6s to 8s, it's all about business-type things. I love to hear about the risks they are taking, what they learn, and how they have overcome their problems.

I know someone who consistently thinks at a 7, and we often feed business ideas back and forth. When I need answers for my problems, I go to my Level 7 and 8 thinking friends, not my 3 and 4 friends. Going to Level 3 and 4 thinking friends with problems always results in conflict and creates resentment.

When a Level 5 thinker initiates a conversation with me about entrepreneurship, I am much more receptive to the discussion because I know he is flirting with the idea and I want to help him. However, if we have many of these kinds of discussions without action, he is more of a talker, so I will make myself unavailable after some time.

Entrepreneurs and business owners tend to relate better with other entrepreneurs and business owners. They can and should network together, help, advise, plan, and collaborate with one another. Sharing failures can be insightful and instructive. There tends to be less judgment then. I have many friends who are 6s, 7s, 8s, and some 9s where we are able to share ideas with each other in a very constructive manner. Many of their insights have helped me, and I know mine have helped them. It is a beautiful thing when you have a go-to person you know thinks on your level whom you can turn to for advice. It often seems he or she has an answer before you even finish asking the question. This is why using the thought-size identification scheme is so useful and efficient.

I personally do not like spending a lot of time with small thinkers because, for the most part, it is a waste of time. I also believe such thought patterns can be contagious and potentially harmful to my focus, much like an empty channel feeding off my river of focus. I want to be around people who inspire me to become better and ignite my mind with inspiration and fire.

How do emotions play into the thought scale?

Everyone has a range of emotions. Some fit very well into the scale. For example, jealousy, I believe, is a very small-sized emotion; however, if it is allowed to grow, it can dominate a person's thoughts entirely.

Fear limits Level 5 thinkers. Level 9A thinkers are filled with compassion for others.

The simple truth is that everyone experiences a range of emotions throughout the day. The main correlation I see between thought size and emotion is that those on the low end of the scale have a much harder time controlling their emotions. Alternatively, those on the upper end of the scale are able to limit or tap into emotion as a tool, depending on the task at hand. Level 7s-9s are particularly skilled at directing and dictating how they choose to feel.

You may be wondering: What more can an individual do to increase the size of his or her thoughts?

Here are some of my top tips to increasing your thought processes, no matter where you may fall on the scale:

1. **Find a mentor or ally** whose thought processes are larger than yours. I have had many, many mentors who guided me along the way, and it would have been impossible without them. Listen very carefully to their advice and how they think. If you can repeat their thought processes, chances are your own thoughts will grow and mature. Bigger thinkers tend to raise you up. If you cannot find a mentor, **read the books of big thinkers.** Many have written books, so we can get to know them and how they think when we read their thoughts. Through his autobiography, Ben Franklin is still affecting the minds of those who read his ideas more than two hundred years after his time. That is so impressive to me. His thoughts were huge, and he put a dent in the universe that is still here today.

2. **Reduce Debt.** When you have tremendous debt, it will be difficult to think of much else, especially as a Level 2 or Level 3 thinker. I've been there. It certainly is not fun thinking or stressing about bills that you have to pay. This forces defensive thinking. Make every sacrifice necessary to get out of debt. Once you do, you will have more time and thought resources to think offensively.

3. **Face and Conquer Your Fears.** Fear prevents us from acting, especially at Level 5. Fear hugely inhibits large thinking. For many years, my greatest fear was of heights. I was terrified of it. I forced myself to skydive to kill that fear. Then it was scuba diving at night in shark-infested waters. I forced myself to do that. As I killed off these fears, I found myself feeling increasingly more courageous. My confidence and self-image improved dramatically. I feel an emotional reward with each fear-conquering success.

I want you to make a list of your Top 5 Greatest Fears, the ones you can safely face and conquer. Pay close attention to how you feel once you do. I promise you if you do kill these fears, you will find courage and discipline to face other fears and your thought processes will expand as fear fades.

Make a list of your Top 5 Greatest Fears here:

Which of them will you conquer in the next week?

How do you feel now that you have conquered a major fear?

4. **Embrace the opportunity to learn from failure.** In the end, this is the most important piece of advice to transition from a 6 to a 7. If you are okay with failing and learning from your mistakes (hopefully inexpensive ones), you will succeed.

5. **Avoid small thinkers**, poo-pooers, and environments that do not ignite your drive to succeed. Smaller thinkers will try to bring you down or rub off on you. Don't let them, and if it becomes a problem, do not associate with them any longer. Yes, ending a relationship can be painful in the short term, but in the long run, it is a wise investment.

In regards to binary decision-making, if you have two different-sized thoughts competing for your attention, go with the bigger thought as often as possible. **Big Thoughts are greater than small thoughts.** Avoid little thoughts, whether your own or others'.

24 – The Blinder

AKA—Minding Your Own Business

I WRITE THIS chapter with hesitation because several times not minding my own business has led to a few of my most personally rewarding experiences. Serving the people of Haiti, Japan, the Philippines, Vanuatu, and Nepal in their times of critical need after major disasters was life-changing for me. Sometimes, service comes in less-risky endeavors; it might be just an open ear; other times, a word of encouragement or emotional support; other times, physical or financial help. Service is a refiner's fire that purifies ego and pride from the soul. Gratitude naturally seems to increase after serving others. I believe that compassion and charity are two of the most worthwhile traits an individual can pursue. All that said, there are some dangers involved in helping others.

Moscow, Russia, 1993—In the middle of a two-year Mormon mission, my missionary partner and I were walking along a street when we passed what seemed to be a typical Russian couple. The woman was in her mid-forties while the male appeared younger—in his late twenties. We didn't think anything of them until a few seconds after they passed us. Then we began to hear her screams for help. As we turned around, the male was standing over her with his fists clenched, triumphantly ripping her handbag from her and walking in our direction.

My partner and I instinctively decided to get involved. But before we could confront the man, the woman yelled, "He has a gun!" The man threw a smug glance in our direction, taunting us to try something, as he casually reached into his coat.

We never saw a gun, but the woman's statement that he had one was enough. We had no interest in getting shot over a purse and walked toward the woman to help her up. She was hysterical and crying. Long story short, the two had been married the week before. They had arrived in Moscow earlier that day. The woman had withdrawn her life savings from a bank, and it was now in her stolen handbag. Husband or not, the man had only been interested in robbing this poor woman. It is amazing what scumbags are out there.

My companion and I spent the next three hours trying to help this woman. She had no money, so we paid for her transportation to the police station and we waited there with her because she begged us not to leave. The police shrugged off the robbery like it was something that happened every day, saying there was nothing they could do. We then traveled with the woman from place to place as she frantically tried to find a friend or relative in the city who could help her. Eventually, from a pay phone, she contacted someone who said he could help. We gave her cab fare and she was on her way.

Later that evening, I would speak about the experience with one of our leaders. While he was glad everything had worked out, he gave a warning that has stuck with me ever since:

"Be careful about making someone else's business your own, especially in cases of domestic conflict. They can get violent quickly, and before you know it, those problems are now in your lap. It is rarely worth the cost."

That experience has really stuck with me. I've thought about it many times—replayed what we could have done differently, and wondered what lessons could be gleaned from it. I think we did the right thing in helping this woman. I also wonder whether we would have gotten shot or worse had we tried to recover the money on her behalf. That is a very thin line to walk with huge implications for error.

Several years later, a friend of mine hit hard times and asked me for money. I felt good about stepping in to help. While I initially believed this was a one-time thing, it wasn't, and the friend returned many times asking for more money. This was a good friend I cared about, so I didn't want to say no and continued to help financially.

This friend did not stop there, asking for a significant amount of my personal time, physical labor, and errand running. I slowly began to realize that this relationship was so one-sided that perhaps I was being used, but I would have felt terrible saying no to someone I had the means to help, especially a "friend." Looking back on it today, there is no question in my mind I was being taken advantage of. I can think of at least a dozen other similar situations. Maybe that has jaded me a little and is why I felt it necessary to write this chapter.

I've come to the conclusion that in default thinking, I should not concern myself with other people's business or problems. This especially includes gossiping or spreading rumors I have heard about other people, stepping into domestic disputes, loaning money to friends and relatives (terrible idea), and the like.

But where do you draw the line between a service project and getting involved in someone else's business?

Service projects are typically planned and temporary in nature. Service projects are such that you can walk away at any time without carrying personal responsibility or consequence for your actions. Generally speaking, you can approach someone who needs help on your own, offer what you like, and then leave. That's what my missionary companion and I did for the woman who was robbed—we offered her moral support and gave her some money—but we did not try to hunt down her husband, regain her stolen property, reason with the man to reconcile him with her, or become enmeshed in her life by going to check on her the next day. It seems that voluntary, temporary, low-risk and impersonal help in times of real need is sufficient most of the time.

Getting involved in someone else's business on a personal level is where problems start. When you try to walk away in these situations, the problem seems to follow you. You may be held accountable and responsible for your words and actions.

Sometimes, these situations will find you, instead of your volunteering of your own free will. That is a really important distinction for me now. Red flags start popping up everywhere when someone has gone out of his or her way to engage me and starts using very high-pressure means of persuasion, including trying to leverage guilt.

Stay in any big city long enough and you will see the homeless and pan handlers. I never give either money, but in many cases, I will give them food. How interesting it is to see the differences in responses between a professional pan-handler (yes they do exist) and someone who is truly hungry. I have had warm meals pushed right back in my face, and other times, watched them instantly devoured.

Yes, there will be extreme, high risk and unusual circumstances when the right thing to do is get involved to prevent something terrible from happening. You must judge for yourself when those times are, as well as potential costs involved. Until then, your default efficiency setting should be "It's none of my business." You have enough problems of your own to worry about. As a binary, it is:

Minding Own Business > Getting into Others' Business

Making other people's business your own can be expensive, time-consuming, and steer you away from "your river of focus."

25 – The Shield of Denial

AKA—Just Say No

A FRIEND OF mine asked me to shoot her wedding when she got married. The problem with shooting friends' weddings is:

1. You aren't initially certain of the date of the wedding. They assume mentioning it to you is the same as booking it.

2. You are expected to charge less than you would charge a regular customer—a lot less.

3. If something goes wrong, it can ruin your friendship.

As fate would have it, when I finally learned of the wedding date, I had already booked a vacation trip to Maui. Because I felt obligated, I cancelled the trip. Then a few weeks later, I was offered another shoot, at ten times the profit of my friend's shoot. I like to help friends out as much as possible, but by agreeing too far in advance, I felt compelled to change plans as well as missed other opportunities. I don't think my friend ever found out about the sacrifice, but I learned from it.

By committing to one thing, you are technically rejecting other possibilities that would occupy the same space or time. I understand the urge to help others; however, our willingness to commit far in advance must be in accordance with what is most important for us. A good rule of thumb is to try to remain as flexible as possible until you have to make a decision.

It is usually better to deny or remain passive to a low priority opportunity and later accept it than it is to commit to it followed by reneging later. In one situation, you have had a change of heart, while in the other, trust is broken.

How to Use the Shield of Denial

Successful use of the Shield of Denial is a delicate balance between who is making the offer and how important the offer is. Unless either of those is great, you should reject as many opportunities and commitments as possible. Here's how you determine whether to commit to something you're unsure you want to commit to:

1. Measure who is making the offer. Tact in delivery of the rejection depends completely on how much interaction you might have in the future. The more interaction and more valuable they are to you, the more careful you should be.

2. Has the person dealt fairly with you in the past? Does he or she have your best interests in mind? Do you owe the person a favor? Are you related to him or her? Is this person a problem magnet just looking to give you his or her problem? Have you answered "I do" after being asked something about living with this person for the rest of your lives, until death do you part?

3. Measure the importance of committing immediately or not. There must be a valuable or beneficial reason for committing early; otherwise, you will lose efficiency. I call early committing to very low priority appointments "constraining," which

means to give yourself unnecessary hurdles to work around later.

4. If you have determined that there is no benefit to committing early, raise your shield! Really...it's okay. You just have to be tactful about how you do this:

    - If you care about the person—Offer a possible alternative date or activity instead of rejecting. Give reasons only when needed. Sometimes, giving a specific reason opens up a line of attack for them.

    - If you know the person, but do not have an emotional connection to him—Be cordial and short. "Sorry; I cannot make it."

    - If it is a stranger—Be polite and strong. No other information is needed. "No, thank you," or "I am not interested," are perfect in these cases.

    - If it is a telemarketer—You can just hang up or tell the person you have registered with the Do Not Call list. (Be sure to do so.)

A very powerful binary here is: "No > maybe." While sometimes we do not want to use the word "no" because many equate it with rejection, it is still incredibly efficient.

"Maybe" means that even if you meant no, you will have to revisit it at a later time, taking valuable time and resources. Saying no and later "reconsidering" also feels like a major win for the other party. All that said, there are times you might need to be more tactful.

Here are some general rules for saying no gracefully:

- When necessary, defer your reason to higher authority or power. This will make you look less like a bad person. I like to use non-living things like "my schedule" or "having tentative plans." These plans can include taking the day off and relaxing. I have friends who always say, "My spouse says no."

- In the same vein, always be honest; never lie. Maintaining your word of honor is important to building trust. Trust is efficient—dishonesty is not.

- Do not volunteer information that doesn't concern the rejected. Give reasons for rejection only on a need-to-know basis. Giving reasons is inefficient because it leads to more questions or arguments about why you should commit.

- Beware of those who pressure you, especially when only they stand to benefit.

- When confronted with a tempting reason to "act now," challenge it. Determine whether the reason is legitimate or just smoke and mirrors.

- Don't let yourself be bribed. If you are, you are no longer making decisions for the right reasons. (i.e., You have a price and can be bought.)

- Plan and prepare while the shield is raised. Time spent behind the shield is an important planning opportunity. Patience doesn't mean to wait; patience means to plan while you wait and fine-tune your options, preparing to strike when the correct window presents itself.

- The selfish are *usually* impatient. Sometimes by denying someone or making him or her wait, his or her true colors become more apparent.

- If the offer could potentially threaten your safety or well-being, do not be afraid to make the rejection count. Sometimes it is necessary to offend.

Day in and day out, you will be presented with hundreds of opportunities. If you are chasing a very specific goal, it will be necessary to say no to the vast majority of those that are unrelated to it. You may feel compelled out of social obligation, but in the end, your river of focus is your most valuable resource for getting stuff done. Don't let others siphon off your time and energy away from pursuing your goal.

26 – The Hot Potato and Problem Magnets

AKA—Side Notes on the Shield of Denial

THE PROVERBIAL HOT potato simply refers to an individual's problems. The more problems you have, the less efficient you become. You already know from firsthand experience that with more problems, your resources are divided.

The fewer debts, commitments, and problems you have, the greater your ability to focus your resources, so the more efficient you become at a single goal.

I always want to do everything myself. In my younger days, this was quite interesting and exciting for me. When I wanted to have a website, I bought a beginner's guide to HTML programming, studied it, and then created my own website. If my truck broke down, I would get a repair manual and learn how to repair it—then I would attempt the repairs, if I could! Looking back on it now, this desire to do everything myself was very inefficient! For every opportunity or issue that arises in your life, you have to make the calculation to determine whether it is worth your time to try to do it on your own.

A *lot* of skilled people out there are looking to take work off your hands, but *you will need to have courage to give your problems to more skilled people.*

When I was getting started as a photographer, I was somewhat broke and could not afford to hire professional models. I would ask friends to pose for me, getting by for a while, but as time progressed, it got harder and harder for me to expand my portfolio and get the same friends to help. Then I realized that for a small amount of money, I could hire very reasonable models almost immediately. I was losing more money by wasting time looking for models than by just paying them.

Hiring others can take away many of your problems, and using various businesses, employees, subcontractors, or automated computer programs can all make the hiring process easier for you. Quality of work will vary, so be sure to measure the cost compared to the benefit.

Find a way to give hard problems to a specialist in a fair exchange.

On the other hand, many people will seek to give you their problems in an *unfair exchange*. This is what I call a **hot potato**. With experience, you will know it as soon as you see it. Do not allow people to give you their hot potatoes. You have enough problems of your own. When you deny a hot potato giver, you are retaining efficiency.

Always seek the win-win. Win-lose is never good, especially when you are on the losing side.

I had a good friend—I will call her Kelly—who was a beautiful model with a kind heart. She couldn't say no to anyone, including her sister, whom I'll call Rebecca.

Rebecca had a young child who needed supervision while she worked. Since Kelly could not say no to her sister she agreed to watch her niece every time her sister asked, for free. Rebecca would always say, "It's only for two or three hours," but it always turned into five to eight hours. Kelly would confide in me how she felt taken advantage of by her sister and how it sapped her free time from working for me or studying. Rebecca successfully gave Kelly her hot potato. She exploited the family relationship to her advantage. I hated seeing Kelly being taken advantage of, especially when she had goals and dreams of her own that she could not focus on when she was babysitting.

I also believe it is wrong to try to give others your problems in an unfair exchange. It's the same as using or taking advantage of someone. If you have a problem you are trying to give to someone else, make sure it is worth her while and she at least feels she can walk away from the exchange with a profit. *If you knowingly take advantage of someone, and that person slowly comes to this realization, you will lose him or her as a business associate or friend.* I know some people who intentionally use others, knowing the consequences and being totally okay with that. I have witnessed others who ride people like waves, and once they are done with one individual, they paddle out and find another one to ride without any hesitation.

Lastly, I want to talk about something I call the Problem Magnet (Level 2 thinkers).

A problem magnet is a person who attracts problems by virtue of his or her poor attitude, poor decision making skills, lack of cost-to-benefit-ratio analysis skills, and inability to pre-visualize consequence. These people are always complaining about something, but from their perspectives, their complaints are well-justified. *They are perpetual hot potato givers.*

Problem magnets have no money or resources; they are constantly sick; their kids need food; they need a ride somewhere. Every time you talk with them, something is wrong and they need your help. They're the ones who will call you to come bail them out at 2 am—

repeatedly. They seem to attract friction of every kind, and then they present themselves as victims of circumstance.

You want to help, right? But when you are dealing with true problem magnets, helping is only prolonging the inevitable, as well as giving the person a sense of entitlement. Some problem magnets are extremely persuasive and charismatic.

Do not help—do not even associate with problem magnets. If you consciously enable a problem-magnet, you are opening yourself to be taken advantage of. It is just a different form of allowing someone to steal from you.

On the flip side, I have learned not to talk about my problems unless it is in regards to discovering or creating a solution. Just talking about our problems for no reason makes no sense and creates negative energy. Chances are, those we whine and complain to have problems of their own and usually do not want to hear it anyway.

In summary, try to minimize taking on other people's problems unless it is a fair and equal exchange. Rely on yourself as much as possible to be self-sufficient. Avoid dragging others into your small problems. When you have big problems you cannot handle on your own, find *good help and compensate those people accordingly.*

27 – Scissors

AKA—Hedging

"One man's trash is another man's treasure."
— Author Unknown

WE SEE IT every year with professional sports. A long-time player is unexpectedly traded away to another team. For whatever reason, the player's value to the original team has depreciated; yet another team still sees the player as more valuable than whichever team it is giving him up.

I compare such situations to using a pair of scissors; metaphorically cutting away something worthless to convert it into something valuable. For example, that papaya tree in your yard that yields so much fruit you don't know what to do with it all. Cutting the fruit down a little early and selling it at a farmers market is a good example of this.

The scissors tactic to me represents a way to create value from what appears to be waste. Another example would be clutter in your garage. There are some things in there you haven't used in years, yet they are still valuable. If seeing this clutter stresses you out, you can literally sell your stress for money.

Any time you can turn disadvantage into advantage, you are being very efficient. There are things you wouldn't want to sell on eBay, like your house or real estate, but for clutter, junk, and valuables you have laying around the house, I can't think of a better way to get some cash from it.

If you don't know how to use eBay or other popular sell/trade websites, you are probably sitting on money.

That old Polaroid Land Camera? eBay. That new car you tried to buy and simply can't make the payments on? eBay. Those cute shoes you bought and never wore? eBay.

When I was in college, I had a box in my closet labeled, "Things to sell on eBay." It had a bunch of random junk—a rust inhibitor, flash diffuser, old camera, pantone color chart, etc. The box sat for a few months until I finally decided either to list the items on eBay or to throw them away. I almost threw them away because I was sick of looking at the box. But I went to eBay and listed them. They all sold within three days. The value—$320. I couldn't believe it! I did this again recently with some old lenses I had stopped using and recouped several thousand dollars.

The potential hazard of the scissors strategy is that it can create clutter if you are not careful. You should have a mechanism that automates the decision to sell; otherwise, it's just junk in a box. Here's the rule I use to determine whether it's worth my time to sell or trash:

If it has been sitting around *unused* for more than two years and its value is more than $20, sell it on eBay. If its value is less than $20, donate it or just throw it away.

Of course, the rule is different for things like photo albums or tax records, obviously, but it should cover almost everything else. If you haven't used something for two years, when exactly are you going to use it? Unless you can think of a specific time and place, and the cost of replacing it would be greater than the expense it is costing you now (i.e., the mentality that clutter is acceptable), you know what you need to do. When you do it, you will have a nice feeling inside—that is flow. Flow can build to momentum.

You can measure the value of your unwanted items on eBay by doing a "completed auction" search.

To see what your stuff is worth, do a normal keyword search and select the "completed auctions" filter. You can then see how much other people are paying for similar things. Would you rather have the money or the clutter?

In addition, eBay is an opportunity to learn and practice entrepreneurship. Just knowing how to use it makes you see and think differently about buying and selling opportunities. As a student, I was once at a campus bookstore sale where they were selling brand new football gloves for seven dollars. Since I played college football, I knew they were *way* underpriced. They had a case of them, forty-three pairs, to be exact. While this wasn't specifically my junk, the concept was applicable: I did some quick calculations.

Let's see; in stores, they cost about forty dollars, but I also know that other people will be selling them on eBay, so I could probably sell them for twenty-two dollars, competitively. Charge another four bucks for shipping, that would be twenty-six dollars per pair. My actual cost would be about two dollars for the auction and PayPal charges, one dollar for shipping, and seven dollars for the gloves. Twenty-six minus ten is sixteen dollars in profit. Sixteen times forty-three is $688. Wouldn't you like to have an additional $688?

Granted, I had to put down more than $300 for the gloves and that was a little risky, but I was *certain* of their value, and the eBay market was so big that I knew they would sell for at least what I had paid for them.

I grabbed the entire case and walked up to the cash register. The manager literally slapped herself on the forehead and said, "You are going to sell those on eBay, aren't you?"

"Yep!" I said with a smile. The student working the register asked out loud why he hadn't thought of it. I sold the entire case and actually made more than the $688 I estimated (because they were auctioned off).

This illustrates an important example of entrepreneurship: *knowing the business you are involved in.* I had a much greater chance of success in this entrepreneurial endeavor because I had an intimate knowledge of the true value of the gloves. Because the manager and the clerk were not familiar with the value and demand for them, *they could not see the opportunity.* When you have expert knowledge of a subject, you will see things others cannot. It is almost as if it is invisible to them.

The advice I give to most entrepreneurs is: stick to what you know, are passionate about, or what you can quickly become an expert at. Venturing into prospects that you are unfamiliar with puts you at a huge disadvantage (known vs. unknown). More so if you are not passionate about them.

Your ability to earn money is directly related to your ability to recognize and exploit value, wherever it may be. If you can find value and match it with a buyer, you have a business.

28 – The Boot

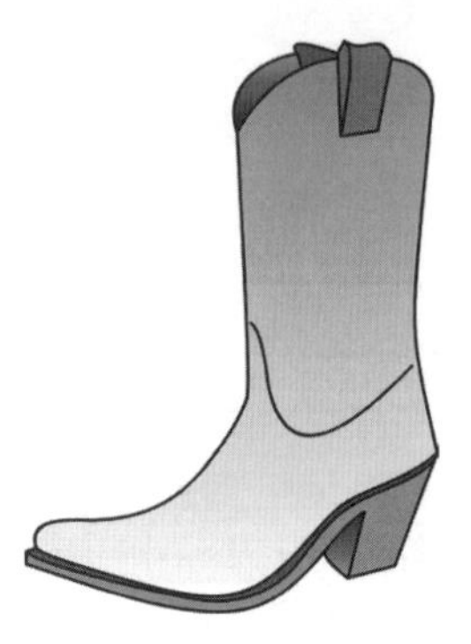

AKA—The Art of Throwing It Away

BIOLOGY PROVIDES MANY wonderful lessons on efficiency. Waste removal systems are found in every single living organism. In every breathing moment of our lives, our bodies are removing CO_2. There are biological storage facilities for waste products resulting from everything we eat and drink, and our bodies remove this waste daily. If waste products were to get into places where they do not belong, we would become violently ill or even die. Because of the great need for efficiency just to live, removing the junk, crap, garbage, and clutter are essential to surviving.

One of the few things that terrifies me is the television show *Hoarders*. I can't watch more than one or two minutes before feeling anxious. I find these episodes more frightening than any horror movie I have ever seen. The show is about people who *only acquire*. They never throw anything away, and as such, their homes fill with trash and useless items, making it impossible even to walk through them.

I believe hoarding usually starts with clothing. We spend a lot of money on something we wear a few times, and then we cannot part with it because we know what it was worth when we purchased it. It would be like throwing away cash. So we hang on to it, believing we will one day wear it—even though we also know that will most likely never happen.

I once dated a woman whose closet was completely full of blue jeans. Completely. Not even hanging because the hanging bar in her closet broke because of the weight. The blue jeans were stacked in neat folds on shelves in her closet. There had to be over two hundred pairs. In her guest room, she had boxes everywhere filled with shoes. Most of them were never worn. When I asked her why she was hanging onto them, she replied, "They are so cute!" She had three dressers in her bedroom with difficult-to-open drawers because they were so stuffed with clothing.

Most of the clothing any individual *really needs for survival*, about a week's worth, can fit into a small duffle bag. I lived out of such a bag for nearly five months on a long road trip across the country. I did my laundry each week at hotels. I never really missed not having certain articles of clothing. For years, if I purchased a new shirt, it meant I had to throw an old one away.

My general rule on clothing now is that if I haven't worn it in six to eight months, I won't wear it in the future, so I usually just throw it away or donate it. I know there are ways to sell used clothing on eBay or at thrift shops, but the amount of time it would take to list, sell, pack, and ship the items usually make it not worth it to me (PTV). Again, you can check eBay's "completed listing" option to find out how much you can sell an article of used clothing for, and if you find it is worth more than your PTV cost to sell it, it might be something to consider.

Clutter is a form of friction. It can create unnecessary thought cycles and stress. We constantly trip over it and it takes up capacity that can be used for other assets.

When something is no longer useful, it must be disposed of. Do not hang onto it.

Sentimentality is clutter's ally.

If something is truly sentimental—it means something to you and is absolutely irreplaceable, so there is no way you are going to throw it away—it's okay. Then organize it in such a way that it isn't affecting your daily life. Extremely special items should probably be memorialized, for example a trophy. You wouldn't hide it; you would find a place where people can see it. If it is affecting your daily life (meaning you trip on it every day), and you haven't used it for two years, it is time to take action.

If you are agonizing over throwing something away, I have found that the following quote helps. I actually said this to one of my favorite shirts that simply wore out and was no longer usable. The best way to go about it is to use the "friends" clause.

"I am sorry. We had a great run, and you have been very effective in helping me on my journey. This is nothing personal. I know you want me to succeed. We will always be friends."

With that, give your piece of property a hug right before you throw it in the trash. It's always nice to end on a positive note!

Keep in mind that this piece of property will scream and beg for you not to do this. It may even call to you from its final resting place.

"Oh please. Please (fill in your name here), don't you remember all the times we (fill in the blank here). You could never possibly throw me away. Let me stay with you forever and ever."

Now, be aware that the shirt or whatever you are throwing away will not tell you its evil plan. It wants to hurt you in the subtlest of ways. You are just going to have to trust me on this. If you fail to throw it away, it will laugh at you and think to itself, “Now who’s the boss?”

29 – The Toolbox

AKA—Findability

"A place for everything, everything in its place."
— Ben Franklin

WALKING OUT THE door for a very important meeting, you look at your watch and judge you will arrive a few minutes early. Terror stops you in your tracks as you suddenly realize you cannot find your car keys. Your mind races to the last time you remember seeing them, a few hours ago. You run inside and begin the frantic search as the seconds tick away—not on the kitchen table, not on the key ring, not by the remote in the living room. As you slowly tear your home to pieces looking for your keys, you begin to accept you will be late. You text the person you are meeting to explain your tardiness, imagining how she is shaking her head in disbelief at your unprofessionalism. Fifteen minutes go by before you finally check the laundry hamper and find the keys in your workout shorts. Unfortunately, the window of opportunity to make a good impression is now past as you race out of the house.

Human nature is such that we are inherently forgetful and error prone. How much time have we wasted...looking for something we literally just had in our hands? Or thought was in a certain place? Or trying to recall an idea we've now forgotten? Or chasing after a child who was there ten seconds ago and is now missing?

Forgetfulness is a form of mental friction. When we forget, we increase the amount of time, resources, and stress required to complete a task.

Findability is the process of making things much easier or much harder to find, depending on your aim.

I have a friend in Alabama whose home is probably the most organized in the world. His family is quite large—last I heard, he had thirty grandchildren, most of whom visit regularly. Every shelf, cupboard, and closet—even in the laundry room, bathrooms, offices, garage, workshop, tool shed, everywhere—is covered in labels that designate what is to go into that space. It is actually quite incredible. I find it soothing to my mind to see the images he posts on Facebook of his amazingly organized home.

You can have the most amazing product in the world, but unless your target customers can find your product—meaning you get your product in front of them—all is for naught, and you will soon find yourself out of business.

Google has created and sustained an empire based on the business of helping make websites findable in its search engine. Businesses can sign up to Google's ad words program and then make bids to pay a certain amount of money every time a potential customer clicks on that ad. The clever part of this scheme is that Google pits business owners against each other for keywords such as "pizza" or combinations such as "Maui pizza." If there are five pizza businesses on Maui wanting to advertise their restaurants to tourists visiting the island, they have to bid against each other, forcing their competitors to bid higher or not bid at all. Whoever is willing to pay the most per ad word will usually find himself at the top of Google's listings, thus making his product more findable.

Stealth also has its advantages. For example, making yourself hard to find when dealing with enemies or predators who intend to harm you is a good thing. No one can doubt what an incredible competitive advantage an individual would have if she could make herself completely invisible. While there is no such thing as a cloak of invisibility yet, we can make ourselves virtually invisible in a number of other ways. If someone cannot see you, he cannot attack or exploit your weaknesses.

This principle was executed in spectacular fashion when the United States unveiled the F-117 Night Hawk during the 1991 Gulf War. Our enemies did not know about this stealth aircraft's existence, much less its angular, black surfaces coated in secret materials, allowing it to give a radar signature no larger than a small flock of birds. The 117s penetrated Iraq's air space unseen, destroyed key targets, and paved the way for larger forces.

If you have something you believe others will want, you must not only make your presence known, but you must make it as easy as possible for people to find and access what you are offering. For years, I struggled to get my training products into one of the largest camera stores in the country. I knew, however, that once I did, it would be easy to sell more of an existing product simply by *positioning* it in the store so it would be easier for photography students to find it.

You have certain skills, knowledge, information, perhaps products, and even unwanted goods that someone else in the world wants. Any product can successfully be sold and marketed with great success simply by knowing how to get it in front of the right audience. The tricky part is connecting the product to the customer.

30 – The Quill

AKA—Memory Systems

THE QUILL IS the tactic of finding ways to capture information in such a way that the data can easily be found later. It isn't enough to capture it. *You have to tag it in such a way that you can find it again quickly.*

The things we need to remember fall under the following categories:

1. To Do Lists
2. Goals
3. Schedules and Appointments
4. Contact Information
5. Computer Files
6. Emails and Messages
7. Inspired Ideas

For years, I have kept my to-do lists in a small notebook, with each item being prioritized from one and up. (Note: Most of my "to-do" lists are for Defensive type tasks, errands and the like, something I'll describe more later.) I focus all of my energy on the most important task at hand, and I cross the items off as they are completed. Once one task is finished, I'll usually start on the next. I try to plan my day in such a way that there is a good probability I can finish early, and when I do, *I enjoy the rest of my day.* "Rewarding" yourself with more work for finishing early will lead to burnout in the long run.

In the evening before bed, I'll recreate a new updated list. While simple, this "to do" allows me to remember, prioritize, as well as track everything I need to do. Imagine the amount of wasted time I'd have if I didn't keep such a notebook and had to re-remember everything I needed to do each day!

Written goals are critical—without them, there is no serious commitment. I like to write my big offensive goals (my "River of Focus") in a place I can see every day, usually a giant dry erase board hanging in my workspace, with the next steps required below it.

I use Excel spreadsheets with my production teams to show them a complex plan's layout. A system of colors on that document designate which stage the individual task is in.

- A white or empty box means we need to shoot a particular segment.
- Yellow means it has been shot and turned over to the editor.
- Light green means editing is complete and ready to be reviewed.
- Dark green means it has been reviewed and is ready to publish.
- Light blue means it is completely finished.

This system has been very effective because we may have 40-50 items that need to be completed, and each team member is working on 2-3 of them at a time. When one task is finished, the colors let each team member know what needs to be focused on, who should be working on it, and when it is done. If a project is very large, I will assign names to each task, so if someone finishes her task early, I can immediately assign her more. This way, everyone is working on something, until we are all finished. It has been a very useful way to track and maintain progress on large video productions.

I no longer keep a daily record of schedules because most of my days are booked working on my own projects. When things were more chaotic, I always preferred written schedules (on paper), but now I use my smartphone with the alarm reminder if something is scheduled in advance. All of my contacts are stored in my iPhone.

As a photographer, I organize all of my computer images as follows:

1. Separate hard drive designated by year, written in marker, for example: 2016.

2. Within each year folder, there are twelve corresponding month folders.

3. Inside the month folders are separate projects with each one's date and name of the shoot, for example Kauai-Vacation-8-1-17.

This system allows me to find any project by date or project name even ten years ago. It has worked wonderfully for me.

Modern email and messaging apps have a search engine that allows you easily to find past conversations with clients.

Some of my very best business ideas come while I am drifting to sleep. I capture these ideas by writing them in a notebook kept beside my bed using a flashlight to see. (There were many years I slept with my iPhone close by, but I am now a believer that it should not be close to where one sleeps, and preferably in another room. This has led to my falling asleep and starting the day with fewer distractions.)

If I am out and about, I will save these ideas into my iPhone. I have learned the hard way that you can have a flash of inspiration, but if you fail to capture it, it can be forgotten forever. Your inspiration-catching system does not need to be anything fancy; it just needs to be consistent and effective.

A number of *memory systems* can also be learned that greatly improve recall. For example, I use the *link* method of association to remember what I need to buy at the grocery store. It works by visualizing the first item and then linking it to the next item in the most ridiculous way possible.

For example, if I needed cereal, milk, apples, shampoo, razors, gum, and canned chili, I would make up a story that goes like this:

"I am riding a giant cheerio down a river of milk. I float into the dark apple forest. If you cut an apple open with a razor blade, you will discover it is full of shampoo. The tree roots are pure bubble gum that feed from cans of chili."

Whenever something else pops up that I need, I just add it to the story in a strange and unusual way. I've used this system for years and only write lists now when they grow very long.

I've used other memory systems to memorize years of information for school tests and thousands of students' names. Memory systems can make you more efficient at remembering. Several memory books will teach you how to use them or develop your own.

Improving how you capture and access important personal data can greatly improve your profits, reduce wasted time and resources, and improve your grades and mental transactions. It can help you elude unnecessary trouble and friction, and overall make your life easier because you will be spending less time looking for lost ideas.

31 – The Piggy Bank

AKA—Frugality

FOR ME, WEALTH is a measure of an individual's freedom. The wealthier an individual, the more she can spend her time and resources on the things she enjoys most.

This definition is different from "having lots and lots of money." I do not believe many financially well-to-do individuals are free. What good is having millions if the person who has them is miserable, depressed, and despises the means by which the assets were acquired?

How happy is the couple that, despite both making six-figure incomes, is buried many times over their yearly salaries in debt? Or, like most of our modern society, how fun is it to wake up every morning having to go to a job just to pay the bills? Living week-to-week is no fun, yet many of us will do it for our entire lives.

I have some more bad news—and this is coming from a single man who has been an entrepreneur for the last thirteen years. Our modern society is set up in such a way that it is nearly impossible to become a millionaire, even through legitimate, hard work.

We are programmed daily to be consumers, pounded over and over to buy the things we do not need or even really want. Advertisers know if they can get into our minds a certain number of times, we will eventually buy their product. Credit card companies target eighteen-year-old college students with high-interest card offers because they know that if they get them hooked young and while in the early stages of freedom, they will own them for the rest of their lives.

We seem to be wired as Americans that the more money we make, the more we spend. I can't tell you how many times I've had a friend who has gotten a $100 per month raise, and spends like he has $200 more per month.

Any time we live beyond our means, we are prostituting our freedom to someone else.

A person is already *financially* wealthy when he does not carry the burden of debt.

Some will disagree with me on this, and that is fine, but I do not believe anyone can be completely wealthy (a measure of freedom) or happy when he or she is in debt.

Excess promotes waste. When you have a lot of something, the natural tendency is to waste it. Waste is the expense of assets without any gain. Waste is inefficient. Therefore, we can also predict that having an excess of anything means it is likely we will be inefficient with those assets.

Chances are that if a person goes from rags to riches overnight, it is only temporary. I strongly recommend an excellent film by the NFL titled *Broke*. It illustrates what happens when young men go from being poor college football players to NFL millionaires. Spoiler alert—as the title suggests, the vast majority spend all their money within a few years of retiring.

This situation isn't limited to football or professional athletes. Look at all the lottery winners who are now broke. It is as common and predictable as gravity. "Coming into wealth" often leaves people much worse off financially than before they had money.

Why is it that a very select few seem able not only to acquire wealth, but to hang onto it for most of their lives?

Frugality: The discipline to say no to yourself and to extend the life of something you already own. I remember a time in college when I was so completely broke. My jeans had ripped, and instead of buying a new pair, I decided to repair them by sewing the hole back together. That ten minutes saved me $50, a small fortune for a struggling college student.

A few years ago, I was faced with the choice of replacing my Prius Hybrid batteries at a cost of $5,000. It was reasonable to tell myself it was time to buy a new car at a cost of $26,000 or more, but I also knew that everything else on my older car was in fine working condition. Replacing the batteries at $5,000 would give me another seven years of use from the vehicle. Saving $21,000 through frugality and driving an older vehicle is worth it to me every time.

I know frugality is not a sexy answer, but it is an eternal truth. You cannot experience long-term financial health without some degree of frugality, no matter how much you make. If you spend more than you make, you are on the road to debt. The more debt you have, the less freedom you have. Frugality limits unnecessary expense waste, leaving you with more firepower to focus on what is truly needed.

Giving millions of dollars to someone who does not have the discipline to save it is like giving a superpower to someone who does not understand the concepts of responsibility and accountability.

He will take that power, abuse it for personal gain, and eventually destroy himself with it.

Let me give you a tip: Practice the magnetic principle of money. The more money you save rather than spend, the faster that money will grow and attract more money.

The rate at which your savings increases is directly related to your discipline not to spend it.

Frugality, like other defensive tactics, is a central cog in long-term financial health, freedom, and personal happiness. Without it, you cannot be efficient.

32 – The Double-Edged Sword

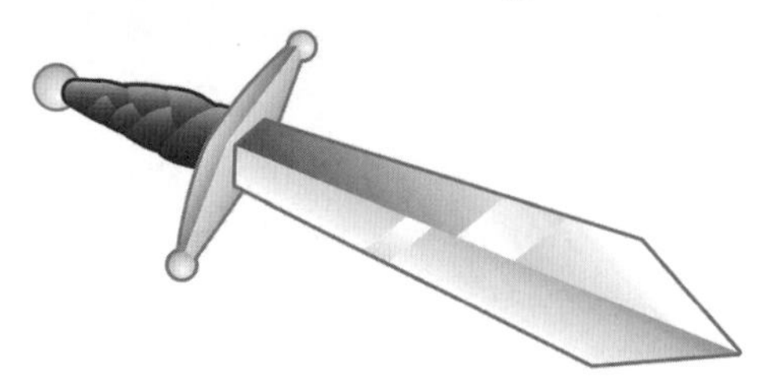

AKA—Killing Two Birds with One Stone

BETWEEN TWO INTERNATIONAL disaster aid trips on my own dime and then investing in and helping produce an independent film, I had missed a lot of work. While I was having the time of my life, sales were way down as competition was rising, and I was running out of cash.

My long-time assistant Kate's job was on the line. Laying her off appeared inevitable in order for me to make ends meet, which would also increase my personal workload.

In addition to all this, I had been developing a secret app that I'll just call Project X. To make matters worse, after enormous financial expense and five years of development, my programmer unexpectedly announced he was done with the project, so I would have to find someone else. After a few months of searching, the new programming team told me it would cost approximately $26,000 for a programmer and a tester over five months to meet the requirements for launch.

Having all of these things come at me at once, I started to look for a way to resolve both issues with the same solution. And then I realized, *Kate is an extremely competent app tester; she knows that app inside and out.*

Long story short, I was able to negotiate with the new development team to use Kate to test the app instead of their employee, which lowered the cost about $12,000 over five months. My new cost was a couple of thousand more per month, which was doable. In addition, I resolved to increase our promotional sales before Christmas. Between the cost savings and the increase in promotional sales, we were not only able to save Kate's job, but we found a solution for two problems.

When attacking with a single-edged sword, you must swing it, then gather it back before swinging again. Double-edged swords allow for a cutting edge to be exposed during both motions of the swing. The double-edged sword is more efficient because its motions are equally deadly, whichever way it is swung.

The double-edged sword is a classic weapon of efficiency; it consolidates two or more problems into a single course of action.

Anyone who makes a shopping list is already familiar with the double-edged sword concept. It is more efficient to make one trip to the store, instead of two. Shopping lists help us remember what we need to buy, so we don't have to make multiple trips; thus, the one trip is killing two or more problems.

While on my church mission in Russia, when we were not actually attending a meeting, we would schedule our afternoons to be able to meet people on the street, strike up a discussion, and invite them to hear one of our presentations about our church. It was very nerve-racking sometimes. We would literally walk right up to a family and say, "Hi. We are representatives of a worldwide church, and we have a message we would like to share with you" or some variant of this, in hopes we could eventually teach them in their homes. We called this activity "contacting."

I cannot tell you how many afternoons and evenings we spent on those cold Moscow streets contacting people without success.

I eventually learned that we were much more effective when we contacted on the way to and from our already scheduled appointments, instead of contacting just to contact. It was more spontaneous and sincere, and we were so successful contacting between appointments that eventually, we no longer needed to schedule time specifically to go contacting.

The secret to using the double-edged sword is to recognize that two seemingly unconnected tasks, chores, errands, or liabilities can, in fact, be connected with a single resource, asset, or solution. As in the case of Kate and my app, using the double-edged sword may not have resolved the situation entirely, but softening the blow of those punches that life throws at you will extend your survivability.

Often, expenses in different areas of your life can be solved with one solution. It is extremely efficient when you can find these opportunities. I remember one summer in college when gas prices were going up; I was sitting in traffic all the time, and I felt like I wasn't getting enough exercise. I realized I was able to ride my bike to and from the school and kill three birds with one stone. And yes.... I was able to get there faster by riding my bike! I was so proud when I found one common solution to three different problems.

My brother Aaron once solved a lack of time, lack of income, and unhappiness issue by quitting his $9 per hour job to look for better employment. Until he quit, he didn't have time to look for another job because he was constantly working to make ends meet. When he quit, he didn't have a job or even an interview lined up, but he found that because he could job search, he could find those opportunities and interview for them, which eventually led to him tripling his yearly income in less than two weeks. Talk about a spectacularly efficient move!

The Double-Edged Sword means to find a common solution to two or more problems.

Assignment: Make a list of your top ten problems and then determine whether two or more of them are connected or can be resolved with the same solution. If so, you have a tremendous opportunity to improve your position:

33 – The Pocket Tool

AKA—Multi-Functionality

ANY SINGLE ASSET that is able to perform two or more valuable tasks is usually more efficient than two similar assets that can each only perform one. Typically, the more functionality an asset has, the more efficient it is, assuming its single function replacement occupies the same space, weight, and cost. Therefore, when acquiring new assets, try to focus on ones that have multi-functional capacity, if those needs exist.

Imagine you are going on a long camping trip. You will need to carry with you all of your food, water, and equipment to survive for the next week in adverse conditions. You need to bring some tools, including a knife, scissors, pliers, a small file, saw, can opener, small screwdriver set, and toothpicks. While you could go out and purchase all of these items individually, you wouldn't, simply because so many products out there combine all of these into a single multi-tool. The multi-tool is probably going to cost less, take up less space, weigh less, and be easier to find and access than all of those other items individually. As long as the multi-tool is able to do all the things equally well, you will conserve more energy and time using it, and, therefore, it is more efficient.

Look at the common smartphone and all its functionality—mini-computer, telephone, mobile Internet browser, media player, camera, video recorder, flashlight, gaming device, navigator, etc. I remember when a navigator alone cost several hundred dollars; now one comes free with my phone. No one in his right mind would go out and buy all of those tools individually and carry them all with him.

Some professions have a very limited number of jobs available. I've seen friends with history, dance, acting, air-traffic control, and other extremely niche educations graduate only to realize no jobs are available, forcing them to go back to school. Contrast this with a business degree, which has applicable skills to every business in the world.

I knew an offensive lineman at BYU who eventually had a solid career in the NFL, not because he was an offensive lineman, but because he could also long snap for punts and field goals. In fact, that became his primary job, but he was still an offensive lineman. NFL teams have a very limited number of roster positions, so when a player can fill two roles, he is a gem of a find.

Adam, one of my longtime assistants, has carved an interesting niche for himself because not only can he edit video, but he has learned other crafts of video production, including special effects, Photoshop, audio engineering, and other related skills. He is a Swiss Army knife in his field, which makes him more valuable and adaptable for our projects than someone who can only edit video. Because of our limited production budgets, having a jack-of-all trades like Adam is more efficient than having four specialists who would require four salaries.

I have another friend who has produced a number of low budget films by simply being able to find and hire crewmembers who have multiple skill sets. Hiring such multi-skilled people keeps his production costs down, while maintaining a high quality product.

The principles of multi-functionality—one person or one tool capable of doing many tasks—seems to conflict with the concept of specialization, which is one person or asset performing only one specific job.

But here's the difference: Multi-functional assets are better for projects or systems that happen infrequently. Specialization (which we will discuss in another chapter) is better applied to projects, patterns, or systems that happen often and predictably.

IV – Automation

34 – The Recycled Loop

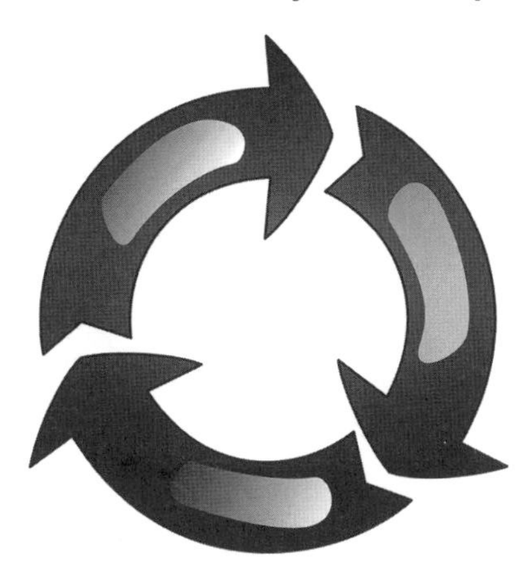

AKA—Thought Cycles

I CANNOT TELL you how many times after shooting an all-day wedding, I have come home and collapsed on my bed, more exhausted than after any football game I ever played.

Decision fatigue is a mental exhaustion that comes from making too many decisions in one day. The casual observer might think, *How exhausting can being a wedding photographer actually be? I mean, you are just standing there and taking pictures, right?* Wrong!

To shoot a wedding, you will have to make somewhere between 5,000 and 50,000 decisions in a single day. You cannot hesitate. Every time you push the shutter button is a decision. On top of that, you must worry about your exposure settings, your lighting, your flash if used, your compositions, directing the bridal party, and your assistant; you need to speak with authority; you must remember their names; and it is expected that you will do this all cheerfully, without any hang-ups, sometimes over the course of ten to twelve hours. It will completely exhaust you because of the number of *thought cycles* you have to go through.

So…what is a thought cycle?

A thought cycle is any set of thoughts or steps that lead us to take action.

The simplest pattern in which ideas in our minds become actions is as follows:

1. Introduction of an idea
2. Consideration of the idea
3. Acceptance or rejection of the idea
4. Plan of action
5. Initiation of action

Thought cycles include two parts: the consideration of the idea (Steps 1-3) and the decision of action (Steps 4-5). They are basically anything that makes you stop, think, and say, "Hey…I need to do that."

There is one fundamental flaw that naturally exists with thought cycles: *Thought cycles have a natural tendency to repeat the entire cycle if they are not completed after deciding to take action.* Lack of action forces us to relive and repeat a decision we have already considered and solved. Over and over. Mentally, this repetition can get expensive.

For example, let's say you need to pay a bill:

1. Rent is due.
2. Should I pay that bill?

3. Yep, need to pay that bill.

4. I'll need to write a check.

5. Let's write that check and send it.

At this point, if real action doesn't happen, guess what? Your conscious is going to remind you at some point about the bill that needs to be taken care of, and you mentally go through each of those steps a second time. Maybe a third, fourth, or fifth time until you actually take care of it.

Let's say this thought cycle has a monetary value related to the PTV it takes to think about it...maybe a dollar ($1). Every time you have that thought cycle, it costs you one dollar in time and stress. If you were to execute your plan immediately, the total cost of this thought cycle from start to finish would look like this:

$1 + any resources needed to complete the task

When thought cycles repeat themselves, the costs could look more like this:

$1 + $1 + $1 + $1 + $1 + $1 + $1 + $1 + $1 + $1 + $1 + $1 +$1 + any resources needed to complete the task + any interest or penalties incurred for waiting or being late

A greater cost comes with re-deciding to act.

The same is true when we go through a partial thought cycle, say steps 1-3 on a specific idea, and when we do not decide what we will do, there is a thought tax if you will re-consider steps 1-3 over and over.

Procrastination is one of the fruits of un-maintained thought cycles. It also increases *thought debt*. In other words, when we fail to have a system for new thought cycles, *we reduce our capacity to think about other things*. Too many thought cycles will eventually overload our thinking process and render us less effective.

Thought cycles are competitive in nature to other conscious thoughts, especially when we have already completed Step Five: We plan to take action.

On a side note, I have noticed that sometimes I have had very creative thought cycles, but I cannot have new ones until the old ones are carried out.

Returning to the number of thought cycles at a wedding, we can also infer that a limit exists to the number of thoughts you can have in a day. That also means that the number of thoughts you will have in a week, month, year, or lifetime are also limited:

You have a limited number of thoughts you can have in this life, and the longer you have already lived, the fewer opportunities you have for those limited thoughts. Make them count!

If that is true and thought cycles have a tendency to repeat themselves, the key to becoming more efficient with your thought cycles is to *automate* them as much as possible.

Defeating the Thought Cycle:

To-do lists or written goals are probably the most common way people deal with thought cycles needing action at another time. The decision has been made; the action has been set-aside for the time being. Writing it down helps us remember the conclusion we arrived at, avoiding the need to repeat the thought cycle later.

This is interesting to me because it shows that most everyone is subconsciously aware of thought cycles and how to reduce their burden. To do lists are very helpful when we are short on time, and sometimes it is the best tool for the job. But is there a more efficient way to deal with thought cycles?

One of the easiest ways to circumvent thought cycles that beat you down is to set up automated responses to the most common ones you face. (As an exception and warning, you must be careful not to allow yourself to fall into predictable tendencies that an intelligent enemy will exploit.)

When you have an automated response, your thought cycles look more like this:

1. Introduction of Idea or Opportunity
2. Initiation of Linked Action

Thought Cycles with automated execution mechanisms produce reduced levels of time, stress, and attention.

By predetermining your thought processes on the matter, and linking a prepared response, you can effectively minimize the cost of repeating thought processes, thus *thinking more effectively.* The following tactics are helpful in defeating recurring thought cycles:

The Link—Means to condition yourself to respond automatically (without thought) to certain stimulus. I use the Link to help me know when I will refuel my car. When it gets to 1/8 of a tank, then I will refuel at the next gas station I see. Been doing that for twenty years. Another example, what do you do when your alarm goes off in the morning? Do you jump out of bed, or do you linger?

Predetermined Decision Making—Similar to the link, this means to prepare a "this or that" response in advance, based on certain data. If two options exist, then those would both be planned for. I use the personal "binaries" I've mentioned as pre-determined decision makers when time is short. Doing so dramatically reduces the amount of time it takes to arrive at a decision. With practice, you will establish your own binaries, or benchmarks for making one choice over another. For example, in stock trading: *Traders will often predetermine when to buy or sell based on a stock hitting a certain benchmark value.* They don't even think about it. When it hits price A, something specific happens (they buy); when it hits price B, something else happens (they sell).

Rejection (The Shield of Rejection)—The most efficient way to kill a thought cycle is to reject it on first contact. Just totally reject the thing. Tell yourself you will never do it, ever, and forget about it. An example of this for me is drug use. It is something I have zero interest in trying or even think about trying.

Isolation or a Barrier—Even more effective than thought rejection is to find ways to prevent them from entering your mind in the first place. If your mind is like a garden, this would be building a greenhouse so the wind won't blow any unwanted seeds into it (like weeds). If you never have to weed, think about all the time you will have to do other, more constructive things.

Delegation (The Hot Potato)—Delegation means giving the assignment or problem to someone or something else. I recommend an assistant once you can afford one—yes, hired help who can put out your day-to-day defensive fires. I have had a full-time assistant for a couple of years now. She makes my life much easier by dealing with all the little things I don't have time for. She is worth every penny. In some cases, you can hire companies or even computer programs to take the work on for you.

Two important rules exist when delegating:

1. You absolutely have to trust that the person or thing you are delegating to will get the job done with an acceptable level of quality, in the allotted time, with the allotted resources.

2. The resources used to have someone else do a task would be less than the resources used if you did it (especially when considering PTV).

Don't Think About It, Feel About It—This example is best described by Malcolm Gladwell in his book *Blink*. The idea is that a person ***trained in a particular area*** **(very important distinction)** has the ability to make correct decisions based on first impressions and instinct with 95 percent accuracy, almost immediately, even if the situation is unique, even without thinking about it. Gladwell refers to this as "Thin Slicing."

Therefore, if you are well-trained in a particular subject, you will know immediately what to do when presented with information regarding that field. This drastically reduces steps for creating a plan of action, and thus, makes you more efficient. The speed and power of "Thin Slicing" cannot be underestimated. (I highly recommend you read *Blink*. It is one of my all-time favorite books!)

When you remove the time required to make correct decisions, your thought efficiency increases.

Removal of Distance—I'm talking about the physical distance of when and how decisions are made. When I used to pick up my mail from the post office, I would always bring my checkbook and stamps. Why? Because if there were any bills, I could write a check immediately and mail it *without bringing bills home, putting them on a shelf, waiting, reliving the thought cycle repeatedly, and eventually writing* *the checks and walking them back out.* Bills are stressful. Why prolong and relive them?

I know this may not seem like a big deal, but not having to think or worry about those bills after first seeing them was a huge advantage, not only in stress and extra steps, but by reducing the number of thought cycles required to complete the task. Today, I am mostly using automated withdrawals for my most common utility bills (cell phone, electricity, Internet, etc.). There may be thought cycles in your life that are determined by two or more points far away from each other. Find ways to shorten that space.

Muscle Memory and Repetition

Do you remember the first time you tried to dribble a basketball or ride a bike?

They were and still are a complex set of processes that, if thought of on a conscious level, are nearly impossible to perform using a thought cycle. However, with the right encouragement, persistence, and repetitive practice, most children can master these skills and retain them for the rest of their lives.

Muscle Memory refers to our innate ability to learn a complex set of processes on a subconscious level through repetition.

Muscle memory is used by pilots, artists, musicians, world-class athletes, soldiers, and many others who make a living performing complex, difficult tasks and making them routine. By circumventing some of the steps normally required of a specific thought cycle, muscle memory allows users to execute their plans faster.

This also means: Any difficult task or process can be made more efficient through repetition.

Thought Speed

Think about the first computer or smartphone you owned and when you connected to the internet using it. There was a joke that "www" meant "worldwide wait." I remember AOL taking several minutes just to connect. Today, I can use my phone to access the Internet instantly. The benefits of fast-thinking computers cannot be understated, and they will only get faster. Keep that in mind the next time you consider how much RAM you should buy for your new computer. Like computers, humans all think at slightly different speeds. If there is a way to train our mind to think faster, in fewer steps, you will have a considerable advantage.

Because the number of thoughts you have in a day is limited, and you have fewer remaining opportunities as time passes, it is critical for you to develop the habit of optimizing your thought cycles, discovering what triggers them, and then establishing systems to minimize their effect on your daily life.

35 – The Link

AKA—The Connection

WHEN I WAS teaching biology to freshmen at the University of Alabama, it was very important to me that I knew my students' names. Name recall is a powerful teaching tool and motivator and improved my ability to connect as a teacher. I could call on anyone in the classroom at any time, and more importantly, I could praise students by name for a correct answer.

That said, while my intentions were good in wanting to remember all my students' names, the process of doing so was very difficult since my classes often had over 250 students. This presented a problem when trying to remember all of their names by the second or third time we met.

The Link is the concept that when something specific happens, another specific thing *should* happen next.

The way I memorized their names was to have everyone introduce themselves in front of a video camera on the way out of the first day of class. I then edited the video down so I had each of them say his or her own name in a one to one-and-half second clip, so the final video was about four or five minutes long. Then I would start playing games with their names.

For example, I pretended that "Alisha Rogers" had a fascination with walking Mister Rogers on "a leash" (as in "Alisha," and Mister Rogers was a famous television children's educator). Once I visually imagined that, it was impossible to unsee or forget it.

"Ashley Adams" had to wash "ash" off of her "Adam's" apple every morning when she woke up. It was a very curious medical condition to say the least.

And so on. By looking at my students' faces, hearing their names, and playing the most ridiculous mind games possible, I found that I could establish a direct link between a face and the visualization I imagined, and I could then decipher names from that visualization. You can imagine how much fun it was to have my students sit down in that second session and one-by-one call them each by first and last name, regardless of where they sat. It blew them away and made them each feel special.

Most of us use defensive links every day. For example:

- When we are hungry, we want to eat.
- When it is ten at night, we might start getting ready for bed.
- When we get a bill, we might feel stressed, or motivated to pay it.

These are reactionary because they are natural, common, and usually happen without any thought at all. Reactions are primarily defensive, meaning that your circumstances or surroundings are dictating how you will respond to threats or needs.

Offensive thinking links match up a strength, asset, or skill to an opportunity or enemy's weakness. They require a little more planning and forethought because they may have no immediate or biological connection. Everyone uses defensive links; far fewer employ offensive links, although I feel this is where the greatest potential for linking is.

When you have a set of predetermined decisions, you skip the longest part of the thought cycle, which, in turn, makes your *thinking more efficient.*

Examples of links are used in football regularly:

If we win the coin toss, we will elect to defer until the second-half.

If the middle-linebacker is blitzing, then I'll pass to the tight-end over the middle.

If the defensive end comes inside, I will try to run around him.

If we only get a field goal with such little time remaining, we will have to on-side kick.

You get the idea. With time, repeated links can become habits that require no thought at all.

By establishing predetermined trigger responses to specific stimuli, we can become more efficient in our thought processes, instead of having to remake the decision over and over, or allowing ourselves to be distracted. The applications of the link are unlimited.

36 – The Fishing Pole

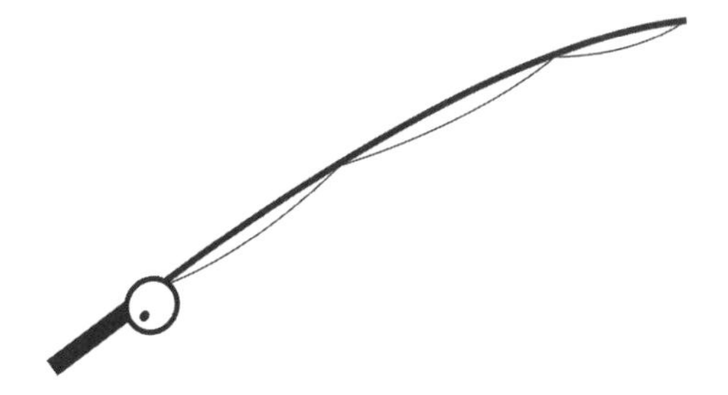

AKA—Self-Maintainers and Self-Regulating Mechanisms

"Give a man a fish and he will eat for a day; teach a man to fish and you feed him for a lifetime."
— Chinese Proverb

WHILE LINKS HAVE more to do with connecting thoughts and plans, the Fishing Pole represents automated ways of actually carrying out the action.

If a behavior is completely consistent and predictable, the correct answer in one instance of that problem will also be the correct answer in another.

Self-maintainers are specialists who automatically handle the same types of recurring problems.

The idea of a self-maintainer is that you set up an automatic mechanism in response to a recurring problem. True self-maintainers will also self-regulate when fulfilling their tasks, so they never require attention.

Here is a good example: I sell training video downloads and I know from experience that the customer who is not tech-savvy will need help or instructions on how to download. Originally, I was the one who would offer customer support. After a few weeks, I got tired of repeating the same steps to different customers.

I decided to create a video I could upload to YouTube that would answer all of my customers' possible questions. I was no longer required to help my customers—the video does it for me, for free. We even send it out *automatically* with every purchase, whether the person needs it or not, because if he does need it, I have already supplied the video and he doesn't need to contact us.

Automatic responses to recurring problems increases efficiency.

Self-maintainers usually take the form of problem solvers responding to specific triggers. They have many forms, including:

- Customer service videos.
- A piece of technology, like a computer, app, or dishwasher.
- A pre-programmed lawn sprinkler system.
- Words, written or verbal—perhaps an email or voice recording.
- Specialists in dealing with specific problems. (I like to think of my personal assistant as such an example.)
- A physical action or way of doing things—workflow is an example.
- Responsibility—pre-assigned areas of concern.

How to develop self-maintainers for recurring problems:

1. **Root Cause Analysis:** If it is a recurring problem that only you can manage, attack the problem at its cause. Try to prevent it from happening. Destroy the enemy before it gains momentum. It is easier to weed seedlings than trees.

2. **Simplify:** If it is a pattern or recurring process, try to reduce the number of 1) steps involved, 2) moving parts, and 3) intermediaries.

3. **Technology and Business:** Thousands of businesses exist solely on the idea that they can do something for you instead of you doing it yourself. If the cost of the technology is less than the cost of you personally performing a task, invest in it.

4. **Delegation:** If technology cannot solve the problem, look for an individual who may be willing to do it for you. This is where a lot of kids make money mowing lawns. This is the concept of employment.

Any time you are faced with a recurring problem, find a way to have a self-maintainer take care of it for you indefinitely, so you don't even have to think about it anymore.

37 – The Assembly Line

AKA—Divide and Conquer by Specialization

PRETEND YOU RUN a pin-making factory in the late eighteenth century. Your task, as manager, is to provide the maximum number of pushpins by the end of each day. For the sake of demonstration, let's assume ten complex tasks are required to produce high quality pins. You have ten unskilled workers just hired off the street. You demonstrate all the steps to all the workers and set them to work making pins individually from start to finish. It doesn't take long to realize that each worker has a very different understanding of the steps involved, works at a different speed, and has a different degree of manual dexterity. At the end of the first day, on average, these ten workers have barely produced ten pins. They each average one pin per day.

The next day, you have a brilliant idea. You have each of the ten workers focus on only one step in the process. You carefully instruct them on a single task, so they become intimately familiar with all of the complexities of one step; then they no longer need to move from one task to the next. All they have to worry about is performing their one assigned task over and over. When they become specialists in their one responsibility, you are delighted to see production reach as high as 48,000 pins in one day, an average of 4,800 pins per worker!

The most shocking thing about the above story is that, in principle, it is real. The concept comes from Adam Smith's *Wealth of Nations*, where he discusses the increase of production using the same number of resources by having workers *specialize*.

When a worker becomes an expert at performing a single task required as part of a complex series of tasks, it is called specialization.

Specialization allows workers to become much more efficient and productive than they would be working alone on many tasks.

Henry Ford later exploited specialization in spectacular fashion, producing cars by means of an assembly line. While many knew of the power of specialization, Ford revolutionized it by having the parts move from worker to worker in an automated system. He was able to narrow both the space and the time each worker needed to assemble a given part, increasing productivity even more.

If you have a system of production, or you are faced with a ginormous task that includes producing something, packing something, or preparing something—any tasks that require continual, repeated steps—it is much more efficient to have specialists at each step, instead of having them all do many steps.

Divide and conquer by specialization will greatly increase your productivity, as well as reduce the time it takes to complete a task.

In the event you are faced with a huge task, consider the option of divide and conquer, breaking up the task into smaller parts. When those parts are assigned to specialists in an assembly line, you are leveraging principles that are potentially thousands of times more efficient.

38 – The Printing Press

AKA—Economies of Scale

ALMOST EVERYONE WHO has taken a basic economics class will be familiar with *economies of scale*, but the principle goes beyond manufacturing and can be intentionally exploited in different arenas.

Let's pretend you have an idea for a gadget and want to mass produce it for profit. You have already spent a lot of time thinking about it, and you will need to spend more time and most likely money to develop a working prototype. This deals mainly with proof of concept, which lets you see whether the thing works and does what it is supposed to.

If you have success, next you will need to spend more time and money to polish your product so it is ready to be delivered to the masses. I tell you these things from experience; this is generally how it is, no matter what you are selling to the public. A lot of time and money is spent in developing any product, like The Maven Adapter, a patented invention I created that allows photographers to attach a camera to the end of a window cleaning pole.

When you finally have something you are proud of and you are sick of making prototypes to be tested, you will take your product to a manufacturing specialist. The manufacturing specialist is typically an engineer who will design or build a machine to create potentially unlimited quantities of your product.

The engineer will charge you, let's say for example, $15,000 for the "tooling," or creation of the mold that the machine will use to create your gadget. Typically, many other fees are involved, such as the time and labor for the set-up of the equipment before each run.

Time and money may also be involved in testing and quality control of the products as they are being produced. There may even be time and money involved in getting the color of the dye right. In some cases, an elaborate assembly line of workers might even be needed to add different parts to make the gadget functional.

Next, we add the cost of materials and labor for each gadget, which is exactly ten dollars per unit—the materials may be rubber, metal, paint, etc. This is just the cost of raw materials and the time it takes to put the gadget together.

Now, after all of this careful planning and set up, if you manufacture one unit, you would pay the cost of all the time that went into the gadget, plus compensating the engineer; in this case, let's say $50,000, plus the cost of the materials and labor used to create the gadget—let's say ten dollars.

So the cost to produce one single gadget in this example is $50,010. Therefore, the gadget would need to sell for at least that much simply for you to break even before taxes.

But having done all of this hard work to create everything we need to manufacture the gadget, what would be our break-even cost if we asked the engineer to make two in a row? After all, a lot of time and resources was invested in getting everything set up.

For this system to create two gadgets, the cost would be:

$50,000 + ($10 x 2 units) = $50,020

Therefore, to break even, you would need to sell each gadget at a cost of $25,010.

By making one extra unit, the cost per unit was dramatically reduced.

Hmm...what about four units?

$50,000 + ($10 x 4) = $50,040 ÷ 4 units = $12,505

This is a simplified version of the economies of scale—*as you produce more units of a given product, typically the cost per unit decreases.* Most of this efficiency is coming from the one-time set-up, research, prototyping, and tooling fees being divided by many units of product.

The same would be true with the printing of a newspaper or magazine. Writing an article, setting up the presses, printing the first issue—these steps take time and money. *But once the presses are rolling, if you continue to let them roll, the cost per unit goes down with each copy printed.*

As the cost per unit decreases, the system becomes more financially efficient.

Assuming you are selling the product for the same price, and you are able to lower dramatically the expense of creating it, the product becomes more profitable. The magic of economies of scale comes from cost savings of setup expenses per unit over time.

Anyone who becomes familiar with a given circumstance or situation will become more and more adept at handling that kind of situation in the future. Thus, experience and repetition have a very similar effect on the economies of scale.

For example, the first time beginning athletes work out, the routine may be confusing. The weights may be heavy or awkward to lift. They may find themselves out of breath. They may feel sore for days. To a non-athlete, the first time training really hard may even be stressful.

But the second time, things seem a little easier. The athletes know what to expect—maybe they aren't out of breath as much; maybe they're not as sore.

With continued workouts, athletes become more adept at dealing with the system and the stress involved, and with time, workouts aren't nearly as hard as the first time.

Similar things could be said about doctors, parents, firefighters, football coaches, chefs, race car drivers, Navy SEALs, sales clerks—all go through this initial learning curve. The first encounter can be stressful and confusing. After repeated exposures to the same situation, it becomes easier for the person involved to perform at a higher and higher level because he knows what to expect and how to react, often without thinking.

On the big scale, it seems that every new experience we gain makes us more efficient in dealing with that same experience in the future.

Experience, when the lesson is learned, *makes us more efficient.*

Bonus Thoughts

I feel lucky to read books written by those who are experienced in given topics. When a mastermind writes a book, it opens a window into how that person thinks.

If you *thought exactly the way a mastermind thinks, you could have a life just like his.* It allows us to gain insights into why they are successful, and gain new thought patterns we can apply to our own lives.

It is said that we are the average of the five people we spend the most time with. And if you can surround yourself with great books written by great people, the thoughts and habits of those people will rub off on you, and you will find your thought processes changing. **Experience is efficient!**

39 – The Greenhouse

AKA—Fertile Ground Doctrine

CONSIDER TWO SEEDS of the same genetic material, each loaded with enormous potential to become a fruit tree millions of times their original size. The seeds are clones, identical in every way. Consider that each of these seeds, once planted, is introduced to the same amount of water and once sprouted, the same amount of sunlight and the same air at the exact same temperatures. The only difference between the two seeds is that one is planted in fertile ground, and the other placed on hard cement, exposed to the elements.

Most plant seeds contain just enough resources to send out tiny roots to anchor themselves into the soil, gather the tiniest amounts of water, grow their first stem to the surface, and grow primary leaves that will allow them to access sunlight and photosynthesize it to create cellular energy. With enough sunlight, water, and relative protection, plants are genetically coded to grow and succeed despite their frail seedling state.

Although the two seeds are genetically identical, we would expect the one planted in the fertile ground to flourish, eventually reaching its full potential, while the other will die off shortly after being placed on the cement.

Without the support of a root anchor, the protection of the soil itself, a frail seedling has no chance of success.

Every seedling is loaded with potential, but that critical phase of when and where it is planted will determine almost all of its success, *regardless of what its genetic material is.* The seedling needs to set its roots to at least have a chance, and it cannot do that on concrete.

I am a firm believer that every person is born with an unlimited and tremendous potential, what I call the Michael Jordan effect; meaning that every person has the potential to become a Michael Jordan in *something*. Maybe not basketball, but something spectacular that he or she was *meant* to become.

Unfortunately, I am also a believer that, for a myriad of reasons, most people never find their calling. It has less to do with their God-given potential and more to do with their environment and surroundings.

- Imagine someone who had the genetic potential of a Michael Jordan on the basketball court, but was born in a country where people simply did not play the sport.

- Or a Bill Gates type mind, born in the early 1100s, raised by farmers.

- Or a Peyton Manning who was constantly surrounded by an inferior offensive line.

- Or the employee with a revolutionary idea, who is then poo-pooed by his or her boss and coworkers.

- Or the entrepreneur who desperately wants to start what would become a booming business but doesn't have the support of his or her spouse.

- Or the Warren Buffet type who constantly had bad business partners who were stealing from the business, or even suing him! (I cannot over-emphasize the importance of good business partners; they are as critical to your business success as anything!)

We are not identical. As individuals, we have tremendous diversity, including genetic and psychological differences. We have been nurtured differently; we have unique thoughts, feelings, and impressions.

Symbolically, this means that no two seeds (individuals) are exactly the same in every way. We each have different, yet valuable fruits we can bring forth if given the right conditions. It seems that often, we gravitate toward wanting to be like others who are highly successful at their God-given Michael Jordan talent. It would be like an orange tree wanting to become an apple tree, only because the apple tree is flourishing. Orange trees cannot become apple trees, and therefore, when an orange tree tries to do exactly that, he or she fails. Orange trees should try to exploit the fact that they are orange trees and are different. I have seen this so many times in the photography industry; a photographer sees another having some kind of success, then does everything possible to copy that person, instead of finding his or her own path.

Additionally, our fates are not constrained to where we are planted or what our surroundings are. We can often dictate and control what kind of life and opportunities we will have for ourselves when we are willing to make the necessary sacrifice.

If you are a seed in infertile ground, do whatever it is you can to put yourself in a situation where you are surrounded by conditions and people that nurture the growth of your given talents, skills, and dreams. This is especially true when you are starting something new—you need to have at least some initial success and traction to grow those roots, get your anchor, and bring in the resources you need to mature in the natural specialty you are wired for.

I should note that "fertile ground" does not mean "easy," nor should it mean "time to run if you don't like how things are going." Fertile ground is usually more like a hammer smashing hot metal, shaping you one day at a time. Chasing dreams is usually a lot of work. Football practice was physically and mentally demanding, but it was *aimed* toward our specific team goals.

It will take some discretion to know the difference between what is constructive progress toward goals versus what is a waste of time and resources when both might be equally difficult in the moment. Knowing the progress you are making is the key.

How will you find your specialty or Michael Jordan type talent?

It is the career or vocation you would do for free because you love the activity so much. It is your form of ideal play, only you are paid for it.

You may know what it is already and have been told by too many people that you cannot or should not pursue it. I can tell you from experience that, most likely, your hidden super talent has to do with that one thing you cannot stop thinking about.

I say this knowing the possibilities are unlimited. If you are a fanatic about coaching football, playing video games, making movies, being a musician, teaching or service, there are profitable careers in all those fields. Follow your gut on this. You have been given these feelings for a reason, and it is part of how you are wired. If you were not naturally wired for those dreams, you would not be having those impressions.

As a young child, I mastered the names and nomenclatures of nearly every single firearm I could learn about. It was easy. I didn't even have to think about it. Once I read the name and saw a picture of it, it stuck.

I had other friends who loved English Literature and could quote lines from a variety of Shakespeare's plays. They could memorize these lines without thinking twice about it. I couldn't if I were threatened under penalty of torture or death. I had other friends who could memorize baseball statistics at a glance. They just stuck with them. They had photographic memories, *but only on specific subjects*. There is huge advantage to pursuing interests we are naturally wired for.

Take two people who are both interested in something like film-making. One is naturally wired for a passion and interest in it; the other is doing it to pay the bills. If you take both of those individuals and put them through the same schooling and environment, the one who is more naturally passionate about film-making will flourish, *even if the soil is fertile for both.* I can speak from experience, spending weeks on a set, working sixteen-hour days, and coming home tired, but still interested enough to look up new filming or lighting techniques just because I find it fun; this passion gives me a tremendous advantage over the filmmaker who is burnt out and ready for sleep. I can go weeks with five hours of sleep a night and be thrilled beyond measure to get up each morning when I am working on a film.

My longtime assistant Adam has a similar infatuation with doing special effects. He can work all day on set, come home, and spend the remaining few hours available studying new editing or SFX tutorials, not because he has to, but because he sees it all as recreation.

Take anyone else who doesn't have that passion for film-making, put him through the same workload and schedule, and he will burn out quickly. I've actually seen this many times on set. After a week or two of shooting, there are those who want to go home early, nap in a trailer, or call in sick. Illness or fatigue would not stop me from coming to the set because I am having so much fun. *Passion is the ultimate paycheck, not money.*

Tremendous efficiency occurs when you match up your naturally-wired potential with the fertile ground for that talent.

I have a good friend on Maui who worked his whole professional life as a carpenter, but his real love was fishing. He is crazy about it—it is all he wants to talk about. Truly a fanatic. He was a carpenter to pay the bills. He eventually realized he could become a professional fisherman on Maui. It was not easy, nor cheap, but he took the courses, got his captain's license, and today makes his living by taking tourists on fishing excursions. He is a very happy man. His dream could not have come to fruition living somewhere like Nebraska or Utah. When he realized his true dream, he made the changes necessary to bring it to fruition, and he *sacrificed for it*. Life is too short to live in infertile ground.

It will simply not be possible to have success at all times and in all places. If you really want true happiness, with the right desire, ambition, and drive, you must be willing to uproot yourself and plant yourself in surroundings more appropriate for helping you succeed.

Stack the cards of your surroundings, opportunities, and mentors in your favor when pursuing a dream.

40 – The Funnel

AKA—The Trap

"WOULD YOU LIKE to have your picture taken with us?" asked the in-full-costume Peter the Great street performer. My good friend Jerry and I were walking across Palace Square in St. Petersburg when we were approached by this man and an-equally-decked-out-eighteenth-century-dressed woman.

"No, thank you," I replied.

"How often can you take a picture with Peter the Great?" he asked in a classic Russian accent as he slapped his heel down and busted a proud pose—chest in the air and chin lifted high. *If Disney ever wanted someone to portray Peter the Great at its theme parks, this is their man*, I thought. The woman following behind him smiled and pinched the edges of her elegantly embroidered dress, doing a little curtsy.

"You can use your own camera, too," he added with a smile and friendly wink.

Really...? Not only was I in St. Petersburg, Russia, but I couldn't help agreeing with him...*How often can a man have his picture taken with Peter the Great...on Palace Square?*

"Sure, why not," I relented, handing my camera to Jerry for the shots.

These two street performers were very good, polished. Not only were their costumes elaborate, but it was clear they had a complete repertoire of poses. They quickly recommended and repositioned me in various positions, with Jerry snapping away at each pose.

"Now you," said Peter, gesturing toward Jerry, who reluctantly played along. It was truly amazing how nice these two were.

Having snapped at least five poses each, we were ready to be on our way.

"Thank you very much," I said, offering to shake the man's hand.

His demeanor suddenly changed from that of a nice, happy street performer to a serious and demanding man as he held out his hand and said, "Now you pay 250 rubles!"

"Chevo?"(*"What?")* I asked loudly in Russian, contesting their demand. They were taken aback that I knew the language, but they still continued their attack.

"Twenty-five rubles for each pose! Ten pictures. You pay now!" the woman joined in. Jerry and I looked around for a cop, but none were in sight. In fact, literally no one was around and we had been duped.

These street performers had designed a very simple, yet effective means of funneling unsuspecting tourists into their trap. I believed I could defend myself if things got nasty, but I didn't know whether Peter the Great was armed, had a knife, or other street performers nearby ready to follow or mug us. From a cultural perspective, if we didn't pay, we ran the risk of having some shady characters believe we had stolen from them. At least that's probably what they wanted us to think.

To be done with it, we grudgingly paid the money and went on our way.

***

It was third and seven. BYU was in a tight game with the Washington Huskies, in Seattle, fall of 1998. As our quarterback dropped back to pass, he read the cornerback blitzing from the short side of the field. There was no one to pick up the blitz, so he had to throw the ball immediately to his "hot" receiver, who also read the blitz and changed his route to a quick slant.

Washington's safety was right there waiting for the slant route. Our receiver caught the pass and was promptly tackled one-and-a-half yards short of the first down marker. BYU would have to punt.

"What you are seeing here," Norm Chow, our offensive coordinator would later say in team meetings, aiming his laser pointer at the screen, "is a very strategic decision to force us to throw the slant, make the tackle, and end our set of downs. If this guy misses the tackle, it is a touchdown (since no other defenders are in the area). *This is what they wanted us to do, and they executed it perfectly."*

***

Funneling is the strategy of knowing a person's tendencies and behaviors so well that you may successfully predict what they will do in a given situation and then steer his decision-making process down a predetermined path toward an intended goal. In short, it is laying a trap. I am teaching you this from a defensive position—*how to avoid being trapped by those who wish to take advantage of you.*

Typically, with more decisions made, funneling becomes harder to get out of; there are few other choices and time is short. When properly executed, it puts tremendous psychological pressure on prey to choose what their predators want them to choose. The premise is to force the prey to choose something he or she wouldn't have initially.

Had the Russian approached me and demanded, "Give me 250 rubles!" I would have immediately said, "No." The more he would directly pressure me, the more I would resist. And he knew that. He also knew that if he set up a funnel (trap) to make me *feel obligated*, the money would be much easier to obtain.

Washington's coach didn't know exactly what play BYU had called, but he knew we would *probably* pass, and from film study, he *probably* knew we used a slant hot route when facing that particular blitz. *By choosing to attack*, Washington baited our reaction, changing who was in control and ending the series of downs—*which was more efficient than attempting to play a safe defense, not knowing which play we were running.*

Funneling is common. You have encountered it or even executed it in your life without knowing it. If you have ever signed up for a credit card, you have probably been funneled. Credit card companies know that it is human nature for people to want something they cannot pay for. Providing a short-term loan in the form of a plastic credit card allows them to exploit this human tendency, and they will make the money on interest and late fees. As a side note, I do not own or use credit cards anymore because of their predatory nature. For me, it is either pay cash or leave the item behind, and that has helped me avoid a lot of purchase temptation.

How "funneling" tactics work:

- Traps involve an intelligent human or business pulling the strings.

- Be **very wary** of accepting anything of value "for free". Whenever someone gives you something, you immediately feel obligated. Many funneling tactics start by making you feel you can gain from the offer with no obligation. It may come in the form of a sample, favor, gift, help, etc. Something-for-nothing should throw up a red flag in your mind immediately, even more so with greater value. No one intelligent gives away value without knowing something greater can be gained in return. *There is almost always a well-planned financial reason why someone is offering you something for free.*

- Beware of any offers that have limited time availability. A good funneling strategy will always introduce scarcity of time, thus adding more pressure on the decision maker. *Why is the offer expiring in ten minutes? What is the specific reason?* If you cannot determine why you need to decide *right this second*, you are probably being funneled. Still, like the blitzing cornerback and angry Russian, the best funneling tactics will involve very real reasons to decide right away.

- Pay close attention when you are on someone else's home field. It may be a physical location, his terms or rules, or even his contract. Having an intimate knowledge of battleground surroundings gives one a distinct advantage.

When you are offered something for free, and on someone else's turf, red flags should be going up all over the place. It will not end well. Keep in mind, you can be baited and trapped on neutral or even your own turf, but the advantage is in the other person's favor when it is on his terms.

So, in conclusion, if you encounter:

A. A person or business,

B. Offering you something valuable for free,

C. With a limited time opportunity,

D. On his or its turf or under his or its rules or contract…

…chances are, you are walking into a trap.

41 – The Incline

AKA—The 1 Percent Rule

WRITING A BOOK is no joke. The first time I tried, I sat down believing I could knock it out in a couple of days of focused effort. I started off quickly, furiously typing my first two pages, and then I ran into "the wall," otherwise known as writer's block. I decided to try harder, really focus, and do my best, writing for at least three or four hours a day. You can guess how that turned out.

I also remember wanting to learn how to play the piano. I figured if I could dedicate four or five hours a day to it, I should be able to learn in a couple of months. I also realized this wouldn't work after about two days.

The ancient Egyptians were faced with the monumental task of moving and lifting enormous stones to construct the pyramids. Many of these stones weighed more than two tons. This task could not be done by simply grabbing the stones, picking them up, and slapping them into place.

The incline is a ramp or path constructed at an angle on which a given load, weight, or task can be moved. The incline reduces the force needed to overcome gravity by distributing that force over greater distances.

While it would be impossible to lift a two-ton stone single-handedly, the Egyptians exploited the incline to a spectacular degree and the proof remains today.

I completed my first book by waking up twenty minutes early every morning and writing. That is exactly how both *3 Weeks in Haiti* and this book were written. Chipping away at them, just a little bit, day after day. There is incredible power in consistency.

If you have a very large task, you can use the incline to break it down into smaller, manageable pieces. If it is a skill set, talent, new business, book, or anything you are trying to create, apply the incline, which I also call the *1 percent rule*:

- Instead of trying to have large chunks of growth immediately, go for very small increments of growth—tell yourself no more than 1 percent per day.

- If you can grow or progress 1 percent each day, in a little over three months, you will be 100 percent better than you were when you started. That is amazing!

A key warning when using the incline: The force required when using the incline must be consistent. It will not work if you do a little one day, then wait a few months before starting again. I've learned that you really have to get into a nearly day-to-day habit in order for this process to be effective. It obviously depends on what you are trying to do, but if you are not actively working on it, you should spend some time thinking about, planning, preparing, or visualizing, even if it is only for a few minutes. That tiny effort over long periods is extremely powerful and efficient in reducing a task's overall friction.

If you have a monumental goal or task, use a disciplined, consistent approach, focusing on smaller steps of improvement.

42 – Dice

AKA—The Law of Variation and Unpredictability

"WE ARE DOING exactly the same things we were last year," said one not-so-popular football coach, attempting to explain the difference between a championship season in 1999, and a catastrophic year in 2000, which eventually led to him being fired.

"It is like a pendulum. When you first see it, its rhythm may confuse you, but if it swings at the same rate, eventually anyone can figure the timing out. You have to change it up, even when you are successful," stated Norm Chow, offensive coordinator and coach of three Heisman trophy quarterbacks.

You may have heard the saying: "If you always do what you have always done, you will always get what you have always got." Unfortunately, it is not true. If you always do what you have always done, at some point, even if you are successful, competitors will copy you; you will run out of time, money, and resources; your customers will get bored; and your enemies will know your plans in advance, making it easier to defeat you. I have also learned that most successes are temporary because the environments in which they happen are constantly changing.

Never allow past success to extinguish your fire for excellence.

Always seek to improve your situation.

Dice is the willful, proactive decision to change things up, even if things are going great.

If I were taking on a giant enemy, one who was far superior and knew exactly what I had done in the past, I would not play how he expects, nor allow him to do what he is best at. *I would try to change how the game was played entirely.*

For example, if I were the head coach of a college football team playing the current juggernaut, I would employ an offense so strange and unusual that the opposing defenders wouldn't even know exactly where to line up. Sure, it might not work, but typically failure is inevitable when the underdog tries to beat the bully at his game. It almost never works. By thinking outside the box; preparing a well thought-out, yet unseen scheme; reducing reaction time; catching them off-guard, and getting him on his heels, you could give your team a chance.

How important is change for success?

On the genetic level, humans are creations of change and variation. Our chromosomes go through extensive gene shuffling called "crossing over" in the early stages of sperm and egg production to ensure genetic variation. Inbreeding, or the mating of similar genetic individuals in humans, leads to developmental defects.

Suppose an evil dictator was successful in creating a clone army where all the soldiers were exactly the same genetically. Perhaps they would have superior strength, speed, vision, intelligence, resistance to disease, etc. However, if they were truly identical genetically, it would also mean that they would all have a *common weakness*, whatever it was. Once that weakness was discovered in one individual, it would apply to all the others as well.

Consider bacteria. When you are infected, your physician may prescribe antibiotics, which destroy bacteria. She will instruct you to take the medication regularly until the medicine is all gone. Why? Because bacteria replicate in an exponential fashion—one becomes two, two become four, etc.

Now assume that during these replications, when one million are becoming two million, just one of them accidentally has a mutation, which makes it immune to the antibiotics what will happen? The non-mutated bacteria will die, and the mutated, bulletproof version will be unaffected by that antibiotic, allowing it to replicate without any trouble. This is essentially how super-bacteria evolve to become resistant to many antibiotics, a real problem the medical field faces today.

Adaptation and variation creates new opportunities.

In my early days as a YouTuber, I would do basic camera reviews. After a while, it seemed more and more photographers started doing similar camera reviews, so my overall subscriptions and views plummeted. Today, YouTube is full of photography channels with the same types of reviews. *Consequently, I had to find something to make myself stand out.* A few years ago, I discovered that if I treated episodes like a TV show and did an array of new tests *showing the results* and not just stating my opinions, I could win more viewers. Since creating my Epic Shootouts channel, I have had great success—and my shootouts are considered by many to be the best camera comparison tests available. I owe so much to that one little change.

Dice is not just adaptation; it is a conscious, focused decision to change tactics, strategy, even the entire game, to evolve or to catch your competition off guard.

43 – The Ace of Spades

AKA—The Competitive Advantage

"If you do not have a competitive advantage, do not compete."
— Warren Buffet

IN LATE 2009, after shooting a photo session, I had a brilliant idea for an iPhone app. Constantly needing model releases signed, and having to use physical paper forms (can you imagine that?), I thought, *What if I could make an app that allows photographers to use their iPhones to create a digital contract, complete with digital signatures signed by the talent right on the screen?* There was no doubt in my mind it would be a hit.

A few months after finding a good developer, my app, Photographer's Contract Maker, launched on the App Store. It was the first of its kind and was a phenomenal success. In the early stages, it climbed to twenty-third on the Photography Apps chart and was selling as many as 100 copies per day.

Just over a month later, something bad happened. A second contract app appeared on the App Store. This one was a little different, with fewer features and no placeholders, but it had something mine didn't—contracts for stock photography releases.

For the next several months, the two apps would battle, each coming out with more features, each being matched by the other. Over time, many more contract apps came out. The last time I checked, at least twenty such contract/model release apps were available, each having varying degrees of success, each essentially knock-offs of earlier ones, and none of them having something that could not be copied by the others.

After some time, I realized this app war was not worth fighting, simply because I was only making $1.99 per sale. There were better ways to spend my time. But a valuable lesson had been learned—a lesson I already knew, but had not executed very well—you need to have a *competitive advantage*.

Whenever I ask people what their understanding of a competitive advantage is, they usually reply, "An advantage?" It is shocking how few people truly understand this gold mine of a secret; it is even more shocking how many business owners are attempting to compete without one.

If we were to look at two business owners trying to compete against each other as a street fight, *neither having a competitive advantage*, we would see two people trying to head butt each other to death. A fifty-fifty chance would exist that either one of them might actually win from a forensic perspective, but in reality, the victor would be equally beaten and bloody.

When my friend's twelve-year-old son Tyler was playing basketball recently, the other team had a mammoth kid on its roster. Even at twelve, he had to be more than six feet tall and weighed 180 pounds. He dwarfed everyone on the court, including the refs. This kid's freak of nature growth had given the opposing team an advantage to which there was no answer. Every rebound he wanted, he got. Every easy shot he took, he made. No one could defend against him because he was just that big. Basketball had no weight limitations like those in little league football. My understanding is this team never lost—ever.

In a knife fight, a competitive advantage is a gun.

In football, a competitive advantage could be that one super-fast and elusive player whom no one else could possibly tackle or defend against.

Michael Jordan in his prime was a competitive advantage.

A competitive advantage—the atomic bomb—is what brought World War II to an end. The Japanese had shown incredible ferociousness against the Allied forces; they were prepared, well-trained, and more than willing to fight to the death. However, the moment Hiroshima and Nagasaki were introduced to this destructive weapon on August 6 and 9 respectively, Japan had no choice but to surrender a mere six days later.

Examples of Competitive Advantages:

- Any valuable asset the competition cannot match or duplicate
- The element of surprise
- A patent, trademark, or copyright
- A formula or trade secret
- A distribution or production monopoly
- Alliances and networks
- A recognized personality
- A strong, recognized brand

Any organization that has a true competitive advantage *knows* the outcome before the game even starts. Any organization that does not have a competitive advantage trains hard and *hopes* it will win. Most of the world seems to cling to the latter train of thought. If you are unsure what your competitive advantages are, you probably don't have any. You are like the street-fighter who wants to head-butt her opponent to death.

When all else fails, competitive advantages often take the form of cheating, and unless caught or policed, will also ensure victory for those willing to do so.

A true competitive advantage is a distinct and specific tool or strategy that cannot be duplicated and allows you to succeed much better than your opponents at a given opportunity. It is rare to have a competitive advantage that can never be copied or defended against, but as long as you have an advantage that your competition does not, you will have much more success.

A lot of confusion exists between differentiation and a competitive advantage. Differentiation means to be different. You can be different without having a competitive advantage. You can be different and be a loser.

Many of the things you read about and learn in this book will help you find your competitive advantage. As I mentioned, many of the best players on our BYU teams kept secret lists of techniques they learned over the years. Most of these players would not share their secrets, even with their own teammates.

Another example comes to mind. Shortly after starting my wedding photography career in Alabama, I made it a point to go out of my way to make friends with other wedding photographers as much as possible, even though they were my competition. Some were receptive, others were not. Something very interesting happened over time.

When I was already booked for a wedding day, I found myself referring potential new customers to my wedding photographer friends. Shortly after, they began to refer customers to me when they were booked for specific dates. Over the period of several years, this group of wedding professionals created a very powerful alliance. Instead of turning away business because of being booked, we were constantly sending new customers back and forth, retaining them within our group. It is a lot of hard work to get a potential customer, but by referring them to one another, we eliminated much of the that initial hard work. There were periods I had every weekend booked for several months because of this competitive advantage through my alliance.

When competing (and you will compete), having a competitive advantage ensures victory and, therefore, is efficient.

V – Communication Skills

44 – The Heart of the Matter

AKA—What Is Most Important

AS A GRAD student in Alabama, I stayed in a super-small studio apartment. Two 10 x 10' rooms, with a very small bathroom. The apartment was so small that in order to have a couch in one room and a desk in the other, the only place for my bed was under my desk. I slept under my desk for three-and-a-half years. But I was willing to do this because rent was $200 per month—a spectacular deal since it was close to campus. Before I made my decision, as part of his pitch, my landlord promised, "I'll do you a special favor and let you keep that rate as long as you stay on." I thought to myself, *Oh, what a deal. I will stay here as long as possible!* And I immediately agreed.

Three years later, he called and said, "Michael, I hate to tell you this, but we need to raise your rent to $300."

"But that's not what we agreed to," I replied. "You said it would stay the same as long as I stayed here."

"I know, but I didn't know you were going to stay so long. You can either pay it or you can move out. I have someone else who can move in right away. I'm sorry. Hey, by the way, what did you think of the game last weekend?"

See what he did there?

A few years later, I realized a business associate would use the same tactic. The way he engaged in discussions was precise. When he wanted to discuss something, it would be very rapid-fire questions that he demanded immediate answers to, or requesting something that needed to happen as soon as possible.

If I had a question about something he didn't want to talk about, he announced he was running late and had to go. Every time I would bring these items up for discussion again, he deferred them to "another time" because he was in a hurry. It became obvious to me that he was only concerned with his wants, so I would have to be extremely careful dealing with this individual. You will meet many people who intentionally avoid the heart of the matter because it makes them uncomfortable to address it head on, or they cannot afford what they know is right.

When we think of Benjamin Franklin, we think of a gifted thinker, statesman, author, inventor, scientist, and founding father. As an American, I can't help but revere the man for his accomplishments.

But Ben, despite his many nobilities, had characteristics most of us never would have imagined: Ben liked to debate. For recreational purposes. While many hate friction and argument, Ben invited it. He liked to get into verbal fights with people, *for fun*.

As Ben matured, he learned a very important detail:

"If you argue and rankle and contradict, you may achieve a temporary victory—sometimes; but it will be an empty victory because you will never get your opponent's good will."

In other words, it is nearly impossible to win an argument by proving yourself right and the other person wrong. But this is how most people argue!

Ben would later change his strategy. Speaking for himself, Franklin wrote in his *Autobiography*:

> While I was intent on improving my language, I met with an English grammar (I think it was Greenwood's), at the end of which there were two little sketches of the arts of rhetoric and logic, the latter finishing with a specimen of a dispute in the Socratic method; and soon after I procured Xenophon's "Memorable Things of Socrates," wherein there are many instances of the same method. I was charmed with it, adopted it, dropt my abrupt contradiction and positive argumentation, and put on the humble inquirer and doubter.
>
> And being then, from reading Shaftesbury and Collins, become a real doubter in many points of our religious doctrine, I found this method safest for myself and very embarrassing to those against whom I used it. Therefore I took a delight in it, practicing it continually, and grew very artful and expert in drawing people, even of superior knowledge, into concessions, the consequences of which they did not foresee, entangling them in difficulties out of which they could not extricate themselves, and so obtaining victories that neither myself nor my cause always deserved. I continued this method some few years, but gradually left it, retaining only the habit of expressing myself in terms of modest diffidence; never using, when I advanced anything that may possibly be disputed, the words certainly, undoubtedly, or any others that give the air of positiveness to an opinion; but rather say, I conceive or apprehend a thing to be so and so; it appears to me, or I should think it so or so, for such and such reasons; or I imagine it to be so; or it is so, if I am not mistaken.

> This habit, I believe, has been of great advantage to me when I have had occasion to inculcate my opinions and persuade men into measures that I have been from time to time engaged in promoting; and, as **the chief ends of conversion are to inform or to be informed, to please or to persuade**, I wish well-meaning, sensible men would not lessen their power of doing good by a positive, assuming manner, that seldom fails to disgust, tends to create opposition, and to defeat every one of those purposes for which speech was given to us, to wit, giving or receiving information or pleasure.
>
> For, if you would inform, a positive and dogmatical manner in advancing your sentiments may provoke contradiction and prevent a candid attention. If you wish information and improvement from the knowledge of others, and yet, at the same time, express yourself as firmly fixed in your present opinions, modest, sensible men, who do not love disputation, will probably leave you undisturbed in the possession of your error. And by such a manner you can seldom hope to recommend yourself in pleasing your hearers, or to persuade those whose concurrence you desire.[1]

What Ben is saying here is that by taking the position of one who is a humble inquirer, or one who was open to being influenced, the end result was that he became an even more effective debater. As he matured further, he learned the heart of the matter when it comes to debate: **The goal is not to win the argument; the goal is to convert thinking, including your own when in error**.

This is a very powerful concept to remember when you meet friction with others. We aren't trying to beat them down with facts, figures, who said what—we are trying to get them not only to see, but

---

1 Franklin, Ben. *Autobiography and Selected Writings. New York*: American Liberty Press (2010). p. 109.

to adopt our position. I can also add that when you sincerely take the position of the humble inquirer, as Ben mentions, you will also become more susceptible to having your own opinions changed and improved.

In the example of debate, the **heart of the matter is discovering truth**. Not so much persuading others to your way of thinking, not so much "winning." Those are less meaningful pursuits. As a binary, it is written:

Discovery of Truth > Persuading Others > Winning An Argument

The Heart of the Matter in general means that an individual can quickly identify the true nature and cause of a particular problem and then stay focused on that issue until the problem is resolved. It is the essence of why anything is worth doing.

The heart of the matter is the opposite of a distraction. Distractions are anything that diverts attention from the real issue or need at hand.

In the case of my sketchy landlord, he was an expert at intentionally diverting attention away from the heart of the matter because he knew he was breaking his promise. He knew that if he could shift someone's attention, even temporarily, away from the heart of the matter, he could escape conflict. You will meet many who will do this intentionally or unintentionally.

When it comes to getting things done and procrastination, I cannot think of a more common and more difficult enemy to defeat than distraction. Distractions can be manufactured intentionally, or they spontaneously appear. They can be used as a tool to your advantage, but more likely, they will come back to bite you in the rear.

Here are more examples of the heart of the matter vs. distraction:

- A dentist repairing a cavity instead of only alleviating pain.
- A business owner re-winning the trust of a disgruntled customer, instead of just giving a refund.
- A companion offering a sincere apology for a wrongdoing and commitment to change, instead of saying something like, "I'm sorry you feel that way."
- A politician making an actual difference instead of focusing only on re-election.

Focusing on the heart of the matter will reduce wasted resources—energy and time—on unneeded distractions thereby *greatly* increasing efficiency.

In the end, there is really only one most important thing at a given time. Being able to identify and stay focused on that one thing will allow for maximum use of resources.

45 – The Lowest Common Denominator

AKA—Finding Common Ground

I HAVE A long-time friend who is a die-hard University of Utah fan. She hates BYU. The strange thing is, she likes to go to BYU football games—and get this...in BYU logoed clothing. When I asked her what in the world she was doing, she told me that she loved to watch football in general. If she couldn't attend a Utah game for whatever reason, she would go to a BYU game just to watch. She would wear BYU apparel to "fit in" and avoid friction with the BYU fans. Her behavior is instructive about the power of assumptions. When other BYU fans see her wearing BYU clothing, they assume she is one of them. They assume she thinks and believes *as they do*. It may even be assumed she has the same religious and political beliefs, when that has nothing to do with the truth. In short, the moment she puts on BYU clothing, she is instantly *more likeable* to other BYU fans (including me!).

We are data-collecting organisms. A **perception**, to me, means data that is available to any of the five senses. Sight, sound, taste, touch, and smell are all means of perception. Another meaning of the word is coming to an understanding, belief, idea, or conclusion based on the information we gather. It means the five senses, as well as understanding.

An **assumption** is what I like to think of as an informational "gap filler." There is a lack of data or understanding, and therefore, we are wired to fill in the gaps automatically, with the best information we have, regardless of the truth. Sometimes assumptions are correct, but often they are wrong, creating conflict.

Assumptions are problematic because there is no standard or predictability on how different individuals "fill in the gaps." When someone is unable to collect information accurately or unable to assemble that information into a truthful conclusion, there is misunderstanding. I have seen many capable and well-intentioned disaster aid volunteers be immediately dismissed as not trustworthy for saying or doing even the slightest wrong things.

In the case of my friend, she was intentionally controlling a *perception* (a visual cue) to influence or play on the *assumptions* (informational gap fillers) of others. By simply wearing BYU apparel, she was immediately able to build on common ground, reduce friction, and believe it or not, increase the trust of those around her. All without saying a word!

This is even mathematical: fractions cannot be added or subtracted from other fractions unless their denominators are the same. Think about that—fractions, in this sense, are incompatible unless they *have some common ground.*

People are like fractions. We have one language we prefer more than others. This language is not limited to the spoken word. The more common ground we can find, the more compatible and efficient the relationship becomes.

Consider the opposite. Try to communicate with someone in a language she does not understand and see how far that relationship will go. Lack of common ground and lack of common language *creates a barrier of friction.*

As with all tools, what I share with you here can be exploited for good or evil. I use these tools on disaster aid trips to speed up the process of bringing relief to victims because I want to ease their suffering. I've also met people who use the same tools to take advantage of others for selfish reasons.

You can build on common ground with those around you by:

1. **Speaking in the language of your audience.** If we are speaking to children, for example, we avoid using words they may not understand. If we are in a foreign land, we may need to hire an interpreter. I also recommend at least trying to learn a few words and phrases of the native language and practicing with the locals at every opportunity because it shows them you are willing to make an effort to speak on their terms. In many cases, this can be a wonderful source of humor as you stumble through the mispronunciations.

2. **Calling someone by his or her first name.** This is far more personal.

3. **Keeping your promises.** Trust increases efficiency, just as distrust increases friction and resistance. Trust is damaged when promises are broken.

4. **Finding and sharing common interests.** Look for things the other person can relate to. Find things you both enjoy talking about. These could be movies, books, food, music, sports, TV programs, etc.

5. **Using problem solving.** When someone has a huge problem and you are able to help him with it, many walls come down. You will need **empathy** to stand in the person's shoes if you really want to understand what he is struggling with. Team-

work in problem solving is an incredible trust builder.

6. **Being willing to sacrifice in service for others.** Sacrificing for others means that you do so without any expectation of return, in the right circumstances.

7. **Showing appreciation to those who have sacrificed for you.** Underappreciation can and will backfire spectacularly when someone feels taken advantage of.

8. **Striving to be sincere and genuine.** Do not try to fake it—it often can be sensed.

9. **Dressing appropriately for the situation.** This also means dressing for your audience, rather than for yourself.

Keep in mind that everyone is different. Use your eyes and ears to find out what is most important to others and build on that. If you are unsure about something, ask...get others to talk about the things they love. Listening to them talk about something they passionately care about is almost as good as liking it yourself.

Some topics are not worth debating because they lead nowhere. If you want to write great dialogue in a screenplay, have two people argue about something they are both individually correct about. This happens in real life all the time.

As for my University of Utah loving friend, I know I cannot convince her to change her favorite football team, and such is the case with many things. Apple vs. Mac. Republican vs. Democrat. Canon vs. Nikon. **Agreeing to disagree** is a subtle and powerful art which discounts friction. I have many friends whom I disagree with on many subjects, but we are still friends because we specifically avoid those kinds of discussions.

"Hey, I like you, but I think we need to just agree to disagree on this." Is something I say when this happens. I wish I would have learned this earlier in life.

I have an entrepreneur friend who will sometimes ask me for advice. I find her mostly *disagreeable*. Meaning, for whatever reason, she likes to take the opposite view, for the sake of taking the opposite view. All the time. It gets old, and I wonder if she realizes that the more it happens, the more I want to avoid her.

One of the most important rules of successful improv comedy is always to *accept or agree* with what the other person is saying and build on that. This can make for engaging and hilarious exchanges. However, even outside of improv, this practice is powerful.

As a teacher, I made a similar rule: *I will never tell a student he or she is wrong in front of the class*. I would find some truth in the student's answers, *and build on that*. This increased the trust my students had in me as an instructor. It made them feel safe and comfortable about participating in class.

Such is true in your relationships with others. Find common ground, common goals, common languages, common problems, common interests, and build on those. When you do, you will strengthen trust and experience improved efficiency in *assumptive* communication.

Finding common ground is a fast and powerful way to help your audience fill in missing gaps of information.

46 – The Golden Pacifier

AKA—Knowing When to Shut Your Mouth

AT LEAST SOME of the stress in our lives is the direct result of saying the wrong thing at the wrong time. Sometimes, we know when we have done so; sometimes, we don't.

Some individuals have fantastically good memories, so once certain words leave our mouths like, "Yes, dear, you do look quite fat in that dress," those individuals will forever use our words against us. They will never forget it—never.

The Golden Pacifier is the concept that we can reduce our long-term levels of friction and stress by not saying something immediately that we will later regret or that can be turned against us.

Silence > Saying the Wrong Thing

Keeping your mouth shut is extremely cost-efficient. When combined with attentive eyes, you will, ironically, be dubbed a master conversationalist. While you may occasionally be regarded as slow or maybe not paying attention, more often than not, especially in high emotion or high stakes situations, not saying anything can be a strategic gold mine.

Here's how to use the Golden Pacifier in your best interests:

- Stand in others' shoes when you communicate with them. How would you feel if you were in their situation? Integrate your thoughts with what you are imagining others would feel.

- Protect the other person's feelings as if they were your own. This includes strangers. Sometimes the truth is not kind, nor good. Simply because something might be true does not mean certain individuals need to hear it. You must learn to measure the cost of your words according to the situation at hand, and determine whether a risky exchange would be emotionally profitable for both parties involved.

- When in doubt, say nothing. This is the key. To master the Golden Pacifier, you must form a subconscious link between feelings of doubt and staying silent. Even if you think you have the answer, it sometimes pays to wait and say, "Let me think about this a little."

Other applications:

- Most people are hungry for someone just to listen to them. They are not seeking advice or your opinion. One of the most satisfying feelings when people are stressed is to feel they are understood and cared for. Learn to listen to others. It is a very powerful tool for building friendships. Sympathize with their pain and be happy when they are happy. Learn to mirror emotions as a gateway to trust. Encourage and tell them you are proud of them when appropriate.

- As a rule, avoid making fun of anyone for the sake of humor. It is simply not worth it. There are many other ways to be funny without breaking trust or hurting feelings. Do not cry wolf. It sows distrust.

Rules of Use:

1. Apply the Abacus (the cost of words) to what you say. Imagine every sentence you say has a positive or negative dollar value. It goes back to what Mom always said, "If you cannot say something nice, don't say anything at all."

2. Sometimes an unexpected pause in the middle of speaking can increase the attention of those listening. If you absolutely must speak in a difficult situation, try sincere gratitude and compassion combined with brevity. An individual is rarely wrong when he or she is expressing sincere gratitude or asking a humble question.

3. Identify those circumstances and those sensitive individuals who may misinterpret what you are saying as an attack. You cannot underestimate how often well-intentioned comments can be hurtful or destructive, especially over texting when tone cannot be heard.

4. Learn to yield the conversation. This happens when two people begin speaking at once. Make it a habit to allow the other person the courtesy of speaking first. You will occasionally meet those who will then go into lengthy, meaningless monologues. Or perhaps they will ask you a question and then cut you off mid-sentence when you try to answer. Individuals who monologue or repeatedly cut others off typically have little interest in what others have to say. Deal with these situations accordingly.

5. Discount your ego in thought and word at every opportunity. Almost nothing positive can happen when one insists on verbally inflating his or her ego. It can be extremely tempting to say something aggressive or provocative just because

> it is clever or to demonstrate your ability to insult. That is not a good investment, and you can never win people over by offending them. Many people have been killed for making provocative, ego-based comments. It isn't worth it.

Keep in mind that there are occasions when not speaking can be much worse than saying anything. As a supervisor, instructor, or parent, we are often required to correct others' errors. This is not an excuse to do so without tact. If you must correct or discipline someone do it in the role of your authority and be as brief as possible. No one likes being lectured once they understand what they have done wrong. Demonstrate the correct behavior and then encourage them to try again. Once the behavior is fixed, praise them. This will build more trust and good vibes. If you discipline someone too much, too hard, or too long without positive feedback, it will sow the seeds of distrust.

47 – The Clear Crystal

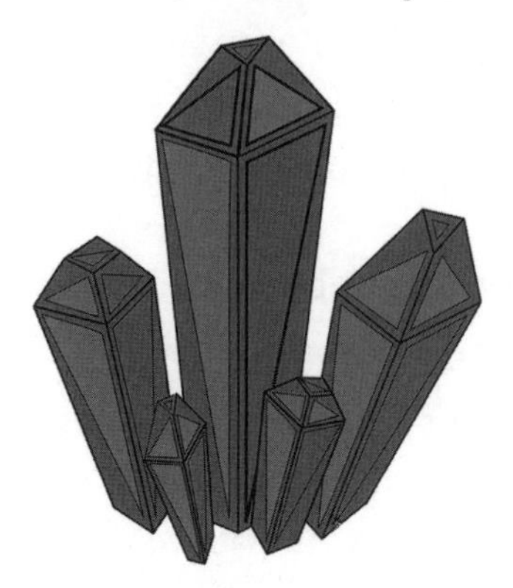

AKA—Become Impossible to Misunderstand

FOR THE LAST several years, I have been an app developer. That means I come up with the idea, design, and funds for an app, and then I hire a team to code it. I have never met any of the programmers in person, all communication is done through email or Skype.

During the course of developing more than twelve different apps, I have had to articulate what I wanted done in such a manner that Andre, the software lead, would understand. I have used diagrams, charts, word descriptions, images, and examples. Despite my very best efforts and knowing how important it is to communicate effectively, Andre often misunderstands what I am saying. I also believe Andre is making the most sincere attempts to receive any information I send him, but his interpretation of it is different, which causes confusion and often conflict.

Together, we created the very first contract and release apps for photographers. Andre would send me prototype apps to test, and while debugging them, I commonly found glitches.

I would email him, "Andre, the app crashes when I sign the contract."

Andre would respond, "That isn't enough information; what are the conditions when it crashes?"

I'd answer, "When I fill out xyz contract."

Andre would implore, "Please list all the steps you have taken so we can recreate the issue here."

I would then meticulously type a long email that would go something like:

1. Open the App
2. Select Contract
3. Select Client
4. Preview Contract
5. Sign App
6. App Crashes

All these steps outline the basic steps leading to signing a contract on the device—all steps he should know.

Andre would then respond, "We have followed your steps here; it is working on our end."

I probably spent a couple of months of my life on these kinds of emails back and forth with Andre, until one day I got so angry and frustrated that I set up a camera and videotaped what was happening. Not only was it much faster than trying to explain in typed words, but when Andre saw the video, he understood the problem immediately.

"We see the problem and are working on a fix now," is typically the answer whenever I send him a video. It has eliminated all the extra steps of trying to re-explain in words.

During my time as a Ph.D. student studying genetics, I would often have to report to my advising professor, probably the smartest person I have ever met, and explain to him what was going on with my research. He would sit very patiently, listening carefully to every word I said, and if I were not *exactly precise* in the words I chose, he would immediately stop me and ask for clarification in such a way that I would understand my error in explaining what I was trying to communicate.

Most of the time, I think he did understand exactly what I was saying, but he was teaching me to deliver *precise* explanations. I was often required to give presentations to large groups of professors and grad students, and any accidental slip would be like blood in the water to a room full of sharks.

Communication becomes much more efficient when it is delivered in such a way that it cannot be misunderstood. This will change depending on your audience.

I believe that my professors' daily correction carried over into my teaching, which led to my success on my YouTube channel and with my training videos.

Recently, I watched another YouTube presenter use an imprecise word in a technical description. He was essentially crucified by his viewers for making the mistake, and then he made it worse by making several "damage control" videos that highlighted the original mistake, explaining what he actually meant and how he was still correct despite his audience misunderstanding what he was trying to communicate. It was an instructive lesson. Precision matters.

While I can't tell you what will work in every situation when communicating, here are some tips that have worked well for me:

1. Be as brief as humanly possible, but not so brief that meaning is lost. Cut to the chase, list the facts and steps, and get out.

2. Give new listeners context and background for the message you are about to deliver.

3. Use precise words listeners know. Speak their language.

4. Be mindful of your tone; it conveys as much information as the actual words you choose. Practice saying the same phrase, "Yes, please" or "Thank you" in different tones until you are certain you can convey most basic emotions.

5. Show rather than tell. You will hear me say this often. Also, having them repeat or demonstrate to you what you have told them will provide proof that they get it.

6. Use stories and analogies when applicable.

7. Avoid absolutes—they cause listeners to start looking for flaws in your statements.

8. Stick to the heart of the matter, not who is correct or incorrect. Avoid tangents.

9. If teaching a class:

    a. Introduce them to the subject you are about to teach them.
    b. Teach them in a clever way.
    c. Review what you have just taught them.

10. Encourage, motivate, and use positive reinforcement. It is usually more effective than nagging, complaining, or punishments.

Be so simple and obvious that it is impossible to be misunderstood. Strive for brevity, precision and be direct; convey all necessary information and nothing more.

48 – The Treasure Map

AKA—Persuasion through Promoting Self-Discovery

"Disappointment is the fruit of expectations."
— My Dad

WHENEVER I USED to treat friends or guests to any of my favorite restaurants, I would ask them, "Are you ready to have your mind blown?" After the meal, in some cases, my friends stated that the food and or experience was excellent, but in many other cases, I was disappointed when they told me, "It was okay, but not mind-blowing." A valuable lesson can be learned here.

Much of our success is based on our ability to persuade, interest, and satisfy others.

It starts at home where you are challenged to satisfy your parents, spouse, children, and relatives in a number of ways. At work, you will be required to satisfy your employer or customers. Friends and strangers will also come looking to you for solutions, and perhaps they can offer you the same.

When we cannot deliver on what we say we can, we are often rejected, abandoned, and viewed as unreliable.

Having taught freshman biology for eight years at the University of Alabama, I became obsessed with the most efficient ways to teach difficult concepts. What penetrated quickly? What was sticky and easy to remember? Several thousand students over that period allowed me to test a variety of approaches and come to some interesting conclusions.

In my experience, nothing is more powerful and efficient in teaching than fostering self-discovery—helping students come to the conclusions you want them to on their own.

If I *told* them a concept or principle, it was about 30 to 40 percent effective—less than half would remember; the rest would immediately forget.

If I *showed* them a concept or principle, it was slightly more effective.

If I *asked* them a question that stumped them, even irritated them a little, and then directed them down a carefully planned path to discover the very answer I wanted them to find, be it through an experiment, test, or trying a hands-on technique, the retention rose to as high as 75 percent memorable.

Self-Discovery > Show > Tell

Later, when consulting friends on their entrepreneurial endeavors, I found their focus and memory retention could almost always be increased when they were *risking* something. Concentration and strategic thinking are naturally increased with greater risks.

I have noticed similarities with setting expectations. When I *tell* someone about something great, I notice that less than half really listen or even care.

If I *show* them my mind-blowing observation, I get better results.

But if they somehow *discover* this awesomeness all on their own, the result, their excitement, and their conversion to the principle is much stronger; even more so when there is personal investment on their part.

A greater affinity for truth results when it is self-discovered.

In many cases, when I invited friends to try a favorite meal, giving my highest endorsement, some seemed hell-bent on shooting me down, no matter what they actually thought of the food.

To tell someone, "You are going to love this place," creates some problems:

1. Your friend may feel a conscious or subconscious desire to prove you wrong, so even if he does like it, he may say he does not.

2. He may truly dislike it.

3. He may have truly liked the place, but by building expectation too high, you caused him to be disappointed no matter how much he liked it.

What I find myself doing now is making a statement that pricks their curiosity: "There's a place I'd like you to try. I don't know if you'll like it or not, but they make this really different dish. Some people like it, some don't, so I'm curious to see what you will think."

This statement sets up an opportunity for your friend or student to self-discover. You personally haven't said one way or the other whether the food is good, so no expectations have been set. If the person greatly likes it, he will emphatically tell you so. If he does not like it, he might say so or not, but at least you don't look like a fool for saying the opposite. You then guide him toward this opportunity, going with him to the restaurant, making suggestions as he orders, and asking follow-up questions.

While the example of making restaurant suggestions represents a very low-level of stress, the same technique of directing someone to self-discovery can be applied to any situation.

Artificially raising a person's expectations offers little to no advantage, unless the goal is to leave him or her dissatisfied.

Artificially lowering one's expectations makes it much easier to establish new expectations and then exceed them.

The only difference between high and low expectations is the person's perception of what is promised. Lowering expectations lowers the requirements needed to reach that level and the resources needed, thus making it easier to exceed expectations.

Light the fire of curiosity in their minds, provide the opportunity to learn, and they will do the rest. They will come to knowledge on their own, and it will never leave them because it is "theirs."

I also know the power of not getting your own hopes up. We cannot always predict what will happen in any given situation. I cannot tell you how many times the very best of my plans did not work at all. Sometimes that disappointment hurts. However, if you are unafraid of failure, you will become fearless in your pursuits. Disappointment can only exist when we *expect* a specific outcome. We have far more to gain when we open our minds to learning, despite pre-conceived notions.

Self-Discovery > Expectations

49 – The Handshake

AKA—Negotiating Skills

FOR THE LAST twenty-three years, my father has run his own pool-cleaning business on Maui. He quickly learned that some pools were easier to clean than others. Logically, he concluded he should be making more money on the difficult-to-clean pools. This was usually not the case. He could charge that same amount for a very easy-to-clean pool, as he could those surrounded with vegetation and in high wind areas, which can take hours to clean. He questioned whether he should clean the difficult ones at all because they were not worth the time.

Instead of just dropping the customer, my father developed a very wise tactic: He simply informed customers that due to the difficulty of cleaning their pools, the maintenance prices would rise. As a result, my father learned something very interesting. Many of his customers quickly agreed to the new terms. With that simple negotiation tactic, he was able to increase revenue from customers who could afford him, and he weeded out those trouble pools where the work wasn't worth it.

"I never voluntarily drop problem pools," my father explained to me. "I simply raise prices on them for what I think it is worth to service their pools."

Any number of valuable lessons can be learned here. My father put the burden of breaking off the relationship on the customer. He was able to earn more money for the difficult pools and developed his "walk-away power."

Walk-away power is the ability to abandon a desirable and valuable goal at the end of a negotiation. The party with more walk-away power is, typically, the most powerful figure in a negotiation and can often demand more. However, the caveat here is that you must be able to walk away without whatever you are bargaining for. (Note: If you ever watch *Pawn Stars* on TV, Rick is a master of walk-away power, as well as negotiating skills in general).

Every day, we encounter situations where someone has something we want. We negotiate with our employers, our customers, our friends, our family, and especially children. It is not uncommon for affluent and powerful individuals to hire lawyers and agents to negotiate on their behalf. Big businesses have teams of lawyers working exclusively for their best interests, handling mergers, acquisitions, and other types of deals.

It seems that in casual day-to-day interaction with others, huge opportunities are missed because most individuals are not trained in negotiating tactics.

I'm talking about specific strategies that would allow you to get more, while offering less, simply by knowing what words to say. If you can increase your profit and production, find more free time, lower expenses, and find new opportunities all by changing a few words, you better believe that learning and executing proper negotiating skills will increase your efficiency.

Negotiating skills include being able to:

- Increase the perceived value of the services or products you are offering
- Change the perception of who has the most power
- Raise the interest level of those with whom you are negotiating
- Seek a win-win solution, so both parties are mutually benefiting
- Enhance your ability to see when you are on the losing end of a negotiation

Teaching you the specific negotiating skills themselves is beyond the scope of this book; however, I can make a recommendation: Read *The Secrets of Power Negotiating* by Roger Dawson. I consider this book one of the best crash courses on the subject. The book is well worth its price and will pay for itself hundreds of times over.

VI – Emotional Management

50 – The Balance of Motivation

AKA—Offensive vs. Defensive Mind-Sets

EXERCISE: WRITE DOWN the top three things you spend most of your time doing and then write down why you do them.

1.

2.

3.

One of the biggest challenges I faced becoming an entrepreneur was becoming Offensive-minded. Most of us are raised to be defensive-minded. From our parents raising and controlling us, to many years of homework given at school, we are taught and conditioned to react.

The goal of this chapter is to help you identify your own offensive and defensive mind-sets by asking yourself the question:

Why am I doing this?

Two main motivating factors exist for why we take action:

1. Stress/Pain (we are compelled to act)

2. Self-Initiative (we want something)

These motivating forces are opposites and can be illustrated as pans on a balance scale. These pans represent what we can control, which is defined in broad terms as defensive (reactive) and offensive (proactive) actions.

The semi-circular indicator represents what we feel. Zero (0) in the middle on the indicator symbolizes equilibrium. Think of it as a state of rest, or comfort.

This indicator might be bouncing back and forth many times a day, depending on which state of mind we are in and what we plan to do about it.

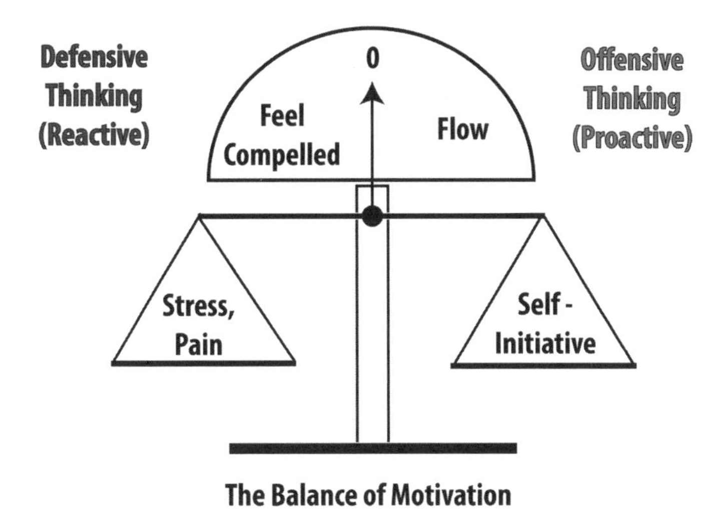

The Balance of Motivation

The left pan is such that life is constantly putting stress into it. If we are not careful, we too can unintentionally add things into the left pan.

This is what it looks like when we have lots of stress in our lives:

The Balance of Motivation

Stress tilts the scale of motivation so we feel compelled to empty that pan and return to a state of equilibrium. When we feel compelled to pay our upcoming bills, we will work forty hours a week, even if we might hate our job.

The further the scale points to the left, the more motivated we are to act. For example, if we have an excruciating toothache, we make it a priority to see the dentist as soon as possible. Once the thing creating stress has been removed, the scale returns to equilibrium:

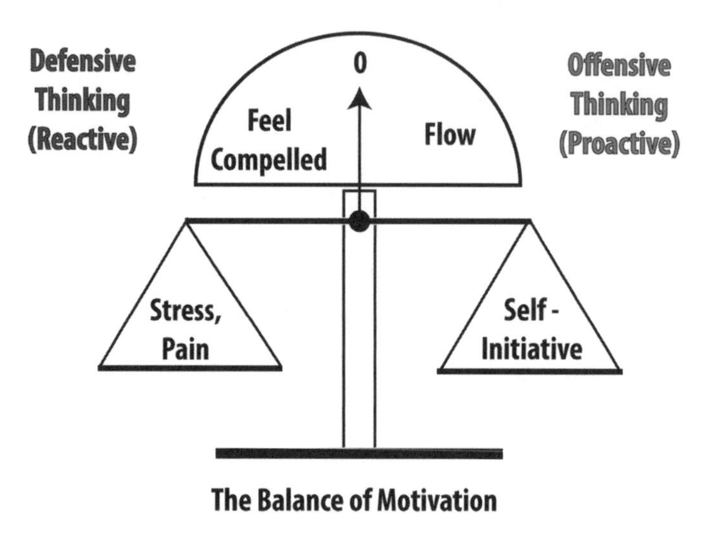

The Balance of Motivation

If a person is only motivated to action by feeling compelled, the motivation stops as soon as the stress is gone. He or she will wait for new stress to occur before taking action again, and so this cycle repeats itself over and over. This is dangerous because it can create a habit of becoming primarily defensive-minded. Some will only act when acted upon first. How limiting!

I think of flow (right side) as any positive goals, worthy feelings, or momentum not motivated by stress or pain. Flow cannot be achieved by removing stress alone. You cannot achieve lasting happiness by going to work only because you have bills. There must be something more.

Once I realized I was mostly defensive minded, I knew I had to find a way to change how I motivated myself. This was a very big step mentally for me that changed everything.

The right pan of this scale, "Self-Initiative," is such that you are the only person who can fill it, and it must be refilled constantly—every single day, every single hour.

Take for example the individual who creates a new business not because she has to, but because she wants something more—maybe more free time or income, maybe to take her kids to Disneyland each year. She has found a way to self-motivate despite weight that may actually be in the left pan. Her offensive drive defeated her defensive mentality. In this case, taking the initiative created a whole new state of mind:

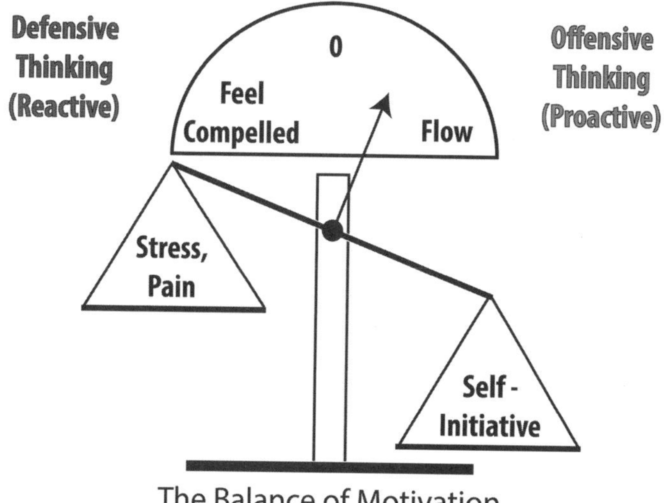

The Balance of Motivation

Flow is an amazing feeling and worth the effort. It is easily achieved when we are focused on initiative instead of removing pain. Taking initiative means that we are no longer on defense. Proactive individuals seek opportunities to thrive, and where none exist, they create them out of thin air. That is the key mind-set of offensive thinking. Removing things from the left pan will always be necessary, however, all successful entrepreneurs I know are predominantly offensive-minded.

When flow is at its greatest, you will not feel stressed about little things. Flow means having all the resources we need to meet all current or future concerns. Bills are stressful when we do not have the money to pay them. I have felt more stress when I didn't have $20 to pay a bill as a poor student than when I had a $10,000 bill I had enough money for as an entrepreneur. That is relativity!

In fact, all big thinkers I know of shift the bar on the scale so it is asymmetrical to the right. It takes much, much more to stress them out than it would a smaller thinker. They live in a perpetual state of:

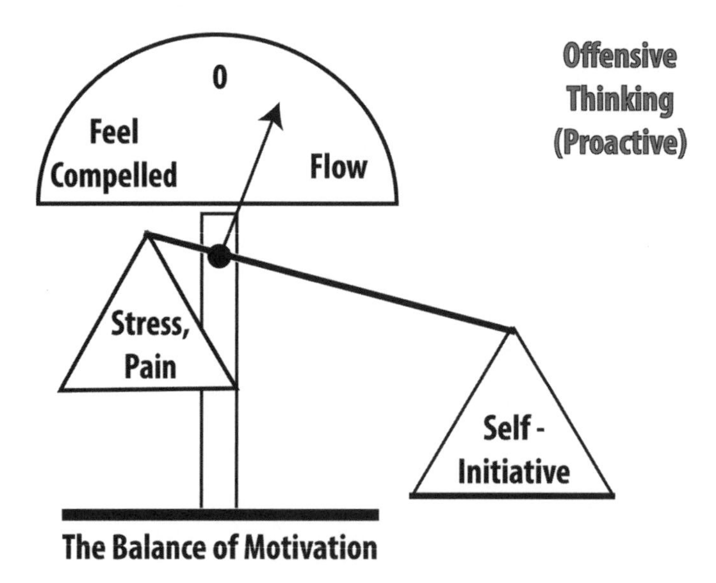

The Balance of Motivation

Big thinkers do this by constantly dismissing small thoughts, people, and problems as miniscule. They have learned to focus on the big picture. Small thinkers have a tendency to shift the bar in the other direction; they magnify little problems and little ideas. Big thinkers, therefore, have a huge advantage in tipping the scales toward the right. Little thinkers are at a huge disadvantage because the smallest of concerns tilts them out of balance.

Find a way to make yourself uncomfortable with being primarily defensive or even at "0." Stay tilted to the right as much as possible. Something I have learned is when I am feeling down or stressed, I can very easily tilt my scale to the right by choosing to be grateful. Gratitude is a form of flow.

To summarize, two general forces balance your motivation—remove stress/pain or take self-initiative. While both actions are necessary, applying the force on the right is usually more efficient, unless the weight on the left is very large.

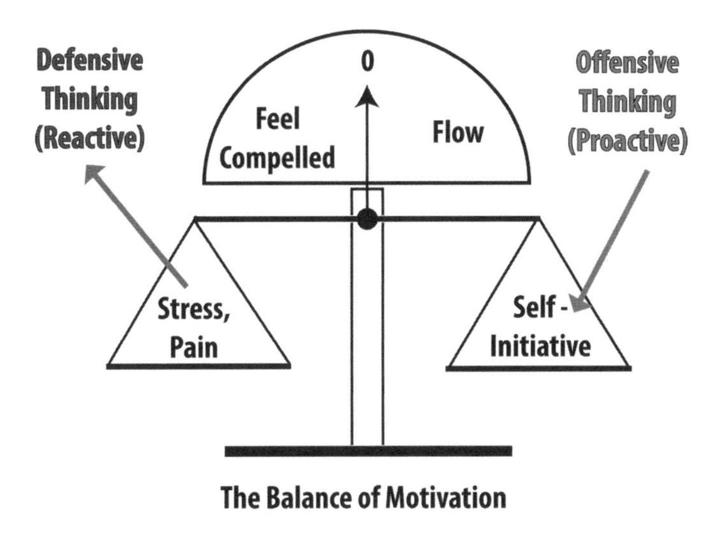

The Balance of Motivation

Unfortunately, our motivations for action are far more complicated and problematic than merely "taking initiative," which is what we will discuss in the next chapter.

51 – The Apple Core

AKA – The Why

"Check yourself before you wreck yourself."
— Ice Cube

A FORMER FRIEND of mine often said the right things for the wrong reasons. He didn't actually mean what he was saying. He was saying these things to say he had said them.

If you have ever heard someone say "Thank you," who then does the opposite of being thankful, you know what I am talking about. If the person's motives are questioned, he will reply, "But I said, 'Thank you'!" as if merely noting it trumps all future action.

After some time, you learn to pick up on that insincerity. It feels hollow and empty. Yes, it was the right thing to say, but if it was for the wrong reason, does it count? Insincerity is like an apple—beautiful and shiny on the outside, but when you take a bite, things are not what they initially seemed. Counterfeit.

I have observed during certain projects that you can have two individuals, with similar jobs, work the same hours and finish the same project, yet one benefits and the other changes for the worse. Not so much for what happened during the project but for the reason they chose to be involved.

For example, on a film production, one assistant can be deeply thankful for the learning experience, while the other might be there so he can be able to brag about working on a movie. The former will be hustling all day long, the other at the snack table talking to the star. They both got what they were looking for, but the Why changed their individual outcome.

The Why is more important than the What.

Why > What

The Why is the foundation of all things we do. The Why is more important than your River of Focus. Your River of Focus is less efficient if it is something centered on the wrong reason. You can do the right thing, for the wrong reason, resulting in a less meaningful experience. Like seeds in the core of our own apples, the Why is the genetic blueprint of who we become, the fruits of our labors, and how we influence others.

Take for example, two medical students wanting to become doctors. One may want prestige and the other to learn to heal the sick (imagine them as two different types of seeds). They can take all the same classes, study the same information, take the same tests, and spend the same time in school (think of this as being planted in a garden and being cared for to maturity), and graduate as two entirely different types of doctors (different fruits). The one may continue to seek prestige throughout his career, the other to heal the sick.

The Why is more important than the ability to hustle and grind. You can spend a decades of hustle on something that won't bring happiness. That can result in a lifetime of inefficiency.

How to Evolve Your What

Your What is how you spend most of your time. Those were the answers you wrote in the beginning of the last chapter.

When I was working on my Ph.D. in grad school, my project ran into a wall. I could not get consistent results, so I was facing the danger of either having to restart my project or drop out. I put my head down and tried to solve an unsolvable problem.

I wasted at least two prime years of my life because I didn't take a few hours to sit down and really ask myself, "Why am I doing this?"

I would have answered: "I am doing this to get my Ph.D." Had I repeated the same question to each answer:

"Why am I getting a Ph.D.?" I would have answered, "To have the knowledge and credentials to start Biotech Companies."

Continuing, "Why do I want to start Biotech Companies?" I would have answered, "To be in a position of influence to help lots of people."

I am satisfied with the Why of helping people, but I should have dug deeper, challenging my current What:

"Why do I think starting Biotech Companies is the only way to help lots of people?"

And as simple as that, I would have had an epiphany. I had become so locked into the habit of grad school that I didn't see any other options. The more I realized there were many other ways to achieve that worthy Why (to help people), my What (getting a Ph.D.) became less critical. (Side note: If you are listing defensive reasons for doing things, your What probably isn't that important and could be easily replaced.)

After those two years of failure, I finally analyzed my Why and dropped out of school without my Ph.D. It was one of the hardest, but best decisions I ever made.

Please learn from my mistake of not asking myself this sooner. I believe I am far happier now than had I stuck it out an additional three more years to restart my dissertation project. My only regret now is not dropping out sooner.

How to Evolve Your Why

The word "tantalize" means to tease and/or torment with something that is not attainable. It comes from Greek mythology, specifically the story of Tantalus, who was punished for various crimes by being placed in a pool beneath a fruit tree. Every time he reached for some fruit, the branches pulled it away from his grasp. Every time he leaned in to drink from the pool, the waters receded. He was forever chasing that which could not satisfy.

And so it is with some Whys. They are temporary, meaningless, or fleeting reasons we waste our most precious resource, time, pursuing that which cannot fill. It is like growing weeds and expecting something good to come from it.

Some tantalizing Whys include:

1. The Inflation of Ego (I am not talking about self-esteem)
2. Glory or Fame
3. Riches & Wealth (For the sake of riches and wealth)
4. Revenge

It is easy to want more pride, more fame, more wealth, and more revenge, even when we have already achieved all of these things. They often result in more emptiness each time they are found.

Some wrong Whys have a worthwhile counterpart that we can consciously choose. What we do can become more meaningful and, therefore, more efficient when we change our Why.

Take for example the single mother working two jobs to pay bills compared to the same woman, doing the same job because she loves providing for her children. By simply changing her why, she dramatically improved her motivating factor.

When I see my reasons for doing something are being influenced by my ego, I try to discount that choice and consider the other motives. If I can't find any, I try to reject that option.

Meaningful Whys > Ego

Instead of chasing temporary glory or fame, I feel better looking for knowledge or wisdom because they do not flee.

Wisdom > Fame or Glory

Instead of looking for riches and wealth, I feel happier working for freedom.

Freedom > Riches & Wealth

Instead of carrying out revenge on those who have hurt me, I have learned it is better to forgive and move forward if the hurt resulted from an honest mistake.

Forgiveness > Revenge

More satiating motivators include:

1. Charity and Service to those in need (this is my go to!)
2. Love (Not Lust)
3. Sincere Expressions of Appreciation
4. Self-Improvement
5. To Inspire others
6. To Praise others (sincerely)
7. Maintaining Good Health, including Exercise

More neutral motivators Include:

1. Preparation
2. Responsibility
3. Good Habit
4. Rest

Choosing the right What to do in life is hard enough, but in the end, the Why is the ultimate reason some find happiness and others cannot. Pay attention to those motivations that fill your soul, and learn to avoid those that leave you feeling empty.

Make it a habit (such as when you eat an apple) to regularly ask yourself, "Why am I doing this?" and repeat that question until you find something that truly justifies where you invest your time and energy.

Abandon meaningless Whats that do not have significant Whys.

Consider more efficient Whats to fulfill your current worthy Whys.

If you are unhappy and cannot change your What, find a way to change your Why to make it more meaningful and significant.

52 – Oil

AKA—Rolling with the Punches

WHEN I WAS four, my dad taught me to punch his hand. I would muster up as much strength as I could and smack him square on his palm. The louder the slapping noise, the louder he would exclaim, "Ouch!" We would sit there for what seemed like hours on end playing this game.

One variant of this game would occur when he pulled his hand away at the last second; it then became more about speed than force. Even as a four-year-old, I realized that when he pulled his hand away in the same direction I was punching, I could not deliver as much force as when he held his hand stationary.

Friction requires an opposing force—the weaker the opposing force, the weaker the friction.

My dad also demonstrated to me what it means to "roll with the punches"—when a boxer is hit across the chin, he consciously rotates his head away from the punch to minimize the damage.

The same is true in life. There will be times when you will be hit across the chin, so to speak. You can roll with it and minimize the damage, or you can roll into it and make it much worse. "Oil" is anything you can do to reduce the friction between two forces.

We are emotional creatures. Something bad happens and we feel it. It may be a feeling that sticks with us for hours or years. If you have lost a loved one, you know this feeling. Often when something goes wrong, even a little thing, it can trigger a negative emotional response and carry over to other aspects of life. If you had a bad day at work, did you direct that energy at someone else? Someone innocent? Did it create more problems? We sometimes find ways to create even more friction for ourselves.

If it is always possible to make your situation harder, it also means you can always make it easier.

Using oil requires the skill of reducing, limiting, containing, or counteracting the causes and effects of unwanted friction.

I believe it is always better to focus on the solution, instead of the pain itself.

Therefore, when experiencing friction, find ways to use oil. For example:

1. Do not let friction cascade into more, unnecessary friction.

2. When you see an unavoidable hit coming, roll with that punch. Providing as little resistance as possible reduces the damage inflicted. The proper "roll-with-the-punch" technique can virtually eliminate all damage in some cases.

3. Reduce friction at the source and prepare for future points of fiction.

Always Be Cool

One night, I was scuba diving in shark-infested waters off Makena on Maui with eleven other divers. I typically go through my air pretty quickly, but my dive buddy, who was also the group organizer, was an experienced dive master, and a much smaller person, had an air supply that lasted forever. Long story short, I was running out of air quickly, and my dive buddy wasn't. Despite my communicating this to him repeatedly, he was taking his sweet time, showing the new divers some nudibranchs and other nocturnal creatures.

At the rate we were moving, I would run out of air far before we got back to shore. Most divers are trained to try to finish the dive with 500 PSI (pounds per square inch) of the original 3,000 PSI left in the tank. Having only 800 PSI left with about half the distance to go, I had two choices:

1. Leave my dive buddy and the group, and try to make it back to shore alone before I ran out of air.

2. Stay with the group and surface just before I ran out, swimming on the surface the rest of the way in. (Since this was feeding time in an area known to be inhabited by tiger sharks, and that recent attacks on humans occurred at the surface in this area, I wasn't really feeling this option.)

I decided to ditch the group and swim directly back to shore underwater, alone. Not a happy feeling, but it felt safer than swimming on the surface like chum. My air reserve continued to drop—700 PSI...600 PSI...500 PSI. I remember reading 400 PSI as I turned the corner of a reef bed. *It'll be close, but I should be able to make it,* I thought.

As I turned the corner of the reef bed, my worst nightmare was realized as I came face to face with a six-foot shark, not more than eight feet away from me. It was moving so quickly that we nearly collided. The shark stopped, turned its attention toward me, and began to circle around, inspecting me. Its pectoral fins turned down, an indication of aggression. I remember thinking *"Be cool...."* But I felt my heart thumping. I positioned the reef to my back, keeping the shark in front of me and holding my camera rig between the two of us. I was aware of breathing much faster. I checked my pressure gauge—250 PSI. I would be out of air in a matter of minutes.

All these little considerations—nighttime, underwater, surprise, shark, alone, running out of air, being circled, each real in its ability to cause me stress—compounded into what I felt was an irresistible desire to panic. I told myself to relax and chill. If I ran out of air, I would have to surface, circling shark or not, so I began to make mental preparations to do so. Eventually, the shark left, and I made it back to shore with almost nothing in my tank. I will never forget that experience.

You will experience many unexpected and stressful situations. Remember that you can make the situation worse by panicking, but if you can just "be cool," you stand a much better chance of success.

Problems are always easier to solve when you (or members of your team) aren't making things worse.
Always be cool.

53 – The Empty Cup

AKA—Capacity

"Empty your cup so that it may be filled; become devoid to gain totality."
— Bruce Lee

IMAGINE YOUR MIND as a cup with limited capacity. The cup represents your ability to hold thoughts. Any time you have a conscious thought, it is the same as having a full cup. That fluid can be there by choice, or it can be forced into your attention. Many other things are also trying to get into your cup; there are beverages you may want to have and some that others are trying to get you to drink.

Your mind's capacity to do new work is inversely proportional to how full your cup is now. If your cup is full of one thing, you cannot use it to do something else. Therefore, you increase your mental capacity, or your mind's ability to do new work, by emptying your cup as quickly as possible.

I like to imagine that when we interact with others, they may pour what they have in their cups into ours, just as we might pour some of what we have into theirs. We must take control of what is in our cups, who is pouring ideas into them, where the ideas came from, the significance of each, and how long they stay in our cups.

Think of conscious thought as a beverage. It may be poison; it may be something wonderful. It might be a big thought; it might be a little one.

I prefer thinking big thoughts. When someone tries to pour little thoughts into my mind, I find I am irritated and left wondering, *Why in the world would this person bring up this minutia?* Big thoughts might not fit into small cups, and little thoughts won't fill big ones. Because we encounter different sizes and types of thoughts throughout the day, it is to our advantage to recognize this and make thought transition fast.

In order to leverage your mind's full capacity, you must become a master of emptying it.

Emptying our cups happens differently from person to person, but I can tell you what works for me: cleaning my home and physical workspace. A relationship seems to exist between the cleanliness of my home and my thoughts. When I am struggling to understand what it is I need to do next, I clean!

My goal is to keep all of my tables, counters, desks, floors, and workspaces as empty as possible because, in some strange way, it feels proportional to my mind and makes me feel ready to work. I believe a clean personal environment is a reflection of your thoughts. Keeping our desk or workspace empty and clean requires discipline and organization. The more we maintain discipline and organization physically, the more disciplined our mind becomes. If we have a thinking flaw or error in organization, it will manifest itself in clutter, and we will see it physically. If we can develop this discipline, we will develop the same habit of controlling and cleaning our thought processes. What I am suggesting is:

The organization and cleanliness of our personal space, often directly reflects the organization of our thought processes.

I also try to focus on my breathing and nothing else as I clean. Just breathe and clean. I do not practice yoga, but my friends who do tell me breathing is a huge part of it. Breathing somehow cleanses the mind. I find that when I engage in very intense exercise, if I focus on breathing, it has a cleansing mental effect. I imagine that different activities also clean the mind for different people. It is up to you to find what works best for you. Maybe it is walking, driving, golfing, etc.

A few months ago a business partner called me upset over a deal that had gone bad. We'd had an offer and were about to close the deal when, unexpectedly, the deal went sour for reasons outside of our control. It was over, but he was rattled about it and couldn't get it off his mind.

I gave him this advice: "We did our part and it is over. Let's move on and focus on what we *can* control, which is finding a new deal and starting our next project." And just like that, our attention shifted away from the negative (and something we couldn't control) to what was important. I cannot stress how important it is to monitor what is in your cup—and how quickly you should get the bad stuff out. Some thoughts, such as regret, jealousy, and envy can become so powerful that they handicap our ability to be proactive.

The faster we can clear our thoughts, the more efficient our minds become to do new work.

54 – Stale Ale

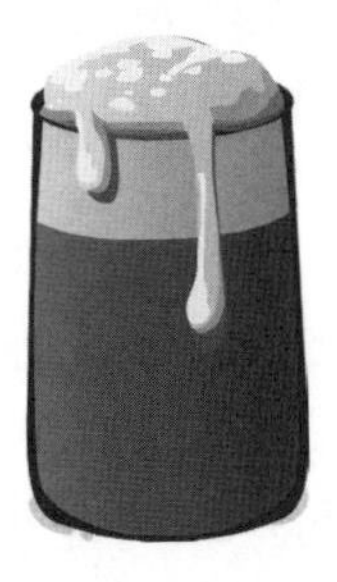

AKA—Thought Abandonment

SOME THOUGHTS ARE good, some are bad, and others change over time. Imagine you have been given a mighty pitcher of the finest ale in all the land, carbonated too! (If you do not drink alcohol, substitute with the best root beer imaginable.) Its sweet aroma, fine color, reputation, and especially the fact that it was free make you feel that it would be the best beverage of your life. Unfortunately, you do not have time to drink it at this very moment, so you set it on your refrigerator shelf, hoping to drink it when you have the chance.

A few weeks later, you spy that pitcher of ale and notice it has a disgusting, pungent aroma, which fills the entire refrigerator. The carbonation is now gone. Faded green mold has formed on the top. Upon closer inspection, you can see hundreds of maggots swimming in it. How about a drink now? Despite being a very fine pitcher of ale at one time, its moment has passed, so it needs to be discarded. Drinking such foulness will only make you sick and miserable—it would be senseless to do so.

Every day, you have hundreds of ideas coming into your brain. Occasionally, there is a really good one that you will write on your "to do" list. Despite it being a fantastic idea, and you thinking about it continually, you never seem to gather the resources to start on it. It just sits there, taking up space and your energy. You still think about it all the time. I think, in general, we tend to want to cling to some of these ideas indefinitely. Whatever it is, a point will come when you should realize the idea has become so stale that even if you were to tackle it now, the benefit would not be worth the cost.

"Stale Ale" or Thought Abandonment is the technique of re-measuring a task you once believed was viable and potentially profitable but has become one of minimal potential return—and then consciously eliminating the thought from your processes, never to look back on it again.

You will need to determine at what point a thought becomes stale, but if it has been years since you first conceived the idea, chances are you do not have the means or willpower to see it through. It may no longer even be a profitable idea; free yourself from it.

The better you become at eliminating thoughts with low return potential, the more time and energy you have to put toward those with high potential.

After a year or two, if you haven't pulled the trigger yet, chances are you never will.

55 – Pins and Needles

AKA—Discipline over Discomfort

WHENEVER SOMEONE COMES to me asking for advice on starting a new business, I make him or her do two things:

- Take out a $100 bill and tear it up, flushing the fragments down the toilet.
- Take a freezing cold shower for ten minutes.

"But why?" they protest.

"Because if you are not able to make yourself do financially and physically uncomfortable things, this business and the friction you will face will beat you down and you will quit, losing far more than $100. You must become comfortable with the idea of risking money with no chance of return."

They almost universally protest the tearing up of money.

"Could you do it with monopoly money or a piece of paper?" I ask.

"Of course," they respond.

"Then why not a $100 bill?" I ask. "It's mostly made of the same kind of material."

"Because it is worth much more and I don't want to waste it!" they exclaim.

"So you believe that a $100 bill has power?" I ask.

"Yes! I can buy many things with it!" they answer.

Usually when I get to this point, I know they won't roll the dice. They're too fearful, too focused on the possibility of loss instead of prospect. They are already in the "making excuses stage." I make a last ditch effort to persuade them: "We all tear up money every day, the only difference is that we do it by wasting time in countless ways. It is far worse to waste time. Money can be replaced; time cannot, and yet we throw it away without a thought. Why do we only feel hesitant to do so if it's in paper form?"

"Secondly, if you are able to demonstrate to yourself in a physical way that you are comfortable with the prospect of losing an investment, that in and of itself is incredibly valuable to an entrepreneur. You will face situations where the outcome is unknown, and you must be willing to take a chance. I can assure you it will be for much more than $100. Your ability to see money as a servant is far more valuable than seeing it as a master. If you cannot grasp these principles, business is not for you."

On a few rare occasions, my friends see through the illusion of money and tear up the $100 bill. I call this "jumping the fence" because once they are on the other side, they see money as a tool, not something that has power over them. Perhaps the lesson is wasteful in the short run, but it always leaves an impression and changes how people think about money. (As a side note, the vast majority of those I have challenged with this task cannot perform it. It is something mental they cannot overcome.)

I'll ask them a few days later, "How was that freezing cold shower?" I love the cold shower test because it is something cheap and easy to access. Almost anyone can at least attempt it. You would be amazed at the number of people who refuse to take a freezing cold shower under all circumstances.

We live in a comfort-based society, where we are constantly seeking comfortable foods, comfortable places, comfortable people, and comfortable things. We may not always get them, but that's what most people want and look for, at least on a subconscious level; a nice comfort zone. The cold shower test is a way to challenge that and safely measure how willing you are to make yourself uncomfortable.

Comfort is seductive and lulls us into a sleep of complacency. When we have comfort, our natural instinct is to stop whatever else we could be doing and enjoy the ride. It is a human tendency.

A deep love of comfort is inefficient.

While we are all limited in similar ways, such as time, the need for sleep and food, and how much information we can process in a given second, an individual's drive and initiative are vastly different from person to person. I believe an individual's drive is inversely proportional to his or her love of comfort.

Many people have dreams and goals they never actually pursue because they are not willing to make the sacrifices necessary to chase them. They are not willing to make themselves uncomfortable to earn what they want.

If an individual's love of comfort is great, you can expect he will have a low-drive output.

If an individual has a very high threshold for discomfort, he does not experience the same mental hurdles and obstacles that those who love comfort do. Therefore, he has a distinct psychological advantage in pursuing goals.

A tremendous opportunity exists in finding those things that make you most uncomfortable, then facing and defeating them. You can train your mind to force a deep love of comfort out of your system. Each time you do it, you will be rewarded.

I'm a big believer in the CrossFit exercise program. While the workouts are fantastic, I am far more interested in the mental discomfort, breathing so fast and hard that I feel like I am about to pass out from exhaustion; with my body screaming at me to stop, I try to find a way to push through it. A gold mine exists in mentally pushing yourself beyond the barriers you believe limit you. Try to visit that place regularly and force yourself to step over the line of where you thought you were limited.

Let's talk about the efficiency of cold showers. Showering is an activity many of us do daily, occasionally twice. The reason I bring this up is because hot showers tend to last much longer than cold ones. Many people take 15-20 minute hot showers daily.

However, when we are forced to take a freezing cold shower, the duration mysteriously decreases to *as fast as humanly possible.* While saving 10-15 minutes a day might not seem like much, over the course of an individual's life it will add up. That compiled 10-15 minutes a day is enough time for me to plan, create, and test market a new product in just a few days or weeks. More importantly, there are other benefits that come with the cost of *discomfort*.

The first time I noticed the positive effects of cold showers was in Russia in 1993, when every summer the government would turn the hot water off for a month or two to repair plumbing lines. We had no choice but to take cold showers since there was no hot water at all. After a few weeks, I noticed I felt amazingly good afterwards. On most of my disaster aid trips, we were forced to take bucket baths or cold showers, so this concept has been reintroduced to me many times over the years.

Instead of listing and referencing all the positive effects of cold showers claimed by scientific research (I'll leave those Google searches up to you) let me tell you what I know for sure from firsthand experience and what my goals are with cold showers:

1. I have never quite gotten used to it. It's still a little uncomfortable to me every time, but it forces me to step outside my comfort zone, and I believe it conditions the mind to adapt better to discomfort in other situations.

2. I always experience a spike in adrenaline. It is as exhilarating to me as sky diving or facing a great fear. This adrenaline spike seems to stay with me for at least a couple of hours.

3. My heart rate becomes elevated and my breathing increases.

4. My electricity bill on average drops about fifty dollars a month when I am exclusively taking cold showers.

5. I feel better in general. It seems my mood is more positive and I am a happier person.

6. Hot showers have a tendency to make me feel hot and sweaty for the next several hours.

Tearing up a $100 bill and taking a freezing cold shower are only two examples of a much larger principle. Each day, find a way to train yourself to overcome the love of comfort. It might be exercise, it might be waking up earlier than usual, it might be something else, but the more you are willing to overcome mental obstacles, the sooner they will disappear from your path, making you better equipped to deal with friction and other obstacles that limit efficiency.

Discomfort Exercise: Find 3 new habits you would *love* have but don't because of discomfort. It is important to distinguish the difference between discomfort and fear. Those are two different things, though they can be related. I see fear as a type of emotion and discomfort as very low-level pain. We had an exercise on fear, and now I want you to start looking at things in your life that make you uncomfortable, and developing the mental fortitude to face them and conquer them.

Follow up with this exercise by describing how you felt once you found the actual strength to maintain these new habits. How did it change your life?

56 – Falling Forward

AKA—Ensuring Your Mistakes and Shortcomings Count Positively

RUNNING BACKS ARE taught early on that a successful running play is three or more yards, with no penalties incurred. If a team gets three or more yards every time a running back touches the ball, theoretically, the team would be unstoppable. For example:

- First down and ten yards to go; three yards gained.
- Second down and seven yards to go; three yards gained.
- Third down and four yards to go; three yards gained.
- Fourth down and one yard to go; three yards gained.
- First and ten, etc.

Any football team on any level that could consistently perform on that simple level indefinitely would be the undefeated champion of its league. Three yards from the line of scrimmage is not a lot, so why doesn't the above scenario happen more often if this is common knowledge?

Defenses are intelligent, determined, and aggressive. Players miss assignments, make mistakes, or get penalties that screw things up.

Offensive play callers get bored. The ball is sometimes fumbled. No team in the history of football has ever made three or more yards on every single play it has attempted. Nonetheless, a huge emphasis is placed on this "three or more yards" strategy.

In order to attain this three-yard-per-attempt average, running backs are also taught always to "fall forward," simply because if the back is hit after a one or two yard gain and is going down, falling forward could still get him to the three-yard mark. That is a pretty amazing concept: If a running back only makes a two-yard gain on each attempt, but falls forward every time he is tackled, and thereby gains an additional yard each time, his team would be unstoppable.

If a running back makes a two yard gain, is tackled, and then crumbles under the force of his tackler, only netting two yards, it completely defeats the three-yard theory of success, and the team would be stopped every set of downs, assuming it continued to run on every down.

Falling forward means to take any failures you encounter in life and gain as much information and experience as possible from them in order to turn failures into long-term advantages.

Over the short term, a two-yard gain before getting hit doesn't look promising. Falling forward and getting that extra yard can be the difference between mediocrity and becoming a world champion.

The mosquito hunts its prey using a falling forward method. A single mosquito will constantly measure the amount of CO_2 in its immediate environment, which is a gas given off by living creatures the mosquito might want to prey on. It will stop in mid-air, measure the CO_2 content, and then move in any random direction, stop, and re-measure the CO_2. It then does one of two things:

1. If there is less CO_2 in the present location than the last, it will return to the previous location, re-sample, and then move in a new direction to resample.

2. If there is more CO_2 in the present location than the last, the mosquito will then move in a similar direction as the last move, then resample.

By repeating those two simple steps, millions of mosquitos successfully track and attain their goals. In other words, if you are closer on this try than the last, keep moving in that direction. If you are farther than you were on the last attempt, go back and try again. It is a simple, incredibly powerful, biologically-proven strategy based on learning from failures.

A couple of years ago, I designed an invention for a friend of mine on my 3D printer. The invention was an ergonomic grip that could be easily placed on the top of a semi-automatic handgun and could then afford more surface area, allowing the slide to be more easily pulled back to load the initial round into the chamber. This is a critical first step in preparing a semi-auto for use, and without the ability to pull the slide back, that particular type of firearm is useless.

For younger people, pulling the slide back usually isn't a problem; for older gun-owners who suffer from arthritis, it is a huge issue. Without sufficient hand strength, it is an impossible task, often resulting in these gun owners abandoning their semi-automatic hand guns for lower capacity revolvers that don't require chambering the first round.

The accessory needed to be light and simple to use. It needed to be easy to place on, and remove from, the firearm, and, most importantly, it needed to stay on indefinitely while shooting, and then be removed without tooling.

Over the course of four months, I created several hundred prototypes—each time learning something a little more from the last design, which then improved the next attempted design. Sometimes, the next design was better; sometimes, it was worse, but using the mosquito strategy, I *learned* from each failure, building on knowledge gained.

In the end, the final product was incredible. It included a rubberized grip around the outside, making the feel even more comfortable. I could fire several hundred rounds through it without it coming off, and when I was finished, I could easily slip it off. I was very proud of this invention.

We searched the Internet for a similar product, and not finding any, we decided to move forward, securing website names, having artwork designed, and investing time and resources to turn it into a business. Then we contracted a legal team and, sure enough, it delivered the bad news: an inventor in Israel had designed and patented an almost identical design three years earlier. Speaking with our engineer and lawyer, we all concluded that the design in its current state was effectively dead. It felt like four months wasted, but there was still an opportunity to *fall forward.*

Some benefits were that we had found a new legal team that was spectacularly good. My previous lawyer sat on my first patent application for five months before asking me for $10,000 to do the work. The new team only charged $299 for the patent search, with another $3,000 fee should the patent application move forward. They also did it within a week from when we contacted them. It was a huge find because since then, I have used this team half-a-dozen times. I also learned the importance of hiring pros to do the patent search for us, instead of doing it ourselves and missing something as we had. I was glad to spend the $300 instead of working four months making hundreds of prototypes before finding out someone else held the patent on the product.

I also gleaned incredible insight into prototyping, including learning the skills of 3D scanning, mold making, casting, and integrating different types of rubber with plastics. It had also given me tremendous confidence in future designs. I have since made many photography accessories using the skills I learned during that experience.

Yes, if we found the existing patent before starting, it would have saved a lot of money, thought, energy, and time, but I learned something even more valuable that is applicable to all aspects of life:

Had I made my mistakes faster, cheaper, earlier, or more often, I could have been much more efficient in coming to the same conclusion. This is the heart of the matter when it comes to failures; there is always gold in them.

To summarize the take home message here on failures:

1. Learn to embrace the possibility of failure as a tool of development. Failure is not the greatest failure—not trying is.

2. Fall forward with each failure, learning valuable insights with each experience and improving on the next attempt, building an arsenal of knowledge.

3. Reduce the expense of failures by making them early, often, fast, and cheap.

What are the three greatest failures of your life? What did you learn from each one?

1.

2.

3.

57 – Power Play

AKA—Dominance

A POWER PLAY is the tactic of altering the actual or perceived level of power, dominion, or authority that one person has over another. When one individual has more power than another, the stronger individual will typically experience greater ease and efficiency in obtaining his goals and desires.

You first experienced the effects of a power play as a child. Your parents, monsters in size and strength, dictated every aspect of your life (when you would eat, sleep, how much, and what you could watch on TV). They made a lot of rules—rules we swore to ourselves we would break once we were old enough. They could punish us physically with spankings and mentally with reprimands. There was not a dang thing we could do about it either. They called the shots because they were bigger, stronger, faster, and wiser than us in every way.

Yet, at church on Sunday, in the middle of a quiet gospel reading, children are able to flip the tables on their parents. Sitting quietly on a bench, many a young toddler knows that once she rips into an ear-shattering wailing, her negotiating power has suddenly skyrocketed to stratospheric heights as her parents offer literally everything they can think of to calm her. (Well, unless you had a parent like mine who would just take you out to the hallway.) Even then, it was a victory.

Growing up, you probably experienced power-play again a few years later when your neighbor Tommy Ferguson brought out his brand new Nerf football that he got for Christmas. Because he was the possessor of said neon orange plaything, he could determine the rules of the game, touch or tackle, who was playing on which team, and occasionally, the outcome of the game itself because it was his ball so the game could not be played without it.

For the same reason, now several years later, when you are driving and a police officer flashes his lights, you immediately pull your car off to the side of the road.

Power play is the reason why we are willing to go to jobs where we are told what to do, when to do it, how to do it, when we may eat, when we may leave, and even when we may take a potty break.

When someone has the ability to provide something we want, or has the ability to inflict punishment, it increases that person's power. When we are willing to approach someone, on his terms, for the price he wants, it is easier for him to make the transaction.

You have probably always been aware of power play, but you may not have made a conscious effort to turn the tables in situations where you are at a disadvantage because of it.

[As an important side note, I am against the immoral use of power to hurt others, which is easy to do once a lot of power is acquired. It is a natural human instinct to exercise unrighteous dominion once great power is achieved. True greatness comes when power and authority are governed by an individual with a strong moral compass, who does not use that power inappropriately to bless himself in a selfish way. Such people, unfortunately, are rare in today's world.]

How interesting it is when the tables are turned on little Tommy; in time, his Nerf Football is lost over the fence, or for your birthday, you are given an Official NFL leather ball.

Several YouTube videos depict policemen, who initially believe they are in the rights of their authority by stopping, for example, a young law student who is openly carrying a handgun on his hip. Many Second Amendment activists, such as this student, know the law very well, and when they can cite it, as well as articulate how their rights are being infringed upon, it is fascinating to watch these police officers backpedal.

Never fired or laid off is the employee who is too valuable to lose. In modern times, more and more freedom, wages, and benefits are given to those who perform and deliver. There are many, many people out there gainfully employed who do not even go to an actual place to work.

If you are in a position of weakness when negotiating with someone (meaning the person has something you really, really, *really* want and you do not have something of equal value to exchange for it), it is typically a mistake to be direct about your wants and needs. Feigning disinterest, or even bluffing that you are walking away, will always achieve more than groveling for someone else's mercy and generosity. (People will only find you pathetic when you do so.) If you can bring yourself genuinely to reject whatever thing it is they believe you want, you will undermine their power over you. Only then can you turn the tables.

If you are in a position of power when negotiating, it is typically easier and faster simply to state what you want in the exchange. Boldness rarely hurts in these situations, and it is usually efficient.

The *appearance* of power and authority is just as important as the real thing.

Without getting into too much detail, I know that the way I look and dress when working in disaster situations has an immediate and direct effect on the assumptions people make about me. Those assumptions have resulted in easier access to people, information, and resources.

It is a subtle and powerful tool to be able to control what others think and conclude about you based on which cards you are showing them.

Fame is another form of power. Movie stars, athletes, and musicians are constantly given exclusive access to people and events that the common man could never dream of. Many rules are bent for the famous.

Wealth is power because almost everyone needs and wants money. There are numerous examples of how the wealthy are treated differently simply because they have money.

As a general observation, I have learned that those who are most fearful of losing power are the ones who overreact emotionally when it is challenged. Those who wield true power do so without emotion or hesitation and are not easily rattled. True power is confident. This is a key distinction to pierce the veil of a false authority.

By becoming aware of what you want, who has it, and how to get it, you should be able to determine quickly who has power over you. By maintaining and controlling assets that others want, you increase your power and, therefore, your efficiency.

58 – The War Horse

AKA—A Positive Mental Attitude

THE LONGER I am on this planet, the more I realize that life just throws you one curveball after another. There are illnesses, betrayals, taxes, and unexpected surprises that will utterly crush your soul. It is especially hard when there is no solution to the problems you face, burying you under a veil of desperation and despair.

When we were children, it felt that most of the resistance we encountered was from either unfamiliarity or rules enforced by our parents. Once we go out into the world and see things on our own, we slowly realize that what we envisioned and expected for our future is not easily attained and our parents were doing their best. We start to face all the things they did and everything that they never told us about because they wanted to protect us from life's realities. We come to the slow realization that all those silly rules they imposed served a wise purpose. *Our parents were right all along!*

Some things I take very hard, especially the death of a close friend. It just destroys me. My appetite disappears, sleep eludes me, I almost go into a trance thinking about the person's family, time we spent together, and what has been lost. The reality that life is fragile comes crashing in. It is like being awoken from a deep sleep, and I wonder about all the time I have wasted and how I haven't lived up to my own expectations. Have you ever felt like that?

It is so easy to have a good day, but when people start having bad days, look out! I had a good friend on the BYU football team who wore his emotions on his sleeve. When he was in a good mood, he was almost giddy with excitement—happy, smiling, laughing, and joking. The guy just wouldn't stop. When things didn't go his way, he was silent, solemn, sad, critical, complaining, and friendless. I don't think he ever realized how emotionally transparent he was.

I started noticing something in practice: When he was in a good mood, practices seemed more fun. When he was in a bad mood, practices weren't fun at all. In fact, his performance diminished. All the players were out there busting their butts, and this one guy, who was having a bad day, seemed to be rubbing off on everyone.

Those of you in the military can attest to the experiences of going on long hikes surrounded by those who are skilled joke tellers versus those who just want to complain about how hard the hike is. A palpable difference can be felt in the actual hike, depending on who you are with. If you are doing something amazingly hard and everyone has a positive attitude, it always goes more smoothly. If everyone is fighting each other, the already hard task becomes impossible.

Maui, where I work part of the year, has some fantastic ocean kayaking. Over the years, I have had a number of guests whom I have taken kayaking. Sometimes, the wind will pick up and require a concerted effort for us to make any progress. You have to paddle as a team. I'm almost always in the back because I have more kayaking experience and can easily steer. I cannot tell you how quickly you can find out about a person's attitude in the face of hardship when you are kayaking with him or her.

One friend, even when the going was easy, just couldn't shut her complaining mouth. Every single stroke she was whining about something—I wasn't paddling enough, I wasn't paddling in perfect unison, it was too windy, it was too sunny, and her paddle was wet. It was just one thing after another. I was trying to be a good host, having taken time off work to show her some of the island at my expense. She couldn't care less. Needless to say, I couldn't wait to get back to shore.

Several months later, another friend joined me on the same outing. The conditions were almost identical. She was happy to be on the water. She commented on how beautiful the scenery was and how she couldn't believe she was so fortunate. When the wind started blowing, she remained positive and upbeat. She encouraged strong teamwork heading back in, and we absolutely destroyed all the other kayakers on the way to the return point. Comment after comment, she was positive and happy. It was an extraordinary and fun way to spend the morning, and I would go kayaking with her anytime.

Again, same conditions, two different people, two different attitudes, two different experiences.

Attitude is a choice—the more positive your attitude, the easier it is to overcome life's frictions.

Imagine picking one day to complain about everything you encounter. Literally everything. Take little things and magnify them as much as possible. Fight with your spouse about every word that comes out of his or her mouth. Flip off every single person you drive by in your car. Complain about every meal you order, asking to see the manager. Find ways to blame other people for your own problems and let them know about it. How would such a day go for you?

What you will quickly come to realize is that when we become problem magnets, life suddenly becomes much, *much* harder. If constantly having a negative attitude makes life harder, why do it at all? Even just a little?

I like to imagine that the attitudes we have are really like horses we ride. Our mind has a stable full of them. There is every single kind of horse in that stable. Some are younger, some are older, some are weaker, and others are stronger. Some are gentle, and some are unbroken and wild.

When we do not choose the horse we will ride, our subconscious will choose for us.

This point takes some time to understand, but when things are going tough we automatically start to feel bad inside. That very feeling should be a trigger for you to walk into the stable of your mind and consciously pick out the best horse for the task: The War Horse.

The War Horse is unlike any other. He is a stallion of the finest breed and has a muscular build that cannot be matched. The War Horse is intelligent and cool under fire; he is not spooked by gunshots, explosions, or screams of pain. The War Horse is able to ride into danger, focused directly on the goal. The War Horse can run for days without tiring. He can sprint, carry heavy loads, move with stealth, and leap over tall fences. The War Horse never complains and loves a good challenge. The War Horse knows that friction and obstacles are opportunities to shine. He is your best friend, companion, and ally in the war of life. If he could speak, he would say, "We will find a way to do this...together!" He will not fail you; all you have to do is choose him as the attitude to ride.

Riding the War Horse is contagious. When others see you riding with such a strong, focused, and positive attitude, they will also seek to change the attitude they are riding.

If you have any sick, weak, old, feeble, miserable horses in your stable, it is time to send them to the glue factory. No reasonable excuse exists to ride them, so they shouldn't even be in your stable. Mentally slaughter them if necessary.

Anyone can have a good day, but only great individuals can have a good day when things go wrong. It is a choice.

The War Horse walks all obstacles under its feet. It doesn't care about mud, rain, or cold. It only cares about one thing...finishing its mission.

59 – The Movie Projector

AKA—The Power of Pre-Visualization

OVER THE YEARS, I have taught many thousands of beginning photographers how to edit their images using Photoshop. Assuming that all of my students know the program's basics, the most common mistake they make is how they think before editing.

A pure beginning photo editor thinks like this:

1. Open Photo.
2. "Hmmm...this is a cool photo. I wonder what cool things I can do to it?"
3. "Let's try black and white. Yeah, that's pretty cool. But maybe I can do better, so let's start over."
4. Re-Open Photo.
5. "Let's try using the levels tool. Move this slider there, that slider there. Hmmm. Not so cool. Let's start over."
6. Re-Open Photo.
7. "Maybe I'll just start opening all these random filters and see

which one is the coolest?" Half hour later... "Okay, those were cool, but not so cool."

8. Re-Open Photo, etc.

Anyway, you get the idea.

A photo-editing student who has mastered pre-visualization thinks this way:

1. Open photo.

2. "Where do I want to take this? What would strengthen this image most?"

3. Quickly runs through dozens of possible edits *mentally*, imagining what the photo should look like when it's finished.

4. Executes the steps required to create the mental image and is finished.

Long before I got into video production, I wanted to make an indie film. I was convinced that the best way to do it was without a plan. Just show up with some actors, a camera, and do everything on the fly. Plans seem to restrict so much. The crazy thing is, I actually shot a few shorts this way. They were terrible, and I wonder now whether I was a borderline lunatic for thinking such a feat would be possible.

From that experience, I came to understand the power of pre-visualization. Any good movie made today is carefully pre-visualized both in script as well as a tool called a storyboard where each individual shot is sketched on individual images. The script and storyboard are how the director communicates her pre-visualization to the rest of the crew and vastly increases the production's efficiency and game plan. Before anything is shot by the camera, everything is pre-visualized. The director has already pre-visualized what the final product of the film will look like when it is shown via a movie projector.

Pre-visualization is the process of mentally creating your end result and working directly toward that goal.

When pre-visualizing, you should be able to screen dozens or even hundreds of possibilities in seconds, without needing to create those individual prototypes physically.

Your mind is the most powerful computer you have access to, and its creative power is unlimited. Use it to your advantage by creating the best mental game plan possible and then executing that plan, instead of moving forward without thought.

Pre-visualization has applications to every type of activity imaginable. Granted, system familiarity will always be required, such as learning Photoshop basics and becoming fluent with your toolsets. However, my experience has been that pre-visualization while learning the basics is much more powerful than just learning the basics.

When learning a new skill, ask yourself what you want to do, how it will look, what is its sound or feel, and then learn the tools that will get you there.

Creative flailing is inefficient.

60 – TNT

AKA—Task, Not Time

PARKINSON'S LAW IS an adage that states: "Work expands so as to fill the time available for its completion." While it is probably intended more as humor than an actual law of nature, its lesson is highly accurate: The more time we give a specific task, the longer it will take that task to be completed.

Time allows us to coordinate with others, set limits when action is required, and even measure progress. Time in and of itself does not do work. Our actions bring about progress. Quantity of time does not equal quality of time.

The goal of working on something for an hour can always be achieved, but it does not ensure that progress will be made in that hour. A false sense of security arises in believing that working on something for a specific time will bring results.

We have a tendency to fall into the trap of correlating time spent to progress. From the time we are young and have to go to school or church or a job for a set period, we are taught that time is work. It isn't. It took years for me to break this type of thinking.

As a college student, I discovered that I was making the same error in my studies, devoting massive amounts of time to memorization, without as much focus on the research and actually understanding the material. I would "spend 2-3" hours each night in the library studying. Friends would visit. We would talk. I might read a newspaper. There was lots of wasted time, but I still managed to "study" for 2-3 hours every evening. Once I started telling myself I could leave as soon as I mastered certain required concepts, I found time spent in the library decreasing and my grades improving.

Exercise has always been important to me, but I nearly always measured the success of my workouts by how much time was spent in the gym. This ranged from one to two hours daily. On one particularly ineffective day, I realized I had spent nearly two hours in the gym, yet I didn't have a very good workout.

"What am I doing in the gym? Why am I there? Where is all this time going?" I learned my true goal—to get in better shape. Burning calories and exercising would help me do this. Not sitting around in a gym.

One day, I bumped into a gym friend I hadn't seen in over a year. He had transformed himself from portly and overweight to fit and muscular. His shoulders and chest bulged with newfound muscle.

"What in the world have you been doing?" I asked.

"Crossfit. It is incredible," he answered.

"I'll be there tomorrow," I replied.

Now, I realize there are some ongoing jokes about how fanatical Crossfitters are. They rave and talk about it to the point of ridiculousness. Once I actually tried it, I understood why: The workouts are so intense that I believe there is a physical addiction that happens afterwards much like a runner's high. The "WODs" or workouts of the day, typically last from **5-20 minutes**, sometimes longer, but they are much more effective and efficient, at least for me. I can't think of any other form of exercise I personally enjoy more.

I have since returned to the gym to lift weights many times, but I can never replicate the intensity or results of a Crossfit WOD. It feels like I am wasting time at the gym, and to think I used to spend two hours at a time there!

In my work as a video producer, I focus completely on *what* needs to be done, not *how long* I should be working on it.

The goal is to complete the task at hand. The time you spend on it is secondary.

This is what **time-only** oriented goals sound like:

- I will work on this assignment for a half hour.
- I will study tonight for three hours.
- I will go to the gym for an hour.
- I will spend the weekend on vacation.

This is what **task-**oriented goals sound like:

- I will master the principles of this assignment.
- I will demonstrate knowledge of the material without using the book.
- I will focus on my chest, arms, and legs tonight at the gym.
- I will go for a hike, camp overnight, and take as many pictures as possible.

Task-oriented goals can be turned into games when we include a way to score:

- I will self-test the principles of this chapter until I score over 90 percent
- I will teach the information from the material to a friend in ten minutes or less.
- I will do three sets of ten reps at 70 percent max capacity for each exercise in less than ten minutes each.
- I will take one spectacular image this weekend while I am camping.

Can you feel the difference between each of these?

The take-home message of TNT is that you set goals based on measureable, completed tasks, not so much a given time frame to work on it. Time in and of itself does not do work.

Focusing on the goals being completed is more efficient than focusing on the time you are working on something.

When Not to Use TNT

TNT should not be used when keeping time to a minimum is the main goal. Examples include, but are not limited to, racing or any other events where time is the final determining motivator. You can use an artificial lack of time to your advantage, such as to create a sense of urgency, or to gamify a process as in the Uncompelled Race, which we will discuss in later chapters.

61 – The Fireball

AKA—A Sense of Urgency

AT BIG TEXAN Steak Ranch in Amarillo, if you can eat a 72 oz. steak (that's 4.5 lbs.) plus sides, in less than one hour, the meal is free. Driving through Texas on a hot afternoon, I stumbled upon this restaurant and decided to give it a go. As the monstrous slab of meat was placed before me, I caught the chef from the kitchen closely watching me. I picked up my knife and fork, began cutting away at the steak, and upon taking my second bite, looked up at the chef and could see him silently mouthing out the words "Too slow."

Upon falling short of the goal an hour later, I looked at the record books and noticed that the fastest eater had consumed the same enormous meal in 8 minutes, 35 seconds; that record was set by the famous champion speed-eater Joey Chestnut. His record would later be shattered by a Molly Schuyler in 2015 with a time of 4 minutes and 18 seconds. *The whole meal.* Molly's feat was more impressive because she ate two additional meals afterwards in under 20 minutes total. While that 72 oz. steak was hard to forget, the thing that stuck most with me was the chef's comment when I had only started eating.

This chef probably watched everyone who attempted the meal, and from his experience, he knew *that without a sense of urgency,* the steak simply cannot be eaten.

I later learned that our bodies have a delayed system of telling our minds when we are full, and that this signal biochemically registers 10-15 minutes after the fact. This means we have a short window from the time we are full to the time we physically realize it. If we are going to try and stuff down 4.5 lbs. of steak, we need to finish eating before this biological signal registers. Champion food eaters know this principle; you can be full and not feel it until several minutes later.

The same is true with thirst, which is why our coaches always told us to hydrate as often as possible. "If you are feeling thirsty, you are already dehydrated." Again, the biological signal takes several minutes to kick in before we physically feel it.

This truth also holds for fatigue. As with most sports, especially when you are in great shape, you do not feel the fatigue until a certain stage far into or far after the workout. There is fatigue delay for all of us; it is just shorter when we are out of shape.

I imagine the same is true for mental fatigue; we expend our best mental strength and energy after a given time, and far before we begin to feel it.

That short window between what is happening and what feels like is happening is a crucial competitive advantage if we are aware of it.

We have all felt a "sense of urgency" at one point in our lives. We are late, have a deadline, and are literally racing against the clock to try to make it. That psychological pressure can be extremely motivating, and it also makes us really fast, really focused, and really efficient at chasing a specific goal. Unfortunately, this feeling seems to be something more imposed, less voluntary, or the consequence of poor planning.

What if there were a way to trigger a sense of urgency artificially? Perhaps in the same way a champion speed-eater would train for a big event? What if there were a way to flip this urgency switch voluntarily, when there was no real need, just to finish ahead of schedule? Surely, if you could find a way to feel a sense of urgency, even when there is no real reason to, it could become a very powerful efficiency tool.

I have lost two close loved ones to ruptured brain aneurisms, which are essentially a weakening of a blood vessel in the brain that can break and cause blood to flow into the brain. In both cases, death was nearly immediate. There were no early indicators, no warnings. They were healthy one moment and gone the next. It can happen to any of us, just as a car accident or any other of the many ways to die. I do not like talking about death or aneurisms, but it illustrates a very important point: We have no guarantee of a tomorrow. One day we will all die, and I think that is sometimes forgotten, and we lose so much on the little, wasteful things. This is a tremendous motivator to me, and I often find myself asking the following questions:

If you were told you had one day to live, who would you call and what would you say to them?

Make a list of the things you would do differently in your daily schedule if you knew you had a month to live:

What goals would you have if you had a year left to live?

I have to wonder: Why is it any of these goals or interactions should be any different than the ones we currently have, *simply because we feel like we have more time, when in reality we may not.*

Knowing that our end is coming should constantly be somewhere in the back of our minds, and it should not take a funeral to remind us how to live.

I have come to the conclusion that if I am not chasing my goals with an extreme sense of urgency, I am living wrong. I want to feel a sense of urgency every day from the moment I wake up, until my work is finished for the day. Of course, I still take time off, relax, and have fun, but when I am working, it is game on. I do not want to be the guy taking his sweet ol' time, not finishing a goal in an hour that others are doing in five minutes.

Find ways to initiate an artificial sense of urgency to motivate yourself to finish the task at hand as quickly as possible. It might be a inventing a game involving a stopwatch, or pretending someone has a gun to your head, but the take-home message here is:

If you think you have plenty of time, you are already at a disadvantage.

62 – The Joystick

AKA—The Gamification of Procrastination

I SPENT THIRTEEN years in college, five years as an undergrad and eight in grad school. That is a lot of classes on a lot of subjects and a lot of tests and studying for those tests. In the beginning, struggling to develop good study habits, I became a victim of procrastination.

When I was an undergrad, my primary method of study was going to the library for several hours to try to memorize everything. The results were sporadic at best. I graduated BYU with a 3.11 overall GPA. It was in grad school that I discovered that I could "gamify" my study habits with the right attitude and a little creativity. I graduated from grad school with a 3.8 GPA and I believe much of it had to do with how I approached study.

To gamify is to turn a dreaded task into a game.

Erin McGonigal, in her book, *Reality is Broken*, beautifully summarizes what makes something a game in the following points:

1. There is a specific goal.
2. There are rules.
3. There is a feedback system (i.e., a score).

4. Playing the game is voluntary.

I personally believe the actual feeling of competing against others or one's self is also incredibly motivating. Competition creates a sense of *urgency.* If you can get into the habit of applying these simple principles to dreaded tasks in your everyday life, you will find yourself much more motivated to start and complete tasks.

Gamification is applicable to almost every task you do not want to do. When you look at tough tasks as a game, it is easier to get things started and easier to make it urgent as well.

I want to share some gaming examples with you that have been very effective for me:

The Uncompelled Race

Racing games are scored by how quickly they are finished. A racing game should not be mistaken with a deadline. True deadlines are compelled races, meaning they are not voluntary and, therefore, not fun. Compelled deadlines also increase stress, which increases the chance of error. Errors are not efficient. It is human nature to put off deadlines for many of the above reasons.

A solution to this dilemma is The Uncompelled Race—a self-imposed contest or game against competition or time. Competition motivates. Motivation increases efficiency by increasing output for invested time. I do not wear a watch for time purposes; I wear one for *speed* measurement—specifically a stopwatch.

How to Use the Uncompelled Race:

1. Instead of waiting for a deadline to motivate you, aim to break personal records or defeat a friend, colleague, or sibling in a friendly contest.

2. Devise a contest where you are scored by how quickly the task is completed.

3. Keep posted scorecards for bragging rights. This motivator can be very effective when PR (personal record) and WR (world record) are added to the high scores. You can use this process for something as mundane as motivating your children to help with certain chores.

Some examples I use the Uncompelled Race with are:

- How quickly I can go from just waking up to being dressed and out the door: 33 seconds

- Shaving my face with a razor, without cuts: 2 minutes, 2 seconds

- Flossing between every tooth without injury: 45 seconds

- Taking a shower and being completely dressed: 4 minutes, 13 seconds

- How quickly I can set up my video lights, tripod, set up microphone, pre-focus before recording a lesson on location: 9 minutes, 33 seconds

A self-imposed race motivates you to perform quickly without much of the stress. When I play these games, I often find myself looking for ways to save more time on each task, in order to achieve a new WR (at least in my world). Something else I have noticed is that when I am aware of specific times to do specific tasks, I refer to the current record as motivation: *this will only take forty-five seconds!* That alone makes it feel easier. You can imagine how funny I look trying to break these records.

"Before You Go" Tasking—(I also call it "dialing up a blitz" for football fans)

It's 4:40 p.m. on a Friday. You are just wrapping up at work and you are about to meet your sweetheart for dinner and a movie. You are excited, have been looking forward to it, and are in a good mood. In order to make it to your favorite restaurant by 5:15, you will need to leave absolutely no later than 4:50. You have ten minutes. If you hurry, you can get at least one thing started you have been putting off for the last few days. In fact, if you hurry, you may be able to finish it completely. *Ready, set, go!*

"Before you go" tasking is a play on the Uncompelled Race. It involves finding lulls (much more on this later) in your daily schedule where you have small gaps of time (five to twenty minutes) immediately before leaving for a mandatory appointment. It doesn't work as well if you are just going home or somewhere there is no expectation for you to arrive at by a specific time. It has to be before an appointment like dinner, a movie, church, the airport, a yoga class, meeting someone, etc. It seems to work better when you are headed to an activity that you enjoy, so you are naturally in an upbeat and positive mood already.

Attacking the task should feel spontaneous and unplanned. You should feel like you just found a twenty-dollar-bill on the street and life is saying, "Here is something you didn't expect, a chance finally to knock this thing off your to do list."

I have had so much success with this technique that I now queue up a list of these extra tasks to have ready for these "before you go" moments; no longer thinking about what I need to get done.

For reasons I do not understand, much of the mental friction of dreaded tasks is eliminated when you simply don't have time to worry. Try packing for a week-long trip in the ten minutes before you must leave for the airport and you will see what I am talking about. We will literally jump up and run around the house as fast as we can to get it done.

"Before you go" tasking typically does not work as well on jobs that require many hours from start to finish or careful calculations, like doing your taxes, attention to detail, like washing and waxing your car, painting a room, and the like. Those are better played with the Uncompelled Race because it ensures you will have time to finish. "Before you go tasks" tend to line up better with *defensive type* work, which we will talk about a little later, but some examples include smaller chores, paying bills, and answering emails.

Divide and Conquer

This is a team game where you have a monumental task and divide it up among several people. They can be friends or employees. Each party races to finish his or her task before the other. There should be some kind of scorecard for all to see as well as a reward for the winner.

Gaming Tactics for Students

One effective study game I called Recon. In studying for a test, I learned that I could gather specific intelligence about what would be on that test by asking the professor certain kinds of questions.

For example, "What is the most important information we need to know for this test?" was the bold and direct way, but it was also very innocuous. It was essentially the same question as, "What will be on the test and what will not?" This gentle probing of the test creator was a simple way for me to know what I should focus my study resources on.

More often than not, the professors described which topics would be on the exam, sometimes in very specific detail, to the entire class. If there were topics they didn't list, I knew I should focus less on them, if at all. I felt this gave me an efficiency advantage over students who were not paying attention to what he said or who studied everything.

The vast majority of professors hold office hours when students can come and ask questions. The vast majority of students do not take advantage of these hours, so when a student does take his or her personal time to visit a professor during office hours, the professor is usually more inclined to answer even more specific questions.

On rare occasion, the professor might say, "Everything. Know everything that was discussed in class." This statement still allowed me to infer that everything not discussed in class, but in certain chapters, would not be on the exam. In some cases, the professor would be even less helpful and disinterested, but I quickly learned that if I peppered him or her with questions about certain topics, I could judge from his or her enthusiasm or the amount of time he was willing to spend on it, the probability that certain material would or would not show up on the test.

Once I had a pretty good idea of what would be on the test, I would study, not based on the amount of time, but rather the understanding of the information I needed to know inside and out. How fast I could learn the information I needed for the test became a game as well. I timed how long it took me to master certain chunks of information.

Another game I played involved linking specific types of information together in the most asinine and hilarious ways possible. The Memory Book by Harry Lorayne and Jerry Lucas outlines the most effective ones. It is a gold mine of information and invaluable to any student.

I spent many hours laughing while studying because I was having so much fun turning memorization into a game.

If the test was more based on practical skills, such as calculating a formula, I would focus more on repetitions and how many I could complete within a given time. Many professors will even hand out old exams with answers to practice on.

When I reached the point where I felt I knew the information, I would then play a game called Professor's Assistant, which involved standing in front of a pure beginner to the subject matter and teaching him or her everything I knew. The beginner was allowed to ask questions about anything that didn't make sense.

Independently teaching someone else an entirely new subject is the best way to know how prepared you are and how well you know the information. If you cannot explain something simply to someone else, you probably do not know it very well. When I couldn't find anyone to teach the material to, I would stand in front of a mirror, or write out everything I knew about the topic on a piece of paper.

(As a final side note on study: It is critical to know if your professor's performance in consideration for tenure is based on a quota of grades he assigns, which was the case in one of my Chemistry courses at BYU. This meant for example, that only the top 10% in the course would receive A's, the next 25% B's, the next 30% C's, 15% D's and 10% Fs. In practicality it meant you might need to spend 30-40 hours a week studying to get an A because you would need to outperform everyone else, or you could spend as little as 5-10 hours a week and still get a B. This is something I wished I had learned the first time I took the course I'm thinking about.)

The heart of the matter about gamification is that whenever you find something that you are not looking forward to doing; find a way to turn it into a game. The game should have a specific goal and a way to keep score (how fast, or a point system of some kind). The task then becomes much easier to start and, therefore, much easier to finish.

VII – Gap Management

63 – The Golden Egg Laying Hen

AKA—The Power of Residual-Based Income

SOCIETY CREATES SO many types of financial friction that we are lucky if we can live within our means. When we look at the cost of a house payment, a car payment, a cell phone payment, insurance and utility bills, food, credit card bills, clothing expenses, tithing if you so choose, and paying what is owed to Uncle Sam, it is nearly impossible to become wealthy as an employee. This isn't to say it is impossible; it is possible for a very small handful of people who have unusual discipline and huge salaries. It is just impossible for the rest of us. As an employee, we are part of a mathematical formula to make someone else more money. The profits from our labor go to the business owner. This is not to say life as an employee is undesirable. If you truly enjoy what you do as an employee, what a blessing that is! Just know the maximum amount of money you can make is more or less fixed.

As a business owner myself, I can also tell you that I have never worked harder in my life than I do for my own business. Even though there are added profits, there are also bigger expenses and bigger problems are associated with running it. Plus, there is the element of risk, which terrifies most employees who just want a steady paycheck they can count on. Risk can be terrifying because it means you can lose everything if a plan doesn't work, which is often the case. This fear is enough to scare away many would-be entrepreneurs from starting a business. The truth is that the security most employees feel is largely a lie. There are no guarantees; any employee can walk into work one day and learn he no longer has a job.

The great secret to financial freedom is *residual-based income*. When I say residual, I mean a business that pays you over and over and over again. When you work as an employee, you get paid once. When you have a residual stream of income, you are paid continually, over and over and over for the work you do. Residual-based income pays you when you are on vacation; it pays you when you are sleeping, and you are also paid on Christmas Day.

At the time of this writing, PewDiePie is one of the most successful YouTube channels. His channel is about him playing video games. His revenue comes from pay-per-click ads that show with his videos and generate five to ten cents per click. In this case, the videos are his employees. But even better, they work for him 24/7/365—and will for years and years to come.

Once a video is uploaded, it becomes his full-time, cost-free employee. When he goes to sleep, that video is generating revenue for him. When he is watching TV, on holiday, driving to the store, those videos are making him money. By the way, it is estimated that he makes about 12-15 million a year. The result of residual-based income is that you get more money, for less work, resulting in more free time.

I realize this example is extreme, the principles remain true; residual-based incomes, when successful, will provide you with more freedom and wealth than being a full-time employee.

I tell everyone I know to make it his or her goal to find a way to escape the employee lifestyle. Find a source of residual, self-maintaining income that will pay you over and over and over again for work you do once.

As a wedding photographer, I was paid handsomely. I could make between $2,000 and $9,000 for a single shoot on a Saturday. The huge problem with this was I would only be paid once and would, therefore, need to work again to make money in the future. I do not believe any non-photographer fully appreciates how much post-production, marketing, meeting with clients, and other business-related expenses are involved.

For the most part, I now shun working on anything for a one-time payment, unless either the pay or opportunity is spectacular, such as learning, networking, or producing an independent feature film. I know that the power of creating something once and selling it over and over again is a much more effective model over the long run. I reject many great one-time-payment offers automatically now because I want to focus all of my efforts on generating more residual income. I would rather invest my time into something that will pay many times over than once. Once you find that niche, you will find yourself saying no regularly and often to everything else.

You maybe be wondering how to find your ideal residual-based income. Nearly everyone is an expert on something. It is a matter of leveraging this knowledge into a source of revenue. I recommend working with the thing you are most passionate about—what you fantasize about doing daily.

Many photographers I am aware of have taken their photography skills and created residual business models:

- One photographer is world renowned for his surf break photography and sells prints and other products containing his images.

- I have a good friend on Maui who prints her island art on hats and bikinis.

- I know of an aerial photographer who recently published a book of his images. He sold 3,000 books at $100 each. (That's $300,000.) Once that book sold out, all he had to do was call the printer to make more copies.

- I know many photographers, myself included, who have created photography apps that sell residually.

- Another photographer is famous for his flash accessories. Every wedding photographer I know is familiar with his products.

- I know many photographers who sell stock photography and prints.

The key to finding a good residual income is to find a product or service that solves a problem in a field you are already an expert in.

Businesses that provide you with residual income usually require at least some maintenance, but very often you can hire a manager or employee to do much of this maintenance work if, and only if, you find good help. The more a residual-based business can "self-maintain," meaning operate itself, the better. There are many, many residual businesses out there that require zero work from the owner. Think about that—indefinite residual income for zero work. Such a form of revenue is very efficient.

Residual-based income is any form of revenue that occurs naturally and consistently over time. They include:

- Wise Investments in real estate and stocks.

- Owning rental property.

- Owning a brick and mortar business run by a paid manager.

Restaurants and storage units are a fantastic example.

- YouTube channel revenues—you can make money publishing videos on YouTube. If the channel is popular enough, you can bet on consistent revenue through pay-per-click ads. You will need many popular videos for this to be sustainable.

- Creating an online business; sell on eBay—I am a huge fan of selling products online. When you sell online, your customer base is *huge*. I have several friends who purchase clothing at low cost and sell it at higher prices on their own websites. If you are able to source a valuable product at a wholesale price, and can sell it online, you have a business.

- Providing complex, valuable, problem-solving types of information. Films, books, PDFs, and how-to videos are all examples of sellable information.

- Software plugins—I have made many of these for other photographers. If the code is outside of my wheelhouse, I have hired programmers to create the software.

- Original content on a blog—If there is enough interest in a particular topic, it can generate a huge volume of revenue through ad space.

- Royalties for published, in-demand work are amazing. Think music, for example. Once the work is finished, you get a percentage on all the sales of that product *indefinitely*.

The Evergreen Factor

Some trees stay green year-round; they are sometimes referred to as evergreens. I use the phrase evergreen to describe a form of residual-based income that generates steady revenue indefinitely.

True evergreens, those residual incomes that require zero maintenance and generate revenue forever, should be the goal; however, they are extremely difficult to set up.

It is much more common for the income from residual-based businesses to fluctuate, but gradually diminish over time.

Whatever your chosen form of residual income, in most cases, it will require some upkeep and updating. Some forms will require extensive maintenance and others less so. With some products, the usefulness of the product expires and must be continually replaced, which demands more work to keep it going.

Some important characteristics to consider when setting up a residual-based income are:

1. How big is the demand for the product I am offering, and how will I find my specific customers?

2. What are the initial costs and time to get set up?

3. How much potential (consistent) daily income can you expect?

4. What is the product's shelf life?

5. How much potential daily maintenance and work can you expect to do?

Finding your residual income niche (preferably with a strong evergreen) is the key to financial happiness.

64 – The Rising Sun

AKA—Why Mornings Matter Most

THE FOLLOWING DEMONSTRATION, which is a simplified version from Stephen Covey's classic; *First Things First*, forever left an impact on my mind when I first saw it:

The Riddle of the Rocks and Sand

1. Get a container, like a bucket or cup.

2. Fill it to the top with rocks or marbles.

3. Add sand slowly until full.

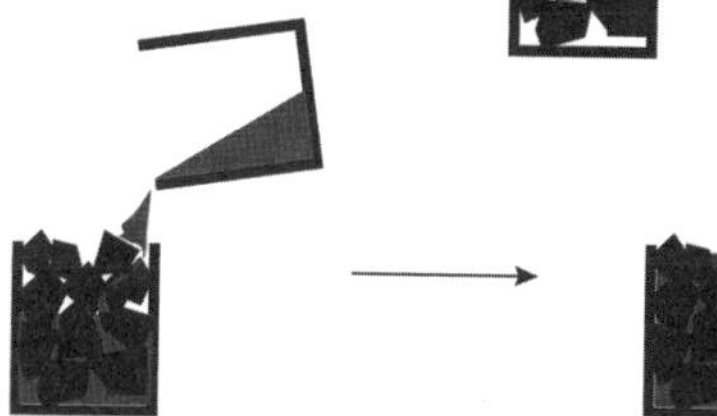

4. Empty container and separate ROCKS from SAND.

5. Repeat, only this time add SAND first, then ROCKS.

6. If done correctly, there will not be enough room for all of the ROCKS.

The point of this demonstration is that if the empty container is a single day, how much you can fit into it will depend on what you focus on first. For what it is worth, Covey's original demonstration included fitting in much, much more. After the rocks came smaller pebbles, followed by sand, followed by water, cramming the container absolutely full. I'm convinced that trying to pack more tasks into our day is a mistake.

The rocks symbolize that big thoughts and important goals should come first. Those thoughts and goals will vary from person to person, but in most cases, they will be duties related to family, work, school, religion, etc. When I am in production mode, my big rock is the one goal I am working on, it is my River of Focus. Symbolically, this would be like using far fewer rocks, only placing one into the container.

The sand symbolizes small thoughts and non-critical things you need to do, small fires that need to be put out, perhaps even recreation; these should be accomplished after the important things have been addressed.

The reason this analogy works so well is because as the day wears on, we typically experience fatigue. When we wake up after a good night's sleep, we should be at our peak-performing level. Our bodies and minds are rested. We feel fresh and energetic. As the day wears on, we get tired. While we are still able to do smaller tasks and errands, even in the late hours, we typically lack the energy and focus needed for heavy thinking and big projects. I've always felt that an hour in the morning is worth three or four in the evening, simply because of how productive I am at the start of the day.

I have applied this simple rule to multiple, enormous projects, including writing this book—just twenty to thirty minutes each morning, consistently. Wake up, write, and then get on with the day. Grab that momentum and ride it like a wave.

In college, I used a strategy called the Sunrise Gambit, which simply meant that if I had a huge test in the morning, I preferred waking up early over pulling an all-nighter, simply because my mind was fresher and faster after a few hours of sleep. The gamble was having enough discipline to be able to wake up at 3:30 a.m.

During times when getting in better shape was my one goal, the mornings would be dedicated to exercise. If I am producing a video or movie, that is the first thing that gets my attention.

Whatever you invest in first has the greatest chance of being finished, regardless of whether the thing is hard or easy.

Harder things should be done earlier, when you are fresh. Easy things should be done later in the day. This is what I call going downhill.

If you start with easy things, you will not find the time to do the hard things.

65 – Gap Management Bar

AKA—Scheduling Income and Time Resources to Your Advantage

THE GAP MANAGEMENT Bar is a very simple graph that demonstrates what we do each day, for what reason, and how we make our money. It is a simple exercise that will allow us to visualize the pattern of our day-to-day efficiency. Patterns allow us to plan and predict when something will happen, which makes it easier to know how to adapt to a less favorable situation.

Note: Being that this book will print in black and white, it will be difficult to distinguish different parts of this tool here. You can find the full color representations of these charts at the following URL:

www.michaelthemaven.com/efficiency

Every person has twenty-four hours in a day, and, therefore, the full length of the bar from side to side, represents twenty-four hours.

Sleep is represented in *solid black*. Assuming you sleep seven to eight hours a night, this would give you a remaining sixteen to seventeen hours a day to work with. I've heard of many entrepreneurs who sleep only four or five hours per night, but for me personally, I cannot sustain that indefinitely. If you are one of the few who can without feeling tired, you have a huge competitive advantage.

Any activity that requires you to go through some type of preparation is denoted with a triangle/ramp and is *gray*. This includes things like waking up, getting ready for work, or commuting. It is everything you need to do in order to start a required activity. I know some people whose morning prep takes up to two or three hours. The longer the gray triangles in your bar, the less efficient you are. I liken preparation to the shifting of body weight back and forth when climbing stairs. It takes time, thought, and energy to "get ready." Too much time can make you lose momentum. The shorter the "getting ready" ramps are, the better. Being in a state of preparation and ready to go is almost always better than being unprepared.

Any activity you feel compelled to do or that results in stress, pain, or artificial constraint is denoted in *red box, above the line*. It includes work or school.

Any gap on the bar is a "lull," a pause or break in the action. Lulls can be good if you have a predetermined plan on how to spend them. (For example, working on creating a form of residual income, or putting out business fires.) Many lulls spaced out randomly are not as efficient as one huge lull.

Everything above the bar represents how you are spending conscious thought. You will notice that if something requires conscious thought, you can only be doing one thing at a time in this space.

Everything below the bar represents activities and systems that do not require conscious thought (AKA automations), specifically, investments that are earning you residual income. These are coded *blue*. The blue bars are active all the time, even when you are sleeping or on holiday.

The number of residual streams of revenue you can have is unlimited, and, therefore, advanced entrepreneurs and investors will have several stacked residual-income bars, all simultaneously earning money. Not all of these investments will be profitable, but entrepreneurs usually have at least one as the "cash cow," which will allow them not to need to work full-time as an employee to pay the bills. They can also use these earnings to fund other investment opportunities.

When we draw it all out, this is what it looks like for students, simple investors, and advanced investors, again it is highly recommended to see this in color on my website:

Gap Management Bar for Employee or Student

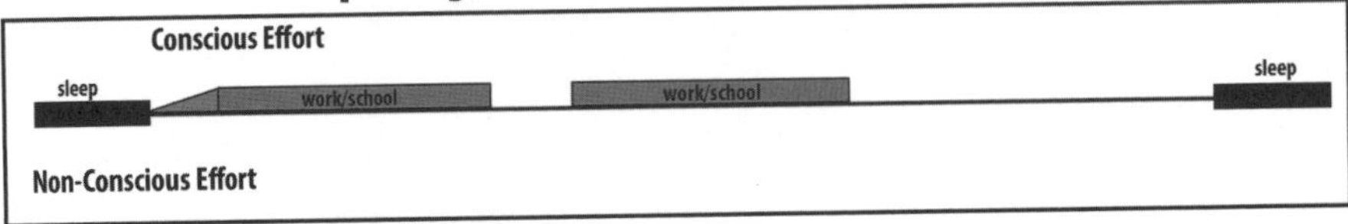

Gap Management Bar for Simple Entrepreneur

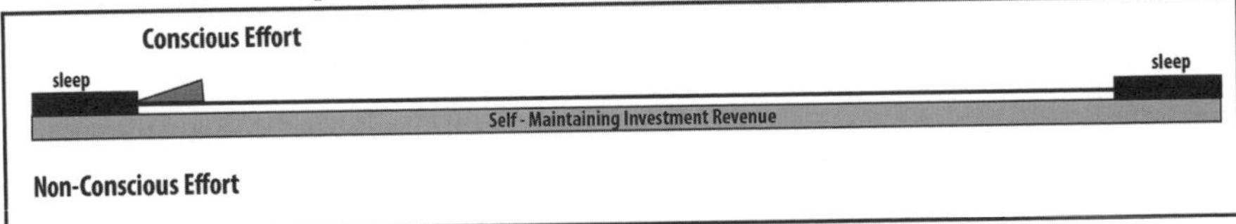

Gap Management Bar for Advanced Entrepreneur

Conscious Effort
sleep
sleep
Self - Maintaining Investment Revenue
Self - Maintaining Investment Revenue
Self - Maintaining Investment Revenue
Self - Maintaining Investment Revenue
Self - Maintaining Investment Revenue
Self - Maintaining Investment Revenue
Non-Conscious Effort

The Gap Management Bar is a powerful way to visualize how you spend your daily time. When you are an employee only, you will be paid once for your work; therefore, you have no residual revenue stream.

I know many people love their day jobs, and I will concede that if you love your job so much that you fantasize about it, you will probably be happy doing it full-time. If you love your job that much, do not change a thing. You have something that 95 percent of the world does not.

You will also notice that in the investor graphs, the conscious effort is left mostly wide open. That does not suggest that investors/entrepreneurs do nothing with their time. Rather, it suggests that someone who is efficient with her schedule has cleared it of as many meetings and commitments as possible, so she has the full force of the day to work on anything she elects to work on. She can choose to take the day off completely, or work on her self-maintaining/residual garden. A clear schedule allows for complete flexibility and adaptability to whatever situation she wakes up to that morning. I even avoid scheduling phone calls when I am working on a heavy project, simply because it introduces a constraint that I must transition to and from. It interrupts my flow. If I absolutely must make or receive any phone calls, it is in the afternoon or evening.

It is possible to get to a state where you never have to work again, but it is rare, not usually sustainable, and takes a heck of a lot of work and effort to reach in the first place. It is also not very fun. There is deep satisfaction in the struggle of a great challenge, and successful entrepreneurs in for the long haul thirst for it.

Most wise investors and entrepreneurs reject many opportunities because they know the value of their time and, therefore, want to keep their schedules as open as possible to focus and work on their self-maintaining incomes or things they enjoy (green polygon) doing.

This is my personal Gap Management Bar Goal when I am writing a book:

Gap Management Bar for Michael The Maven

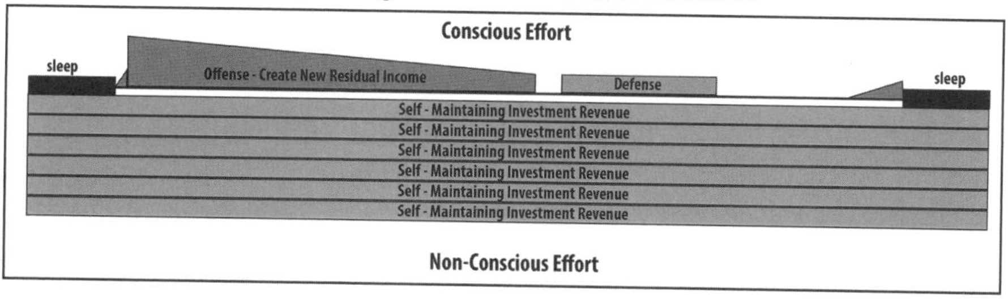

Conscious Effort
sleep
Offense - Create New Residual Income
Defense
sleep
Self - Maintaining Investment Revenue
Self - Maintaining Investment Revenue
Self - Maintaining Investment Revenue
Self - Maintaining Investment Revenue
Self - Maintaining Investment Revenue
Self - Maintaining Investment Revenue
Non-Conscious Effort

This isn't exactly what happens every day, but it is what I aim for. I give myself complete flexibility to change and adapt the day's plans as needed, without feeling any type of guilt. There are some important distinctions:

Offense

To me, offense means how you will impose your will on a situation or opportunity. It is prospect and capitalism. It is not the kind of work you feel compelled to do but work you self-initiate as I explain in the chapter "The Balance of Motivation." It is offense because it is focused on generating new revenues or opportunities.

I focus on offense first and for most of the day, preferring to start as early as possible after a good night's rest. I do not have a rigid schedule or time to wake up; *I like to keep things flexible according to the task at hand and adapt as needed.* Suffice it to say, I get the rest I need, wake up, and get to work as early as possible. I also usually have at least one workout break during the day, but again, it can happen anytime I choose.

At least 60-80 percent of my work time is spent creating new forms of self-maintaining, residual income, simply because once that new stream of revenue is created, it is stacked along with the other residual revenues in the Non-Conscious Effort side of my day for months or years to come. In my personal model, offense for me means doing the things that only I can do (which I call the Exclusivity Principle). In the case of training videos, it would be scripting, practicing, or recording new training videos. Or offense could be producing independent films, creating apps, or writing this book. Knowing the difference between what only you can do and what you can farm out will make a huge difference in your productivity.

Many offensive tasks I personally do not need to do, such as editing or posting a video. I send recorded assets to an editor who then puts them together and handles the rest. If I do not need to do it personally, I will find someone with quality skill sets who can.

You will notice that the offense bar is higher on the left than on the right. This means that I like to do the most demanding tasks as early in the day as possible because my energy and thinking power are at their highest. Mornings where I live are quieter (often needed for recording videos or voiceovers), there is less traffic, fewer people around, fewer distractions, fewer phone calls, etc. It is the prime time and opportunity to attack the type of work I do.

When I am on offense, I put my cell phone in a drawer in another room so I cannot even see it to respond to text messages or surf social media. I often will not check my phone until noon or later. It all comes down to that one piece of offensive business in front of me until it is finished.

Offensive thinking for me means I focus on tasks, not how long I am working. For example, I much prefer to "write a new chapter" than "write for thirty minutes," even if writing a new chapter takes thirty minutes.

It is not unusual for me to focus on just a few offensive tasks for the day, and when I finish those, I am finished with offense for the day. I think it is a mistake to reward ourselves with more work for having finished a hard job early. If I am working on something really demanding, I usually set a cut-off time around when I will eat lunch. I can usually *feel* when I have lost my offensive mojo for the day, so I try to stop working *before* I get to that point, keeping myself a little hungry for tomorrow.

Defense

When I say "Defense," I mean all those tasks required to run a business, but not necessarily for the sake of generating residual income. As the day wears on, I find myself more and more fatigued mentally and physically, and, therefore, I prefer to do less strenuous work during that part of the day—those tasks that require little to no mental or physical effort.

My personal defensive work has three characteristics:

1. Exclusive—Meaning only I can do it.
2. Important—It must get done in order for the company to continue to thrive.
3. Urgent—It needs to happen as soon as possible.

I think where many people get caught in the weeds is personally trying to deal with every urgent issue—things that need to happen soon, such as a customer service inquiry. So what happens is self-employed entrepreneurs spend the morning answering customer service emails, and by the afternoon, they are too mentally exhausted to create that new product. *Well...maybe tomorrow,* they think, and repeat the situation the next day. That is an efficiency error.

Most defensive work can be farmed out to third-party vendors. Farm out as much as possible, whenever possible.

For example, when I first got started making training DVDs, I actually made them at home on my computer. I literally burned the DVDs from my hard-drive and even printed the DVD covers on my home printer. I would then handwrite each envelope, place the postage, and personally take them to the post office.

After a very short period, I realized this production and delivery process was taking up a lot of my time, and it also took me away from creating new videos. I found it was much more efficient to hire a DVD-replicating company and a shipping-fulfillment company to fulfill the orders for me. Getting shipments out was both urgent and important, but it wasn't something I personally *had* to do.

Most of my customer service today is handled by a third-party vendor, available by email, Facebook, or even by phone. I don't hear customer concerns or requests 98 percent of the time because I have given this support company full authority to do whatever it needs to do to help the customer with his purchase. I give as much work as I possibly can to my support team, opening up my day for offensive tasks, which allows me to spend more time on offense rather than defense.

Transition Periods

As the day winds down and I get ready for bed, I like to prepare for the next day, simply because a long preparation period in the morning can slow me down. If you have too many tasks to do before actually getting into the work, it stifles momentum. It is a great feeling to wake up and get into whatever your one big task is. Laying out your clothing, packing your lunch and important documents, charging your batteries, prepping your gear, etc. the night before can also save you by allowing time to remember things you didn't do earlier. How many times do we rush to get ready right before leaving and forget something because we are in such a hurry? If it requires low-level thinking, do it in the evening the night before, and you will have better momentum starting your next day.

Side Notes about Rest, My Days and Time Off

I set aside the hours 6 p.m. to 9:00 p.m. not to do any work. I can spend those three hours any way I choose, including the gym, eating, movies, going to the beach, etc. If I need a mental break during the day, I can also work out anytime I want. It is also true that when I am feeling burnt out, I find a way to play. Because my schedule is under my control, I can drop everything and go scuba diving or on a three-day trip whenever I want. I secretly despise and avoid scheduling any kind of meeting if I can help it because I lose a little control over my schedule when I do.

I try really hard not to work on weekends, and I try to get out and do something that gets me out of my workplace. It is very important to have scheduled rest and play time daily, weekly, and monthly. Otherwise, you will burn out. Avoid attempting to do more than what was planned for that day. What this means is if I have a day where I am ahead of schedule, *I typically will not give myself more work.* More work is the path to eventual burnout and getting discouraged. Know your one goal, pursue it consistently, reach your daily goals, and *then go have some fun and reward yourself after!*

This is a marathon. A good pace is 75-80 percent of total capacity. Yes, I will sprint when I am close to a finish line, but unless I am a day or two within finishing, that 75-80 percent consistent pace is what I am going for. No more, no less. No adding new unexpected work.

What if you are an employee or student and do not have time to work on any kind of residual-income business? I understand this is often reality. I was there. My suggestion is to shift your sleeping schedule permanently so you wake up thirty to sixty minutes before you normally would. The real trick there is going to bed earlier. If you are getting enough sleep, waking up earlier isn't an issue at all.

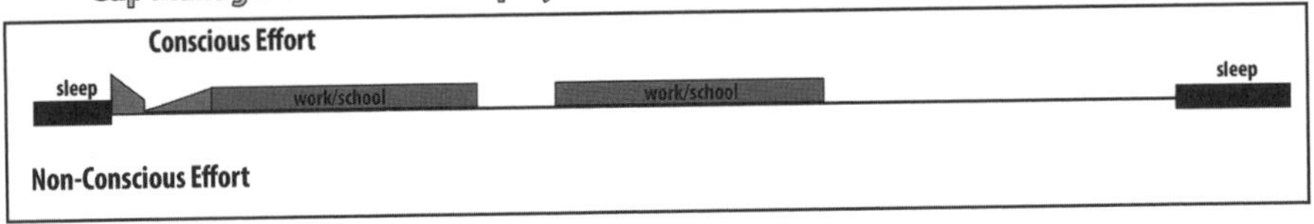

While it may not seem like much, if you can go to bed a little earlier, wake up earlier, and invest in yourself first, at the beginning of the day when you are at your best, that is the easiest way to spark a new business with limited time. If you can't get up, you probably do not want it bad enough.

In the end, the Gap Management Bar isn't a rigid plan, but rather a tool to help you visualize, organize, and find opportunities in your daily routine to convert over into a residual-based income lifestyle. While it isn't easy, creating residual income is the ultimate goal of an entrepreneur—freedom.

66 – The Wedge

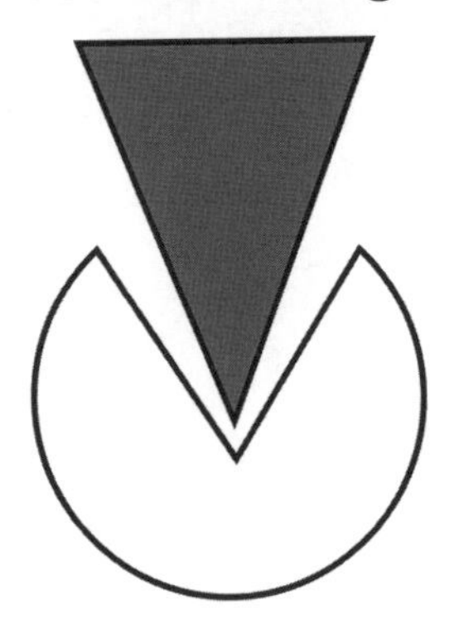

AKA—Attack the Gap

SEVERAL YEARS AGO, while visiting the Louvre in Paris, my mind's eye was opened to a spectacular possible shot located at the glass pyramid bottom inside the museum. It had everything I wanted in an abstract image, including a strong sense of symmetry and contrast. The problem was its location—it was a popular photograph spot, so dozens of people were standing around, waiting to have their pictures taken with it. I realized that even with all this coming and going of people, if I were patient, there would be at least a split second at some point when no one would be standing in my shot. I composed my image, dialed in the exposure settings I wanted, took a few test shots, and waited with my camera held against my face. Forty-five minutes later, there was a random, split second in which, despite all of the chaos of visitors coming and going, no one was in my frame. I fired away, and the resulting image hangs on my wall today as one of my favorites.

We all practice the Wedge in one way or another, but not as much on the conscious level as exploiting it as a tool of efficiency. It was after the Louvre that I made a specific effort to try to understand how to exploit opportunities based on predictable patterns. The wedge works best, not so much by putting your head down and just working, but by using your powers of observation to identify a predictable pattern of weakness that can be exploited to your advantage.

A handful of YouTube photographers will, whenever a new camera is announced, rush as fast as they can to make a "preview" video. Many of these videos will come out within an hour or two of a camera's announcement. Each video is basically a summary of the photographer's personal thoughts about a piece of gear he or she has never even touched. These photographers make these videos hoping that by being the first to publish an opinion on a camera, they will get more views, earn more subscriptions, and gain more pay-per-click ads on their channel. Something curious happens, however, once the camera is actually released. These preview videos become obsolete, and the number of views earned drops off sharply because better videos are made by photographers who have actually used the equipment in question—also referred to as "hands-on" experience. Regardless, more and more YouTubers make these preview videos, increasing the number of competitors for that topic of temporary interest. Such is also the case with companies that offer products and services already available. Competition creates friction.

If you commute, you know traffic is worse at certain times. If you go out to eat, you know certain restaurants are busy at 6:00 p.m., but not so much at 4:30 or 5:30. You know there will be lines at movie theaters on Friday night when the latest and greatest movie is released, but not so much for the matinee. If you are a firefighter chopping your way into a wall, you know it'll be faster to avoid the studs. If you are a running back, you know you will usually have more success running through a path your teammates have opened for you.

The Wedge is the offensive mind-set of finding predictable patterns of weaknesses in regards to resistance or friction and concentrating all of your energies and resources on that point of weakness.

If you find yourself competing with others for a limited resource or opportunity, identify a predictable pattern of least competition, and focus your plan of action on that window, instead of trying to compete with everyone else for the same space or resource. There is a saying "Is it better to be a big fish in a small pond or a small fish in a big pond?" Obviously, the pond size and its resources matter, but small fish in a big pond have one huge problem that those in a smaller pond don't—*the predatory behavior of bigger fish.*

When your efforts have less resistance, the efficiency of your actions increase.

Many times these windows of opportunities can be artificially created in such a way that they cannot be easily copied. In the photography world, the dynamic range of an image is the number of shades the camera can capture. In the midst of many similar camera reviews, I devised a cheap but effective way to test a camera's dynamic range. I believe this specific test helped my videos get more views and attention because I found an opportunity no one else was exploiting.

You want your best player or asset matched up against the enemy's or opportunity's weakest point. This is called a "mismatch." We had several plays at BYU that used this concept to exploit a defense's weaknesses. We loved to get our very fast running back lined up one-on-one with a bigger, but slower linebacker. If the quarterback had protection, that play almost always worked. Even in high school, when we figured out which of our opponent's defensive linemen was the weakest, that was exactly in whose direction we would run the ball on third and short.

The same concept applies to life; you want your very best assets, strengths, and skills lined up with the best opportunities to exploit them, not against the strength of the defense or the strongest point of resistance.

You will have more success focusing your strengths on the problem's weaknesses than focusing your strengths on others' strengths in those same circumstance. This is the heart of the matter when it comes to offensive thinking. *Strength on Weakness* or *Strength on Opportunity.*

Use the power of observation to determine where the weaknesses are, and then apply your unique strengths and abilities to that opportunity. This is what it means to "attack the gap."

67 – The Lull

AKA—A Pause in the Action

"WHEN YOU ARE in the middle of a gun fight, when do you reload and get situated with your magazines?" I asked my friend Mark Forester, a combat controller with the U.S. Air Force.

"Even in intense gun fights," Mark replied, "there are these little lulls, a brief moment where the fighting seems to pause. That is the time you should be getting your ammo or anything else you need squared away."

A **lull** is a temporary pause or stop in the action that surrounds you. It can last from seconds to years, depending on what you consider action. It is often unexpected and unpredictable. A lull can feel like nothing is happening, or you may feel a sense of frustration for having your time wasted intentionally by a business, system, or life in general. You may find yourself asking, "What am I going to do now?" Or you feel a sense of confusion because there is not a predicated, immediate plan at hand. It is like being given an opportunity with which you don't know what to do.

Efficiency during lulls builds upon the wedge principle of strength-on-weakness. The wedge is a means of attack. A wedge can line up perfectly on a lull if there is some kind of plan in place. Without a plan for these little interruptions in our day, we can lose precious hours and opportunities.

A classic offense-on-lull military example was the retaliatory attack of the Texan Army (after the Alamo) against the Mexican General Santa Ana at the Battle of San Jacinto. General Santa Ana ordered his weary soldiers to take a nap, at which time the Texans attacked. The resulting battle lasted eighteen minutes, with the Texans quickly defeating Santa Ana's troops.

In Mark's case, a lull in a battle can be an unexpected opportunity for preparation, if one has a preemptive plan in place to take advantage of a short lull. Mark was trained that, "If A (a lull in fighting) happens, you will B (reload and get situated)." There is an automatic link there, so he doesn't have to think about what to do when it happens.

An "imposed lull" can be a form of defense used to stop your opponent's momentum. You force the opponent to break his action up into smaller pieces, even when he does not want to. In modern football, coaches have learned to call a time out when their opponent is marching down the field, gaining too much momentum, or immediately before they attempt a game-winning field goal. This is referred to as "icing the kicker." I have witnessed these time-outs to be effective many times. And yet, when we watch kickers during these time-outs, they almost all are taking practice kicks or otherwise mentally preparing.

Preparing for the next action is a great plan to exploit lulls for efficiency.

In a life-and-death scenario, two soldiers, each armed with the same model rifle, are in a combat situation. One of the weapons is clean and well taken care of. The other is dirty and frequently jams. The soldier with the better-prepared asset will have a better chance of survival. The higher the stakes, the more important and efficient it is to be prepared.

Imagine two runners of equal ability at the start of a race. One is squared away in all respects. The other's shoelaces are untied, but she doesn't realize it until immediately before the starting gun fires. Those few seconds of kneeling down to tie her shoes will cost her the race when competing against her equal.

Any asset in a superior state of preparedness is more efficient than a less prepared asset.

While most of us are not engaged in combat or track and field competition, we are all fighting our own battles, and we all have enemies of sorts. Whatever the situation you are engaging in against competition—a test, trial, problem, lack of time, friction—you will always fare better when you are prepared for the conflict.

There is tremendous advantage in always being ready to go. Those who are ready to go do not have to "get ready." Getting ready means you have more steps, time, and processes to go through before you can get into the meat of the action.

Is it not enough that someone out there will take every advantage of you, even kill you, if given the chance? Why would anyone want to put him- or herself at any disadvantage in the event that you were to meet an enemy like this face to face?

When we fail to prepare, we put ourselves at a disadvantage.

I remember studying in college for an advanced genetics class. All I did was go over the study problems over and over. I knew walking into that test that there was nothing the professor could throw at me I wouldn't have the answer to. Preparation brought confidence and knowledge—fear disappeared. I look at fear as a form of friction. It makes us hesitate, but we know how to kill fear. We prepare.

Fear is mental friction that is inversely proportional to an individual's preparation.

On the flip side, a few years later, I would be teaching freshman biology at the University of Alabama. My classes were large, so there were always a handful of very young students who would show up to a test, get this, without a pencil! They would come to a major exam without anything to write with!

They would approach me with their dilemma, asking for assistance. Anticipating this, I had a little box of golf pencils at the ready. You know, the very short kind (less comfortable), that would need to be sharpened (more lost time), the ones without an eraser (can't change their answers easily).

If they protested about not having an eraser, I would say, "Oh no... well, better make sure it is right the first time you write it down."

On one occasion, a student protested after the exam, to which I responded, "Coming to a major exam without a pencil is like trying to play football without a helmet. There is no excuse for it, and that responsibility is yours alone." I wasn't interested in coddling or enabling the student's lack of preparation.

I wanted my students to learn by experience that they were putting themselves at a disadvantage so they would never do it again.

Your chances of failure are increased when you are not prepared.

Lulls are an opportunity to prepare, and, therefore, can increase efficiency, as well as decrease fear.

Time Shifting Through Preparation

I've often wished there was such a thing as a time bank, where we could deposit our idle time and, when we needed a few extra minutes or hours, we could withdraw that time and use it—say when we are running late. While time banks don't exist, the next best thing does—using idle time to prepare.

For example, making a full-length movie is incredibly complex, expensive, and difficult. Something a production will do to save time and money is to shoot scenes out-of-sequence. What this means is, if a movie you and I were making required multiple scenes in a restaurant throughout the film, we would shoot those scenes all on the same day, or consecutive days, even though they do not appear in that order in the final film.

For *Love Everlasting*, we shot our first four or five days at a high school, even though the school doesn't appear in the film until a third of the way into the movie. We did this because it takes a tremendous amount of time and effort to move the production team from one location to the next. These transitions are referred to as a "company move," which is packing up and driving four RVs, multiple equipment trucks, and dozens of people to a new location—that can take hours. It made more sense to shoot at the school once and never go back.

To make it even trickier, some of the actors, especially the famous ones, require payment for every day on a shoot, including the days they are not personally in front of the camera. In such an instance, it makes sense to schedule all of their days consecutively, even though the scenes they appear in are not consecutive.

It is estimated that this shooting-out-of-sequence can save a single production up to 30 percent in costs. That is an incredible savings for small productions with shoestring budgets.

On a twenty-six-day shoot, every single hour of every single day was planned. The script was broken down into locations and required actors and then grouped together to exploit any cost savings possible, avoiding company moves or off days. We removed the transitions and lulls in shooting to make everything as consecutive as possible. When we began shooting, it was twelve hours on set, plus additional work before and after. I personally averaged about five hours of sleep each night. The work pace was brutal with very few breaks in the action. If we weren't actually shooting, we were setting up the next shots. In the end, there was no way we could have shot the film on our budget without this kind of planning.

It was the two to three months of *pre-production lull* before we started shooting that made it all possible, and much of it was focused on removing shooting lulls during production.

Taking advantage of a lull illustrates the principle of time-shifting, meaning that you can use extra free time now to prepare for when time will be short.

If you were that soldier in battle whose gun was jamming, you would wish to have just a few minutes of peace and quiet to disassemble your weapon, clean and inspect it, reassemble it, check the sights—is it not so? And if you know there is an attack coming, you can shift the time needed to clean and repair your weapon to *now*. This principle applies to every future battle you will face.

Side note: On our productions, we also planned breaks into our schedule in the form of a single day off every five to six days. In the event that we needed to reshoot (which happens), we could use that day and we did. Having twelve, one-hour lulls over a week was not as useful to us as having a free twelve-hour day over the same period.

Many lulls spaced throughout a schedule are generally less efficient because they force more transitional periods to get back into the action. This is what I call a "Constrained Schedule," which is the inefficient planning of activities resulting in more lulls spaced out throughout the day.

When we look at it with the gap management bar, it looks like this:

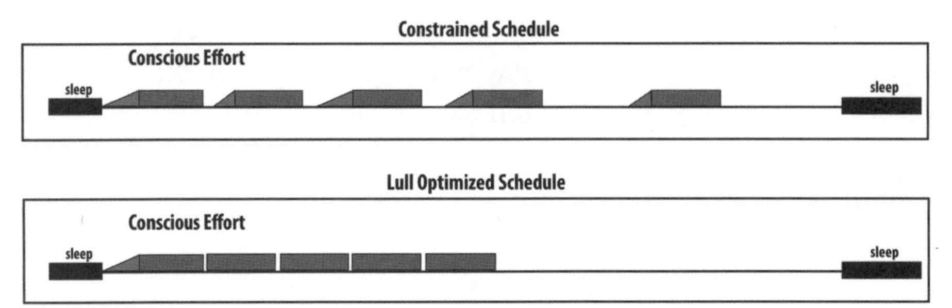

Lull optimization means to consolidate transitional periods in your schedule. If you can reduce the number, length, frequency and space between activities, you can expect to see either a gain in efficiency, or an increase in free time or both.

As an example, consider the music instructor who travels and visits each of her students ("Constrained Schedule" because time is lost traveling to each student) versus the music instructor who requires her students to come to her, one after another on a tight schedule ("Lull Optimized"). Both teach the same number of lessons, to the same number of students, for the same amount of money, but because the latter strategically reduces the number of lulls, she has much more free time later in the day.

Despite the very best of planning, there are always going to be some lulls in your action daily. You will recognize the following:

- Being placed on hold during an important phone call
- Sitting in traffic

- Standing in line
- Waiting for an important response from someone else, like a coworker or supplier
- Rendering out edited video or special effects for your video business
- Uploading assets or footage over a slow Internet connection
- The overly-friendly person who always wants to show you dozens of pictures of his newborn
- Waiting for your significant other to "get ready"

You cannot always control when lulls will happen. Learn to identify them for what they are and exploit them to your advantage.

Michael's Thoughts on Multi-Tasking

For the most part, I am a single "river of focus" kind of guy, and I have had great success being so. Focus on one thing at a time and nothing else until it is finished. If there are small lulls, it is okay just to rest and prepare mentally to attack the next big task. This happens a lot on set.

I almost universally reject multi-tasking as a strategy for efficiency, but there are some exceptions. Most normal people cannot have two conscious and deep thoughts simultaneously, and, therefore, both tasks usually suffer when you try to do both at the same time, creating inefficiency. There are "lull-like" activities when you are doing something that takes such little concentration it is almost like you aren't really doing anything.

For example, certain types of exercise (walking or hiking), driving, and cleaning around the home are all low-concentration tasks. I've found audio books are quite enjoyable for me during these activities. Sometimes, I will hike for four or five hours or drive ten hours, so fitting in an audio book is not a problem and makes sense.

The shorter the lull encountered and the more important the action at hand (risk), the less efficient it will be to exploit that lull for secondary purposes.

Being Prepared and Ready for Big Things > Multi-Tasking for Minute Time Savings

If a huge risk is involved, such as driving your car in heavy weather or operating a large machine that might kill someone, it is probably better not to try to do anything that would distract you. I think texting, social media, etc. while driving is a terrible idea because the risk is too high. It isn't worth it.

At one time, I would wake up and check my email, answer messages, make phone calls, etc.—all while still in bed. It was easy to waste two to three hours of my most productive morning time doing this. Often, I would end up aimlessly surfing the Internet. I later realized all these, low priority, low-risk defense type tasks should be done later, when these little lulls presented themselves. That was a revelation to me.

My aim in the mornings is to jump out of bed and get at it—whether exercise or work—ASAP. That kind of momentum will carry through to a great day. I'll check emails later, when a lull presents itself—because I know lulls are always coming—or in the late afternoon when I'm on defense.

In summary, you will experience many lulls throughout the day, irrespective of whether or not they are something you can control.

I guarantee it. I strongly recommend to have pre-planned lull options. Try to line up the length and difficulty of the task to how long the lull is:

1. Use **short** lulls (1-10 minutes) to address small **defensive** fires that need to be put out. My default is returning emails, but it can be anything quick, fast, and easy that needs to be done. My smartphone is often involved. I mentally link the idea of standing in a line or waiting on hold to answering emails. If there is something really big and important about to go down, I will not try to do something else. I standby *ready.*

2. Use **medium** length lulls (10-30 minutes) to **prepare**, preferably for the next set of coming actions. This means you don't have to prepare later. It can be cleaning, packing, organizing, charging batteries, laundry, research, self-improvement, stretching, and even rest. (I use medium length lulls in disaster zones to power nap because some days in the field I don't know when I'll have the chance to sleep again.) You will know what you need to prepare for most, and medium-length lulls are an opportunity to address that.

3. Use **long** lulls (30 minutes or more) to focus on your one thing, offense—especially if you are looking to transition from employee to business owner. Long lulls in the evening are ideal for rest and relaxation. Have some fun! Note: While I prefer offense in the morning, I will not hesitate to do some offense if it is needed and I get an unexpected opportunity. I try to have 2-3 hours every evening (from 6-9 p.m.) to spend anyway I choose (relaxation, dinner, reading, exercise, movies, etc.). It's very important to have planned time and days off; otherwise, you will burn out.

As a final thought, be careful not to create unforced lulls of your own. Lingering and hesitating when you have better things to be doing leads to lulls. Unforced lulls are the equivalent of a running back fumbling. It means to surrender tremendous opportunity for no good reason.

68 – The Forked Path

AKA—Options Theory

"Two is one and one is none."
— Navy SEAL Saying

IT WAS AN important engagement shoot. I switched my camera on, and quickly realized something was wrong. My camera would not power up. This shoot had been booked weeks in advance, the couple had paid, and this would be their only chance in the next several weeks to get the pictures they wanted. Without a camera, there was absolutely nothing I could do. On a wedding day shoot, such a breakdown would be catastrophic. Luckily (well not "luckily"), I had a second camera body in my bag and was able to continue the shoot without any hiccups. The couple did not even know about the first camera.

All football plays have varying degrees of sophistication. In Pop Warner (youth-league), they are simple, such as handing the ball to the running back and letting him run where his team is blocking.

In high school and college, sophisticated football plays have a number of different ways they can be executed as the play develops. Good coaching includes teaching the running back to adapt to opportunities as the linemen blocking develops, or a quarterback to throw to any of his five receivers, depending on what kind of coverage the defense is showing as well as how they attempt to cover the offense. Advanced players are taught to read specific indicators, such as where a defender lines up, or how a lead blocker might try to hit an opponent, and those indicators will determine the adjustments. Not so much, "run or pass in this direction."

Options Theory is the idea of planning for and increasing your viable plans as the attack develops.

To have one, strict, rigid plan is extremely risky, simply because many well thought-out plans fail on first contact with opposition.

Napoleon, the legendary French general who nearly conquered Europe, really shook up how wars were fought up to his day. In the past, armies would line up several rows deep in overly systematic firing lines. But not Napoleon's army—he gave them a set of guidelines to follow, and they had the autonomy to be flexible and change their tactics on the fly. This strategy threw a wrench into what other commanders were used to at the time, and in the heat of battle, they found it difficult to deal with the French army's adaptability because it was outside of the conventional rules.

I'm not a great chess player, but I enjoy the game and the philosophies it teaches. My dad always tried to ingrain in me that with every move, you should try to:

1. Increase your options
2. Increase your mobility
3. Increase control of the center
4. Decrease your weaknesses

Creating a plan with flexibility to adapt and make changes as you progress is more efficient than trying to stick with one plan from start to finish. The *forked path* tactic understands that the ends justify the means.

From this we can derive that "The What" of our actions is more important than "The How". We also know that from the chapter on Motivations, that "The Why" is more important that "The What". This leaves us with the very powerful binary of:

Why > What > How

Efficiency advantages to our decision-making processes are generally going to favor that prioritization.

Funneling, which I discussed in a previous chapter, removes your opponent's choices as the engagement develops. Think of options theory as the opposite—you are trying to improve the number of viable options at your disposal, so as the battle progresses, there are more opportunities and tactics you can employ.

If you have an important piece of equipment, or a weak link, have a backup for it in case it fails. If you are making a strategic plan, do so with adaptability in mind. As Mike Tyson eloquently described: "Everyone has a plan 'til they get punched in the mouth."

Remember, the goal is to win, not so much to stick to the game plan. Always have a plan B ready and be open to plan C, D, E, etc.

VIII – Conclusion

IT'S BEEN OVER twenty-five years since I climbed those stairs as a BYU freshman. I have returned several times to that exact staircase, and I always take a moment to re-climb them, feeling ***that burn*** and reflecting on what triggered my fascination with efficiency. *How I wish I would have had these insights as a young man,* but how excited and grateful I am to share them with you! These are the same tips and suggestions I give to very close friends who come to me for first-time coaching or business advice, and I am absolutely confident they will give you a tremendous advantage in a very competitive world.

There are many other tactics and principles I have not included in this book. Dozens of chapters were painfully removed for the benefit of focusing on the heart of the matter. I have a feeling many of these subjects will be released as articles or even video on my blog, www.michaelthemaven.com.

There are many other tactics and principles I have not included in this book. Dozens of chapters were painfully removed for the benefit of focusing on the heart of the matter. I'm still learning every day, keeping my eyes peeled for every tip, hack, or opportunity available, and sifting through the ones that are legitimate game changers versus passing fads. Whether it is streamlining a motion during exercise or running, or some new technology that saves me time, if it is tremendously useful, I cannot be stopped from sharing it. I have a feeling many of these subjects will be released as articles, podcasts or even video on my blog, www.michaelthemaven.com/efficiency

I *really* hope to hear from you about how *The Efficiency Playbook* has improved your life. The best way to connect with me is in the review section at Amazon.com. I will personally respond to each of the first 1,000 reviews, and look forward to speaking with you there.

Again, thank you so much for your support, and I wish you the best of luck until next time. Best wishes!

Michael

Appendices

Appendix A
A List of Friction

FRICTION'S FACES ARE unlimited, but the following are a few examples I want you to recognize as forces that will continually resist you:

Gravity requires us to work to overcome its effects.

Fatigue: How many times have you come home after a long day and been too tired to do anything more than veg in front of the television?

Lack of Time: How often do you have enough time? The value of many assets will depreciate with time. Money has a time value. Information has a time value. Problems in your relationships can be compounded with time. Time brings age.

Physical Aging will bring friction. You are aging, and yes, one day you will die. As you get older, it will be harder to move around, harder to see things, harder to function than when you were younger. Aging will bring *forgetfulness, disease*, and *death*—not happy thoughts, but reality. As the friction of aging increases, efficiency's power becomes more important.

Physical Distance increases friction. How many hours of our lives are spent traveling from one location to another? The longer the distance between steps in a process, the longer it will take to complete that process. Therefore, typically, with an increase in the number of steps in a process, the process becomes exponentially less efficient.

Resistance can slow machines down and generate **heat,** or **entropy,** which is a form of used, unharnessed, and lost energy. It can even generate sound—like the proverbial squeaky wheel, or frustration, like a lid that cannot be opened.

Lack of information: Decision-making is harder and sometimes terrifying if you don't have all the facts. And yet, these decisions still need to be made.

Bills: How much of what we do for a career is influenced by bills to pay?

Add on Fees: Any traveler knows all the nickel-and-diming that adds costs and frustrations to any trip—things like paying for an extra bag, trip insurance, etc. At every turn, there is another fee. This is one of the ways airline businesses use friction to their advantage.

Debt dictates the amount of freedom you have, and it creates a constant, unrelenting pressure that will never leave you alone until it is gone.

The more **stressed** a person feels, the harder it is to think straight, stay focused, and stay on track.

For the spiritual, ***sin** is friction*. It impedes spiritual growth, self-value, and enlightenment. It can destroy meaningful relationships. It can bring doubt, hesitation, and regret.

Diversion, or anything that distracts from the primary purpose or goal, will stand as resistance.

Attitude can add or reduce friction. Your attitude will take many blows. Life will throw you curveballs that will bring you down and rob you of your will. Your *ego* can guide you down aimless paths if you are not careful.

Clutter, in all its forms, is friction. It steals space and initiative.

Unpreparedness for limited, desirable opportunities is a form of friction. How many opportunities have most of us missed because we were not prepared?

Rate-limiting factors are friction. In cooking, chemistry, and countless other processes, rate-limiting factors are the ingredients required to achieve the specified outcome. The presence or absence of just one ingredient or tool can cause any recipe, experiment, or process to fail.

Activation energy is required to begin a process. If the activation energy is too high, the process will never move forward. Lowering the activation energy of a system makes it easier to get things started.

Dishonesty adds friction. Dishonesty destroys trust, and trust is efficient.

Misunderstandings increase friction. Misunderstandings and breakdowns in communication can turn molehills into mountains—instead of enjoying life with those around you, you find yourself fighting with them.

Positioning can add or subtract friction. Being in the wrong position at the right time is inefficient.

Incompatible Relationships: How much time, arguing, and heartache has been spent because two people do not get along?

How much time has been wasted looking for something because we were **forgetful or lost** something?

Appendix B
Michael's Notes on How to Be More Efficient

Here are some basics for becoming more efficient. If you master just a few of these, you will see huge gains in efficiency. The opposite truths can be inferred from each.

- Doing things faster is usually more efficient because it saves time, as long as the minimum acceptable quality is maintained.
- Keeping things simple reduces complexity.
- Calculating the cost of options before starting a process increases productivity.
- Removing or reducing a repeated process' number of steps improves efficiency.
- Speeding up how early or soon needed tasks start, usually improves efficiency.
- Repeating a skill makes difficult tasks easier and faster.
- Focusing on one thing improves the chances it will be completed.
- Being prepared saves time and stress in the moment of conflict.
- Gathering reliable information allows us to make better choices. The earlier that information is received the better.
- Reducing complex decisions to a binary determination makes it faster to identify the heart of the matter.

- Inferring correct information when a complete picture is not available helps in making better decisions when in doubt.
- Giving knowns and probabilities more consideration than unknowns is usually more accurate.
- Making things easy to find and access usually increases performance speed.
- Automating processes and systems usually increases efficiency.
- Multi-functioning tools improve efficiency when the task performed is rare.
- Using specialists or specific tools increases efficiency when a task is performed often.
- Hiring others with better skill sets than your own usually increases efficiency, especially when you pay them less than you earn per hour.
- Finding patterns allows us to predict and exploit certain types of behavior.
- Focusing strength on the defense's weakness is a hallmark of a good offense.
- Disrupting an opponent's ability to execute its plans is a hallmark of a good defense.
- Having an offensive mind-set is generally more powerful than having a defensive mind-set.
- Maintaining a positive attitude will make a huge difference during trial.

- Negotiating tactics can greatly improve profitability.
- A deep love of comfort makes us undisciplined.
- Maintaining a consistent, residual form of income that requires little maintenance can give us much more time and freedom than being paid as an employee.
- We can always decrease our efficiency through self-sabotage.
- Using modular components allows us to swap out broken parts of a system when things go wrong, without needing to rebuild.
- Making decisions based on a pre-determined model is generally faster.
- Exploiting lulls for defense and preparation is a powerful use of downtime.
- Starting with fertile ground offers a better chance of initial success.
- Working smart is usually more efficient than working hard, though both are needed.
- Showing generally requires less persuasion than telling does.
- Moving extremely fast in a general direction is usually better than moving slowly in a perfect direction.
- Being consistent over long periods is usually more efficient than occasional high intensity sprints, when the task is very large or burdensome.

Appendix C
Michael's Short List of Favorite Binaries

(including some inferred from the reading and others not found in this book):

Few Steps > More Steps

Known > Probability > Unknown

Control > Reliant on Others

Heuristics Now > Perfection Later

Proof > Unsupported Assumption

Showing Evidence > Spoken Opinion

Big Thoughts > Little Thoughts

Offense > Defense (At least in my mind!)

Minding Own Business > Getting into Others' Business

No > Maybe

Focus > Distraction

Direction > Position

Discovery of Truth > Persuading Others > Winning an Argument

Silence > Saying the Wrong Thing

Self-Discovery > Expectations

Meaningful Whys > Ego

Wisdom > Fame or Glory

Freedom > Riches & Wealth

Forgiveness > Revenge

Producer > Consumer

Opportunity > Stagnation

Sincere > Insincere

Genuine > Fake

Evergreen Residual Income > One-Time Pay (unless it is very large)

Quality of Relationships > Quantity of Relationships

Freedom > Money

Time > Money

Discipline > Comfort

Profitability > Cool or Ego-Driven (in a business)

Playing Smart > Going Hard

Passion & Fun > Compelled & Boring

Fertile Ground > Adverse Conditions

Actual Demand > Assumption of Need

Being Prepared & Ready For Big Things > Multi-Tasking for Minute Time Savings

Why > What > How

Appendix D
Your Notes on Efficiency

Which of the principles in this book were most helpful?

Connect with Michael

The best way to connect directly with Michael is in the review section of this book on Amazon.com. He has committed to personally checking and responding directly to the first 1,000 reviews posted there.

Michael is available for private efficiency coaching, business consulting, speaking engagements, and workshops. For business inquiries only, he can be contacted directly at: **support@michaelthemaven.com**.

Michael's Daily Blog: www.michaelthemaven.com.

If you are interested in one of Michael's photography camera training videos, they can be browsed at: **www.michaelthemaven.com/products**.

Michael's YouTube Photography Channel: MichaelTheMaven.

Michael's Facebook, Instagram & Twitter: @michaelthemaven.

About the Author

Known in the photography world for his camera "Crash Course" training videos and Epic Shootouts on his YouTube Channel, Michael Andrew, aka Michael The Maven, earned three varsity letters playing football for Brigham Young University (95-98). Michael holds degrees in Zoology (BS), Russian (BA), Molecular Biology (MS), and Business Administration (MBA). He dropped out of his Ph.D. program in Developmental Genetics at the University of Alabama after five years to focus on entrepreneurial endeavors and credits his success to his personal study of efficiency, which is outlined in this book.

Michael is also the CEO of the non-profit charity group, Red Lightning, and has served volunteer international disaster aid missions in Haiti, Japan, the Philippines, Vanuatu, and Nepal. He travels year round, but he can be found working mostly in Arizona, Utah, or reading under a tree on Maui, Hawaii.